Java 7 New Features Cookbook

Over 100 comprehensive recipes to get you up-to-speed
with all the exciting new features of Java 7

Richard M. Reese

Jennifer L. Reese

PUBLISHING

BIRMINGHAM - MUMBAI

Java 7 New Features Cookbook

First published: February 2012

Production Reference: 1160212

Published by Packt Publishing Ltd.
Livery Place
35 Livery Street
Birmingham B3 2PB, UK.

ISBN 978-1-84968-562-7

www.packtpub.com

Cover Image by J.Blaminsky (jarek@jblaminsky.com)

Credits

Authors

Richard M. Reese

Jennifer L. Reese

Reviewers

Jacek Laskowski

Deepak Vohra

Acquisition Editor

Amey Kanse

Lead Technical Editor

Hyacintha D'Souza

Technical Editors

Ankita Shashi

Lubna Shaikh

Copy Editor

Leonard D'Silva

Project Coordinator

Michelle Quadros

Proofreader

Mario Cecere

Indexer

Rekha Nair

Graphics

Manu Joseph

Valentina D'silva

Production Coordinators

Arvindkumar Gupta

Melwyn D'sa

Cover Work

Arvindkumar Gupta

About the Authors

Richard M. Reese is an associate professor teaching Computer Science at Tarleton State University in Stephenville, Texas. Previously, he worked in the industry for over 16 years in the aerospace and telephone industries. He earned his Ph.D. in Computer Science from Texas A&M University and served four years in the Air Force, primarily in the field of communication intelligence.

Outside of the classroom, he enjoys tending to his vegetable garden, maintaining his aquariums, and running with his dog, Zoey. He also enjoys relaxing with an episode of Firefly and is ever hopeful for the return of the series.

He has written numerous publications and has also written the EJB 3.1 Cookbook.

Jennifer L. Reese holds a B.S. degree from Tarleton State University. She currently works as a software engineer for Local Government Solutions in Waxahachie, Texas, developing software for the county government. Prior to graduation, she worked for the Center for Agribusiness Excellence at Tarleton, where she used Java in conjunction with GIS software to analyze crop and weather data.

In her free time, she enjoys reading, cooking, and traveling, especially to any destination with a beach. She is also a musician and appreciates a variety of musical genres.

Acknowledgement

No book can be written without the help of others. To this end we are thankful for the support of Karla, our wife and mother, whose patience and reviews have made this effort possible. In addition, we would like to thank the editorial staff of Packt and our reviewers for their input which has resulted in a much better book than it might otherwise have been.

About the Reviewers

Jacek Laskowski has over 15 years of IT experience, focusing on software development and architecture design with open source and commercial product offerings. He's interested in Service-Oriented Architecture (SOA) with Java Enterprise Edition (Java EE), Business Process Management (BPMS), and Business Rule Management System (BRMS) solutions. He is a seasoned technology professional with a strong software development and advisory track record. His interests revolve around Java Enterprise Edition and supportive solutions like Enterprise OSGi, Service Component Architecture (SCA), WS-BPEL, and WS-BPMN to name a few.

He is a founder and leader of Warszawa Java User Group, and has been a speaker at local and international conferences. He has been organizing Confitura (formerly Javarsovia), Warsjawa, and Eclipse DemoCamp conferences for the Java community in Poland. He contributes to open source projects—Apache OpenEJB and Apache Geronimo. He envisages himself using functional languages in projects and the decision to learn Clojure (a little bit of JRuby, Scala, F#, and Dart lately) influences his current self-learning activities. It's been quite recently that he's got into Android, too.

Knowledge sharing is his passion. He mentors students, and is an author of IBM Redbooks publications and has also contributed to a few other books as a technical reviewer. While supporting business partners and customers with their use of IBM WebSphere BPM products, he regularly runs courses and workshops. He is a member of the NetBeans Dream Team— highly-skilled and motivated NetBeans users.

He actively blogs at `http://blog.japila.pl` and `http://blog.jaceklaskowski.pl`. Follow `@jaceklaskowski` on twitter.

I'd like to thank my family—my wife, Agata, and my three kids, Iweta, Patryk, and Maksym, for their constant support, encouragement, and patience. Without you, I wouldn't have achieved so much. Love you all immensely.

Deepak Vohra is a consultant and a principal member of the NuBean.com software company. Deepak is a Sun Certified Java Programmer and Web Component Developer and has worked in the fields of XML and Java programming and J2EE for over five years. Deepak is the co-author of the Apress book Pro XML Development with Java Technology and was the technical reviewer for the O'Reilly book WebLogic: The Definitive Guide. Deepak was also the technical reviewer for the Course Technology PTR book Ruby Programming for the Absolute Beginner, and the technical editor for the Manning Publications book Prototype and Scriptaculous in Action. Deepak is also the author of the Packt Publishing books JDBC 4.0 and Oracle JDeveloper for J2EE Development, Processing XML documents with Oracle JDeveloper 11g, and EJB 3.0 Database Persistence with Oracle Fusion Middleware 11g.

www.PacktPub.com

Support files, eBooks, discount offers and more

You might want to visit www.PacktPub.com for support files and downloads related to your book.

Did you know that Packt offers eBook versions of every book published, with PDF and ePub files available? You can upgrade to the eBook version at www.PacktPub.com and as a print book customer, you are entitled to a discount on the eBook copy. Get in touch with us at service@packtpub.com for more details.

At www.PacktPub.com, you can also read a collection of free technical articles, sign up for a range of free newsletters and receive exclusive discounts and offers on Packt books and eBooks.

http://PacktLib.PacktPub.com

Do you need instant solutions to your IT questions? PacktLib is Packt's online digital book library. Here, you can access, read and search across Packt's entire library of books.

Why Subscribe?

- ► Fully searchable across every book published by Packt
- ► Copy and paste, print and bookmark content
- ► On demand and accessible via web browser

Free Access for Packt account holders

If you have an account with Packt at www.PacktPub.com, you can use this to access PacktLib today and view nine entirely free books. Simply use your login credentials for immediate access.

Instant Updates on New Packt Books

Get notified! Find out when new books are published by following @PacktEnterprise on Twitter, or the *Packt Enterprise* Facebook page.

Table of Contents

Preface

With the release of Java 7, numerous new features have been added that significantly improve the developer's ability to create and maintain Java applications. These include language improvements, such as better exception handling techniques, and additions to the Java core libraries, such as new threading mechanisms.

This cookbook covers these new features using a series of recipes. Each recipe addresses one or more new features and provides a template for using these features. This should make it easier to understand the features along with when and how they can be used. Step-by-step instructions are provided to guide the reader through the recipes and are followed by an explanation of the resulting code.

The book starts with a discussion of the new language enhancements, which is followed by a series of chapters, each addressing a specific area such as file and directory management. The reader is assumed to be familiar with the features of Java 6. The book does not need to be read in sequential order, which enables the reader to choose the chapters and recipes that are of interest. However, it is recommended that the reader cover the first chapter, as many of the features found there will be used in subsequent recipes. If other new Java 7 features are used in a recipe, then cross references are provided to the related recipes.

What this book covers

Chapter 1, Java Language Improvements: In this chapter, we examine the various language improvements introduced as part of Project Coin. These features include simple improvements such as using underscores in literals and the use of strings with switch statements. Also, more significant improvements such as the try-with-resources block and the introduction of the diamond operator are detailed.

Chapter 2, Locating Files and Directories Using Paths: The Path class is introduced in this chapter. It is used in this and other chapters and is the basis for much of the new file-related additions to Java 7.

Chapter 3, Obtaining File and Directory Information: Many applications need access to specific file and directory information. How to access this file information is addressed here, including accessing such information as the basic file attributes, Posix attributes, and a file's access control list.

Chapter 4, Managing Files and Directories: In this chapter, the basic mechanisms for managing files and directories are covered, including such actions as creating and deleting files. Also addressed are the use of temporary files and the management of symbolic links.

Chapter 5, Managing File Systems: Here a number of interesting topics, such as how to obtain the filesystem and file store information, the classes used to traverse a file structure, how to watch for file and directory events, and how to work with a ZIP file system are presented.

Chapter 6, Stream IO in Java 7: NIO2 is introduced. New techniques for performing asynchronous IO are detailed along with new approaches for performing random access IO and using a secure directory stream.

Chapter 7, Graphical User Interface Improvements: There have been several additions to Java 7 to address the creation of a GUI interface. It is now possible to create windows with different shapes and windows that are transparent. In addition, numerous enhancements are explained such as the use of the JLayer decorator, which improves the ability to overlay graphics on a window.

Chapter 8, Handling Events: In this chapter, new methods for working with various application events are examined. Java 7 now supports extra mouse buttons and precision mouse wheels. The ability to control a window's focus has been improved and secondary loops have been introduced to mimic the behavior of modal dialog boxes.

Chapter 9, Database, Security, and System Enhancements: Various database improvements such as the introduction of the new RowSetFactory class are illustrated along with how to take advantage of new SSL support. In addition, other system improvements such as additional support for MXBeans are demonstrated.

Chapter 10, Concurrent Processing: Several new classes have been added to support the use of threads, including classes that support the fork/join paradigm, the phaser model, an improved dequeue class, and a transfer queue class. The new ThreadLocalRandom class, used to generate random numbers, is explained.

Chapter 11, Odds and Ends: This chapter demonstrates many other Java 7 improvements such as new support for week, years, and currency. Also included in this chapter is the improved support for dealing with null references.

What you need for this book

The software required for this book includes the Java Development Kit (JDK) 1.7 or later. Any integrated development environment that supports Java 7 can be used to create and execute the recipes. The examples in this book were developed using NetBeans 7.0.1.

Who this book is for

This book is designed to bring those who are familiar with Java up-to-speed on the new features found in Java 7.

Conventions

In this book, you will find a number of styles of text that distinguish between different kinds of information. Here are some examples of these styles, and an explanation of their meaning.

Code words in text are shown as follows: "We can include other contexts through the use of the `include` directive."

A block of code is set as follows:

```
    private void gameEngine(List<Entity> entities)
{

    final Phaser phaser = new Phaser(1);
    for (final Entity entity : entities)
{

        final String member = entity.toString();
        System.out.println(member + " joined the game");
        phaser.register();
        new Thread()
{

            @Override
            public void run()
{

                System.out.println(member +
                    " waiting for the remaining
participants");
                phaser.arriveAndAwaitAdvance(); // wait for
remaining entities
                System.out.println(member + " starting run");
                entity.run();
}
}.start();
}
        phaser.arriveAndDeregister();      //Deregister and continue
        System.out.println("Phaser continuing");
}
```

When we wish to draw your attention to a particular part of a code block, the relevant lines or items are set in bold:

```
private void gameEngine(List<Entity> entities)
{
    final Phaser phaser = new Phaser(1);
    for (final Entity entity : entities)
    {
        final String member = entity.toString();
        System.out.println(member + " joined the game");
        phaser.register();
        new Thread()
        {
            @Override
            public void run()
            {
                System.out.println(member +
                        " waiting for the remaining
participants");
                phaser.arriveAndAwaitAdvance(); // wait for
remaining entities
                System.out.println(member + " starting run");
                entity.run();
            }
        }.start();
    }
    phaser.arriveAndDeregister();     //Deregister and continue
    System.out.println("Phaser continuing");
}
```

Any command-line input or output is written as follows:

```
            Paths.get(new URI("file:///C:/home/docs/users.txt")),
Charset.defaultCharset()))
```

New terms and important words are shown in bold. Words that you see on the screen, in menus or dialog boxes for example, appear in the text like this: "clicking the **Next** button moves you to the next screen".

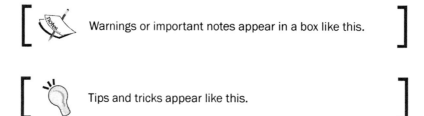

Warnings or important notes appear in a box like this.

Tips and tricks appear like this.

Reader feedback

Feedback from our readers is always welcome. Let us know what you think about this book—what you liked or may have disliked. Reader feedback is important for us to develop titles that you really get the most out of.

To send us general feedback, simply send an e-mail to `feedback@packtpub.com`, and mention the book title through the subject of your message.

If there is a topic that you have expertise in and you are interested in either writing or contributing to a book, see our author guide on `www.packtpub.com/authors`.

Customer support

Now that you are the proud owner of a Packt book, we have a number of things to help you to get the most from your purchase.

Downloading the example code

You can download the example code files for all Packt books you have purchased from your account at `http://www.packtpub.com`. If you purchased this book elsewhere, you can visit `http://www.packtpub.com/support` and register to have the files e-mailed directly to you.

Errata

Although we have taken every care to ensure the accuracy of our content, mistakes do happen. If you find a mistake in one of our books—maybe a mistake in the text or the code—we would be grateful if you would report this to us. By doing so, you can save other readers from frustration and help us improve subsequent versions of this book. If you find any errata, please report them by visiting `http://www.packtpub.com/support`, selecting your book, clicking on the **errata submission form** link, and entering the details of your errata. Once your errata are verified, your submission will be accepted and the errata will be uploaded to our website, or added to any list of existing errata, under the Errata section of that title.

Piracy

Piracy of copyright material on the Internet is an ongoing problem across all media. At Packt, we take the protection of our copyright and licenses very seriously. If you come across any illegal copies of our works, in any form, on the Internet, please provide us with the location address or website name immediately so that we can pursue a remedy.

Please contact us at copyright@packtpub.com with a link to the suspected pirated material.

We appreciate your help in protecting our authors, and our ability to bring you valuable content.

Questions

You can contact us at questions@packtpub.com if you are having a problem with any aspect of the book, and we will do our best to address it.

1
Java Language Improvements

In this chapter, we will cover the following:

- Using string literals in switch statements
- Using underscores in literals to improve code readability
- Using the try-with-resources block to improve exception handling code
- Creating a resource that can be used with the try-with-resources technique
- Catching multiple exception types to improve type checking
- Re-throwing exceptions in Java 7
- Using the diamond operator for constructor type inference
- Using the @SafeVarargs annotation

Introduction

Java 7 was released in July of 2011 and introduced a number of new features. In the Java SDK documentation, you may see it referred to as **Java 1.7**. This chapter will focus on those that have been grouped as part of the Project Coin (`http://openjdk.java.net/projects/coin/`). **Project Coin** refers to the small language changes in Java 7 that are designed to make programs more readable by removing extra text when possible. The changes to the language do not involve modifying the **Java Virtual Machine** (**JVM**). These new features include:

- The use of strings in switch statements
- The addition of binary literals and the ability to insert underscores into numeric literals

- ▶ The use of a multi-catch block
- ▶ The try-with-resources block
- ▶ Improved type inferences using the diamond operator
- ▶ Improvements in the use of methods with a variable number of arguments

Since the inception of Java, only integer values could be used to control a switch statement. Strings can now be used and can provide a more convenient technique for controlling the execution flow that is based on a string. The *Using string literals in switch statements* recipe illustrates this feature.

Underscores can now be used with literals as examined in the recipe *Using underscores in literals to improve code readability*. These can make a program more readable and maintainable. In addition, binary literals can now be used. Instead of using a hexadecimal literal, for example, the literal bit pattern can be used.

New to Java 7 are the improved try-catch block mechanisms. These include the ability to catch more than one exception from a single catch block, and improvements in how exceptions can be thrown. The *Catching multiple exception types to improve type checking* recipe looks into these enhancements.

Another improvement in exception handling involves the automatic closure of resources. In earlier versions of Java, when multiple resources were opened in a try block, it could be difficult to effectively close the resources, when an exception occurs. Java 7 provides a new technique as discussed in the *Using the try-with-resources block to improve exception handling code* recipe.

To take advantage of this technique, a class representing a resource must implement the new `java.lang.AutoCloseable` interface. This interface consists of a single method, `close` which, when implemented, should release resources as needed. Many core Java classes have been augmented to do this. The recipe: *Creating a resource that can be used with the try-with-resources technique* illustrates how to do this for non-core classes.

Java 7 provides the capability to re-throw exceptions in a flexible manner. It provides a more precise way of throwing exceptions, and more flexibility in how they can be handled in a try/catch bock. The *Re-throwing exceptions in Java 7* recipe illustrates this capability.

When generics were introduced in **Java 1.5**, it became easier to write code to address a number of similar problems. However, its usage at times could become somewhat verbose. The introduction of the `diamond` operator has eased this burden, and is illustrated in the *Using the diamond operator for constructor type inference* recipe.

When a method uses a variable number of generic arguments, sometimes an invalid warning is generated. The `@SafeVarargs` annotation has been introduced to flag a method as safe. This issue is related to heap pollution and is discussed in the *Using the @SafeVarargs Annotation* recipe.

In this and the other chapters, most of the code examples will be written to execute from within a main method. While no specific **Integrated Development Environment** (**IDE**) is needed to use the new features of Java 7, the examples in this book were developed using **NetBeans 7.0.1** and **Windows 7**, unless otherwise noted. At minimum, a version of the **Java Development Kit** (**JDK**) **1.7** or later is needed.

Also, note that the code examples provided do not include import statements. These are not shown here to reduce the number of lines of code. Most IDEs make it easy to insert these imports, but you need to be careful that the correct imports are used.

Using string literals in switch statements

The ability to use string literals in switch statements is new to Java 7. Previously, only integer values were the valid arguments in a switch statement. It is not uncommon to need to make a decision based on a string value, and the use of a switch statement to perform this task can simplify the series of if statements that would otherwise be needed. This can result in more readable and efficient code.

Getting ready

A selection based on a string value may occur in an application. Once such a situation is identified, do the following:

1. Create a String variable to be processed via the switch statement.
2. Create the switch block, using string literals for the case clauses.
3. Use the String variable to control the switch statement.

How to do it...

The example demonstrated here will use a switch statement to process an application's command line arguments. Create a new console application. In the main method, we will use the args argument to process the application's command line arguments. Many applications allow command line arguments to customize or otherwise affect the operation of the application. In this example, our application will support a verbose mode, logging, and provide a help message regarding the valid command line arguments for the application.

1. In this example, create a class called StringSwitchExample that possesses three instance variables to be set by the command line arguments, shown as follows:

```
public class StringSwitchExample {
    private static boolean verbose = false;
```

```
private static boolean logging = false;
private static boolean displayHelp = false;
}
```

2. Next, add the following `main` method, which will set these variables based on the command line arguments provided:

```
public static void main(String[] args) {
    for (String argument : args) {
        switch (argument) {
        case "-verbose":
        case "-v":
        verbose = true;
        break;
        case "-log":
        logging = true;
        break;
        case "-help":
        displayHelp = true;
        break;
        default:
            System.out.println("Illegal command line
argument");
    }
    }
            displayApplicationSettings();
}
```

3. Add the following helper method to display the application setting:

```
private static void displayApplicationSettings() {
        System.out.println("Application Settings");
        System.out.println("Verbose: " + verbose);
        System.out.println("Logging: " + logging);
        System.out.println("Help: " + displayHelp);
}
```

4. Execute the application using the following command line:

```
java StringSwitchExample -verbose -log
```

5. If you are using an IDE, then there is usually a way to set the command line arguments. For example, in NetBeans, right-clicking on the project name in the **Project** window, and selecting **Properties** menu will open a **Project Properties** dialog box. In the **Run** category, the **Arguments** textbox allows you to set the command line arguments, as shown in the following screenshot:

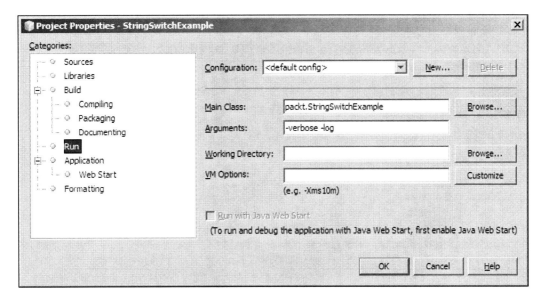

6. When the application is executed, your output should appear as follows:

Application Settings

Verbose: true

Logging: true

Help: false

How it works...

The application setting variables are all initialized to `false`. A for-each loop iterates through each command line argument. The `switch` statement uses a specific command line argument to turn on an application setting. The `switch` statement behaves like the earlier Java `switch` statements.

It is interesting to note that the Java Virtual Machine (JVM) currently provides no direct support for switching with strings. The Java compiler is responsible for converting strings in `switch` statements to the appropriate byte code.

When the for loop completes, the `displayApplicationSettings` method is invoked. This displays the current application setting, reflecting the configuration specified by the command line arguments.

It is important to note, however, while a `String` variable may be passed to the `switch` statements, as with the other data types used in `switch` statements, the strings used in the case clauses must be string literals. The general rules regarding `switch` statements apply when using string literals. Each statement within the `switch` block must have a valid non-null label, no two labels may be identical, and only one default label may be associated with each `switch` block.

There's more...

When using strings, you need to be careful about the following two issues:

   ▸   Null values for strings
   ▸   The case of the string

Using a string reference variable that is assigned a null value will result in a `java.lang.NullPointerException`. See the *Handling null references* recipe in *Chapter 11, Odds and Ends*, for more information on how to handle a `NullPointerException`. This is also true when used with a `switch` statement. Also, the evaluation of a case expression is case sensitive in a `switch` statement. In the previous example, if the command line argument is different from what appears in the case expression, then the case is skipped. If we had used the following command line instead, where we capitalized the word verbose:

```
java StringSwitchExample -Verbose -log
```

Then the verbose mode will no longer be used as indicated in the following output:

Application Settings

Verbose: false

Logging: true

Help: false

Using underscores in literals to improve code readability

Numerical literals can contain underscore characters (_) in Java 7. This is intended to improve the readability of code by separating digits of a literal into significant groups at almost any arbitrary place that meets the needs of the developer. The underscore can be applied to primitive data types in any supported base (binary, octal, hexadecimal, or decimal), and to both integer and floating-point literals.

Getting ready

The first step is to identify instances where it will be beneficial for the developer to format literals in such a manner. Typically, you will want to identify longer numbers or numbers that would have significant parts in their external form, such as debit card numbers. The basic steps include:

1. Identify a literal to use with underscores.

2. Insert underscores at appropriate places within the literal to make the literal more readable.

How to do it...

This example illustrates using underscores to clarify the inherent gaps found in most debit card numbers, and demonstrates their use with floating point numbers.

1. Create a new console application and add the `main` method as follows:

```java
public static void main(String[] args) {
    long debitCard = 1234_5678_9876_5432L;
    System.out.println("The card number is: " + debitCard);
System.out.print("The formatted card number is:");
    printFormatted(debitCard);

    float minAmount = 5_000F;
    float currentAmount = 5_250F;
    float withdrawalAmount = 500F;

    if ((currentAmount - withdrawalAmount) < minAmount) {
        System.out.println("Minimum amount limit exceeded " +
minAmount);
    }
}
```

2. Add a method to display the credit card number properly formatted for output, as follows:

```
private static void printFormatted(long cardNumber) {
    String formattedNumber = Long.toString(cardNumber);
    for (int i = 0; i < formattedNumber.length(); i++) {
        if (i % 4 == 0) {
            System.out.print(" ");
        }
        System.out.print(formattedNumber.charAt(i));
    }
    System.out.println();
}
```

3. Execute the application. The output will appear as follows:

The card number is: 1234567898765432

The formatted card number is: 1234 5678 9876 5432

Minimum amount limit exceeded 5000.0

Notice that in the first output line the displayed number does not contain underscores, but our second line is formatted to use spaces where the underscores were. This is to illustrate the difference between how the number looks internally, and how it needs to be formatted for external display.

How it works...

The debit card example partitioned the number into four sections making it more readable. A `long` variable was needed due to the length of the debit card number.

Next, a minimum limit was placed on the amount of money in a bank account. The variable `minAmount` of type `float` was set to 5,000.00 using the underscores to denote the location of the comma. Two more `float` called `currentAmount` and `withdrawalAmount` were declared and set equal to 5,250.00 and 500.00, respectively. The code then determined whether the `withdrawalAmount` could be subtracted from the `currentAmount` and still maintain a balance above the `minAmount`. If not, a message to that effect was displayed.

In most applications involving currency, the `java.util.Currency` class would be a more appropriate choice. The previous example used floating point literals only to explain the usage of underscores.

The only purpose of the underscore is to make the code more readable to the developer. The compiler ignores the underscores during code generation and during any subsequent variable manipulation. Consecutive underscores are treated as one and also ignored by the compiler. If the output format of a variable is important, it will have to be handled separately.

There's more...

Underscores can be used for more than base 10 literals. In addition, underscores can be misused. Here, we will address the following:

- Simple underscore usage mistakes
- Using underscores with hexadecimal literals
- Using underscores with binary literals

Simple underscore usage mistakes

Underscores may generally be placed arbitrarily within the literals, but there are guidelines limiting their use. It is invalid to place underscores at the beginning or end of a number, adjacent to a decimal point when used in a `float` or `double`, prior to the D, F, or L suffix, or where a string of digits is required.

The following are the examples of invalid underscore usages:

```
long productKey = _12345_67890_09876_54321L;
float pi = 3._14_15F;
long licenseNumber = 123_456_789_L;
```

These will generate the syntax error, **error: illegal underscore**.

Using underscores with hexadecimal literals

Underscores can be particularly useful when dealing with binary data expressed in hexadecimal or binary. In the following example, an integer value representing a command to be sent to a data port was expressed as a hexadecimal and as a binary literal:

```
int commandInHex = 0xE_23D5_8C_7;
int commandInBinary = 0b1110_0010001111010101_10001100_0111;
```

These two numbers are the same. They are only expressed in different bases. Here, we used base 2 and base 16. The base 16 representation may be more readable in this example. Base 2 literals will be discussed in more depth in the next section.

The underscores were used to more clearly identify parts of the command. The assumption is that the first four bits of the command represent an operator, while the next 16 bits are an operand. The next 8 bits and 4 bits could represent other aspects of the command.

Using underscores with binary literals

We can also use underscores with binary literals. For example, to initialize a device we may need to send a specific 8 bit sequence to the data port. This sequence may be organized such that the first two bits specify the operation (read, write, and so on), the next three bits may specify a device resource, and the last three bits could represent an operand. We may encode this sequence using a binary literal with underscores as follows:

```
byte initializationSequence = 0b10_110_010;
```

Use of the underscores clearly identifies each field. While it is not necessary to use the variable `initializationSequence`, it allows us to use the sequence in more than one place in a program. Another example defines a mask where, in this case, the first three bits are eliminated during an **AND** operation as follows:

```
result = inputValue & 0b000_11111;
```

In a bitwise AND operation, each bit of the operands are Anded with each other. These examples are illustrated as follows:

```
byte initializationSequence = (byte) 0b01_110_010;
byte inputValue = (byte) 0b101_11011;

byte result = (byte) (inputValue & (byte) 0b000_11111);
System.out.println("initializationSequence: " +
        Integer.toBinaryString(initializationSequence));
System.out.println("result: " + Integer.
toBinaryString(result));
```

When this sequence is executed, we get the following output:

initializationSequence: 1110010

result: 11011

The byte cast operator was needed because binary literals default to type `int`. Also, notice that the `toBinaryString` method does not display leading zeroes.

Using the try-with-resources block to improve exception handling code

Prior to Java 7, the code required for properly opening and closing resources, such as a `java.io.InputStream` or `java.nio.Channel`, was quite verbose and prone to errors. The try-with-resources block has been added in an effort to simplify error-handling and make the code more concise. The use of the try-with-resources statement results in all of its resources being automatically closed when the try block exits. Resources declared with the try-with-resources block must implement the interface `java.lang.AutoCloseable`.

This approach enables a better programming style as it avoids nested and excessive try-catch blocks. It also ensures accurate resource management, which you may see referred to as **Automated Resource Management (ARM)** in literature.

Getting ready

When working with resources that need to be opened and closed, the `try-with-resource` block is implemented by:

1. Creating the try block and declaring the resources to be managed.
2. Using the resource within the try block.

How to do it...

1. Create a console application and add the following `main` method to it. Create a text file in the working directory called `users.txt` and add a list of names to the file. This example opens up that file and creates a backup, while demonstrating the use of the `try-with-resources` technique, where a `java.io.BufferedReader` and `java.io.BufferedWriter` objects are created with the try block:

```java
public static void main(String[] args) {
    try (BufferedReader inputReader = Files.newBufferedReader(
                Paths.get(new URI
                    ("file:///C:/home/docs/users.txt")),
                Charset.defaultCharset());
            BufferedWriter outputWriter = Files.newBufferedWriter(
                Paths.get(new URI("file:///C:/home/docs/users.bak")),
                Charset.defaultCharset())) {
        String inputLine;
        while ((inputLine = inputReader.readLine()) != null) {
            outputWriter.write(inputLine);
            outputWriter.newLine();
        }
        System.out.println("Copy complete!");
    }
    catch (URISyntaxException | IOException ex) {
        ex.printStackTrace();
    }
}
```

2. Execute the application. The output should be as follows:

   Copy complete!

How it works...

The resources to be managed are declared and initialized inside a set of parentheses between the `try` keyword and the opening curly brace of the try block. In this case, two resources are created. The first is a `BufferedReader` object associated with the `users.txt` file and the second is a `BufferedWriter` object associated with the `users.bak` file. The new IO techniques using the `java.nio.file.Path` interface are discussed in *Chapter 6, Stream IO in Java 7*.

The first file is then read line by line and written to the second file. When the try block is exited, the two IO streams are automatically closed. A message is then displayed showing that the copy operation is complete.

Notice the use of the vertical bar in the catch block. This is new to Java 7 and allows us to catch multiple exceptions in a single catch block. The use of this operator is discussed in the *Catching multiple exception types to improve type checking* recipe.

Bear in mind that the resources declared with a try-with-resources block are separated by semicolons. Failure to do so will result in a compile-time error. Also, resources will be attempted to be closed, regardless of whether the try block completes normally or not. If the resource cannot be closed, an exception is normally thrown.

Regardless of whether resources are closed or not, the catch and finally blocks are always executed. However, exceptions can still be thrown from these blocks. This is discussed in more detail in the *Creating a resource that can be used with the try-with-resources technique* recipe.

There's more...

To complete our understanding of the `try-with-resources` technique, we need to address two other topics as follows:

- ▸ Understanding suppressed exceptions
- ▸ Structuring issues when using the `try-with-resources` technique

Understanding suppressed exceptions

In support of this approach, a new constructor was added to the `java.lang.Exception` class along with two methods: `addSuppressed` and `getSuppressed`. Suppressed exceptions are those exceptions that are not explicitly reported. In the case of the try-with-resources try block, exceptions may be thrown from the try block itself or when the resources created by the try block are closed. When more than one exception is thrown, exceptions may be suppressed.

In the case of the try-with-resources block, any exceptions associated with a close operation are suppressed when an exception is thrown from the block itself. This is demonstrated in the *Creating a resource that can be used with the try-with-resources technique* recipe.

Suppressed exceptions can be retrieved using the `getSuppressed` method. Programmer created exceptions can designate an exception as suppressed by using the `addSuppressed` method.

Structuring issues when using the try-with-resources technique

It may not be desirable to use this technique when a single resource is used. We will show three different implementations of a sequence of code to display the contents of the `users.txt` file. The first, as shown in the following code, uses the try-with-resources block. However, it is necessary to precede this block with a try block to capture the `java.net.URISyntaxException`:

```
        Path path = null;
        try {
            path = Paths.get(new URI("file:///C:/home/docs/users.
txt"));
        }
catch (URISyntaxException e) {
            System.out.println("Bad URI");
}

        try (BufferedReader inputReader = Files.
newBufferedReader(path, Charset.defaultCharset())) {
            String inputLine;
              while ((inputLine = inputReader.readLine()) != null) {
                System.out.println(inputLine);
            }
}
}
catch (IOException ex) {
            ex.printStackTrace();
}
```

This example is predicated upon the need to catch the `URISyntaxException`. This can be avoided by creating the `java.net.URI` object inside of the `get` method as shown below. However, it does make the code harder to read:

```
        try (BufferedReader inputReader = Files.newBufferedReader(
            Paths.get(new URI("file:///C:/home/docs/users.txt")),
Charset.defaultCharset())) {
            String inputLine;
            while ((inputLine = inputReader.readLine()) != null) {
                System.out.println(inputLine);
            }
}
}
catch (IOException | URISyntaxException ex) {
            ex.printStackTrace();
}
```

Notice the use of the multiple catch block as discussed in the *Catching multiple exception types to improve type checking* recipe. Another approach is to avoid the `URI` object altogether by using the `get` method with a `String` argument as follows:

```
        try {
            Path path = Paths.get("users.txt");
            BufferedReader inputReader =
                    Files.newBufferedReader(path, Charset.
defaultCharset());
            String inputLine;
            while ((inputLine = inputReader.readLine()) != null) {
                System.out.println(inputLine);
    }
    }
catch (IOException ex) {
            ex.printStackTrace();
    }
```

The methods that are used and the structure of the code affect the readability and maintainability of the code. It may or may not be feasible to eliminate the use of the `URI` object, or similar objects, in a code sequence. However, careful consideration of alternative approaches can go a long way to improving an application.

See also

The *Catching multiple exception types to improve type checking* recipe and *Creating a resource that can be used with the try-with-resources technique* recipe provide further coverage of the exception handling in Java 7.

Creating a resource that can be used with the try-with-resources technique

There are many resources in Java libraries, which can be used as part of the `try-with-resource` technique. However, there may be times when you may wish to create your own resources that can be used with this technique. An example of how to do this is illustrated in this recipe.

Getting ready

To create a resource that can be used with the `try-with-resources` technique:

1. Create a class that implements the `java.lang.AutoCloseable` interface.

2. Override the `close` method.

3. Implement resource-specific methods.

Any objects created with the try-with-resources block must implement the `AutoCloseable` interface. This interface has a single method, that is, `close`.

How to do it...

Here, we will illustrate this approach by creating three classes:

▸ One class that contains the `main` method

▸ Two classes that implement the `AutoCloseable` interface

1. Create two classes called `FirstAutoCloseableResource` and `SecondAutoCloseableResource`. Within these classes, implement a `manipulateResource` and `close` method, shown as follows:

```
public class FirstAutoCloseableResource implements AutoCloseable {
    @Override
    public void close() throws Exception {
        // Close the resource as appropriate
        System.out.println("FirstAutoCloseableResource close
method executed");
        throw new UnsupportedOperationException(
                "A problem has occurred in
FirstAutoCloseableResource");
    }

    public void manipulateResource() {
        // Perform some resource specific operation
        System.out.println("FirstAutoCloseableResource
manipulateResource method executed");
    }
}

public class SecondAutoCloseableResource implements AutoCloseable {

    @Override
    public void close() throws Exception {
        // Close the resource as appropriate
```

```
        System.out.println("SecondAutoCloseableResource close
method executed");
        throw new UnsupportedOperationException(
                "A problem has occurred in
SecondAutoCloseableResource");
    }


    public void manipulateResource() {
        // Perform some resource specific operation
        System.out.println("SecondAutoCloseableResource
manipulateResource method executed");
    }
}
```

2. Next, add the following code to a `main` method. We use the `try-with-resources` technique with the two resources, and then call their `manipulateResource` method:

```
        try (FirstAutoCloseableResource resource1 = new
FirstAutoCloseableResource();
                SecondAutoCloseableResource resource2 = new
SecondAutoCloseableResource()) {
            resource1.manipulateResource();
            resource2.manipulateResource();
    }
catch (Exception e) {
            e.printStackTrace();
            for(Throwable throwable : e.getSuppressed()) {
                System.out.println(throwable);
    }
    }
```

3. When the code executes, the `close` methods throw an `UnsupportedOperationException` shown as follows:

FirstAutoCloseableResource manipulateResource method executed

SecondAutoCloseableResource manipulateResource method executed

SecondAutoCloseableResource close method executed

FirstAutoCloseableResource close method executed

java.lang.UnsupportedOperationException: A problem has occurred in SecondAutoCloseableResource

    at packt.SecondAutoCloseableResource.close(SecondAutoCloseableResource.java:9)

    at packt.TryWithResourcesExample.displayAutoCloseableExample(TryWithResourcesExample.java:30)

at packt.TryWithResourcesExample.main(TryWithResourcesExample.java:22)

Suppressed: java.lang.UnsupportedOperationException: A problem has occurred in FirstAutoCloseableResource

at packt.FirstAutoCloseableResource.close(FirstAutoCloseableResource.java:9)

... 2 more

java.lang.UnsupportedOperationException: A problem has occurred in FirstAutoCloseableResource

How it works...

Within the resource classes, the `manipulateResource` methods were created to perform some resource-specific operation. The resource classes were declared as part of the try block, and the `manipulateResource` methods were called. This was illustrated in the first part of the output. The output has been highlighted to clarify the process.

When the try block terminated, the `close` methods were executed. They were executed in an opposite order than expected. This is the result of how the application program stack works.

Within the catch block, the stack was dumped. In addition, we used the `getSuppressed` method to return and display the suppressed methods. Support for suppressed exceptions was introduced in Java 7. These types of exceptions are discussed in the *Using the try-with-resource block to improve exception handling code* recipe and later on in this recipe.

There's more...

Within the `close` method, one of the following three actions is possible:

- Do nothing if there is nothing to close or the resource will always close
- Close the resource and return without error
- Attempt to close the resource, but throw an exception upon failure

The first two conditions are easy enough to handle. In the case of the last one, there are a few things to bear in mind.

Always implement the `close` method and supply specific exceptions. This provides the user with more meaningful feedback concerning the underlying problem. Also, do not throw an `InterruptedException`. Runtime problems can occur if the `InterruptedException` has been suppressed.

The `close` method is not required to be idempotent. An **idempotent** method is the one where repeated execution of the method will not cause problems. As an example, reading from the same file twice will not necessarily cause problems. Whereas, writing the same data twice to the file may. The `close` method does not have to be idempotent, however, it is recommended that it should be.

See also

The *Using the try-with-resources block to improve exception handling code* recipe covers the use of this type of try block.

Catching multiple exception types to improve type checking

Within a try block, multiple exceptions can be generated and thrown. A corresponding series of catch blocks are used to capture and then deal with the exceptions. Frequently, the action needed to deal with one exception is the same for other exceptions. An example of this is when the logging of an exception is performed.

In Java 7, it is now possible to handle more than one exception from within a single catch block. This ability can reduce the duplication of code. In earlier versions of Java, there was often a temptation to address this issue by catching a higher-level exception class and handling multiple exceptions from that block. There is less need for this approach now.

Getting ready

Using a single catch block to capture multiple exceptions is achieved by:

1. Adding a catch block
2. Including multiple exceptions within the catch blocks' parentheses, separated by a vertical bar

How to do it...

In this example, we wish to deal with invalid input from the user by logging an exception. This is a simple approach that will suffice to explain how multiple exceptions can be handled.

1. Create an application with two classes: `MultipleExceptions` and `InvalidParameter`. The `InvalidParameter` class is used to handle invalid user input, and the `MultipleExceptions` class contains the `main` method and example code.

2. Create the `InvalidParameter` class as follows:

```
public class InvalidParameter extends java.lang.Exception {
    public InvalidParameter() {
        super("Invalid Parameter");
    }
}
```

3. Next, create the `MultipleExceptions` class with a `java.util.logging.Logger` object as follows:

```
public class MultipleExceptions {

    private static final Logger logger = Logger.getLogger("log.txt");

    public static void main(String[] args) {
        System.out.print("Enter a number: ");
        try {
            Scanner scanner = new Scanner(System.in);
            int number = scanner.nextInt();
            if (number < 0) {
                throw new InvalidParameter();
            }
            System.out.println("The number is: " + number);
        }
        catch (InputMismatchException | InvalidParameter e) {
            logger.log(Level.INFO, "Invalid input, try again");
        }
    }
}
```

4. Execute the program using a variety of input. Using a valid number, such as **12**, results in the following output:

   Enter a number: 12

   The number is: 12

5. Using invalid input like a non-numeric value, such as **cat**, or a negative number, such as **-5**, will result in the following output:

   Enter a number: cat

   Invalid input, try again

   Aug 28, 2011 1:48:59 PM packt.MultipleExceptions main

   INFO: Invalid input, try again

   Enter a number: -5

Invalid input, try again

Aug 28, 2011 1:49:20 PM packt.MultipleExceptions main

INFO: Invalid input, try again

How it works...

The logger was created and when an exception occurred, an entry was made in the logger file. The output created by using NetBeans also displayed these log messages as they occur.

When an exception was thrown, the catch block was entered. Notice that the two exceptions of interest here, `java.util.InputMismatchException` and `InvalidParameter`, occur within the same catch statement and are separated with a vertical bar. Also, notice that there is only a single variable, `e`, used to represent the exception.

This approach is useful when we need to handle a few specific exceptions, and need to handle them in the same way. When a catch block handles more than one exception, the catch block parameter is implicitly final. This means that it is not possible to assign new values to the parameter. The following is illegal and its use will result in a syntax error:

```
}
catch (InputMismatchException | InvalidParameter e) {
            e = new Exception();  // multi-catch parameter e may not
be assigned
            logger.log(Level.INFO, "Invalid input, try again");
}
```

Besides being more readable and concise than using multiple catch blocks, the generated bytecode is also smaller and does not result in the generation of duplicate code.

There's more...

The base class or classes of a set of exceptions impact when to use a catch block to capture multiple exceptions. Also, assertions are useful in creating robust applications. These issues are addressed as follows:

- ► The use of a common exception base class and the `java.lang.ReflectiveOperationException`
- ► Using the `java.lang.AssertionError` class in Java 7

The use of a common exception base class and the ReflectiveOperationException

Catching multiple exceptions in the same catch block is useful when different exceptions need to be handled in the same way. However, if the multiple exceptions share a common base exception class, then it may be simpler to catch the base class exception instead. This is the case with many `IOException` derived classes.

For example, the `Files` class' `delete` method may throw one of the following four different exceptions:

- `java.nio.file.NoSuchFileException`
- `java.nio.file.DirectoryNotEmptyException`
- `java.io.IOException`
- `java.lang.SecurityException`

Of these, `NoSuchFileException` and `DirectoryNotEmptyException` are ultimately derived from `IOException`. Thus, catching the `IOException` may be sufficient as illustrated in the following code:

```
public class ReflectiveOperationExceptionExample {
    public static void main(String[] args) {
        try {
            Files.delete(Paths.get(new URI("file:///tmp.txt")));
}
catch (URISyntaxException ex) {
            ex.printStackTrace();
}
catch (IOException ex) {
            ex.printStackTrace();
}
}
}
```

In this example, notice that a `URISyntaxException` exception is potentially thrown by the `URI` constructor. The recipe *Deleting a file or directory*, in *Chapter 4, Managing Files and Directories*, details the use of the `delete` method.

In Java 7, a new exception, `ReflectiveOperationException`, has been added to the `java.lang` package. It is the base class for the following exceptions:

- `ClassNotFoundException`
- `IllegalAccessException`
- `InstantiationException`
- `InvocationTargetException`

- ▸ `NoSuchFieldException`
- ▸ `NoSuchMethodException`

This exception class can ease the handling of reflection type exceptions. The use of the multiple exceptions catching mechanism is more appropriate for those sets of exceptions which have no common base class.

 As a general rule, it is better to catch the exception that is as specific to the problem as possible. For example, it is better to catch a `NoSuchFileException` as opposed to the more broad `Exception`, when dealing with a missing file. This provides more detail about the exception.

Using the AssertionError class in Java 7

Assertions are useful in building an application that is more robust. A good introduction to this topic can be found at `http://download.oracle.com/javase/1.4.2/docs/guide/lang/assert.html`. In Java 7, a new constructor was added that allows a message to be attached to a user-generated assertion error. This constructor has two arguments. The first is the message to be associated with the `AssertionError` and the second is a `Throwable` clause.

In the `MultipleExceptions` class developed earlier in this recipe, we tested to see if the number was less than zero, and if so we threw an exception. Here, we will illustrate the use of the `AssertionError` constructor by throwing an `AssertionError`, if the number is greater than 10.

Add the following code to the `main` method near the original test of the number:

```
if(number>10) {
        throw new AssertionError("Number was too big",new
Throwable("Throwable assertion message"));
}
```

Execute the program and enter **12** again. Your results should be similar to the following:

Enter a number: 12

Exception in thread "main" java.lang.AssertionError: Number was too big

at packt.MultipleExceptions.main(MultipleExceptions.java:28)

Caused by: java.lang.Throwable: Throwable assertion message

... 1 more

Java Result: 1

Prior to Java 7, it was not possible to associate a message with a user-generated `AssertionError`.

See also

The use of the `Files` class is detailed in *Chapter 4, Managing Files and Directories*.

Rethrowing exceptions in Java 7

When an exception is caught in a catch block, it is sometimes desirable to rethrow the exception. This allows the exception to be processed by the current method and methods that called the current method.

However, prior to Java 7 only a base class exception could be rethrown. When more than one exception needed to be rethrown, you were restricted to declaring a common base class in the method declaration. Now, it is possible to be more restrictive on the exceptions which can be thrown for a method.

Getting ready

In order to rethrow exceptions in Java, you must first catch them. From within the catch block, use the `throw` keyword with the exception to be thrown. The new rethrow technique in Java 7 requires that you:

- Use a base class exception class in the catch block
- Use the `throw` keyword to throw the derived class exception from the catch block
- Modify the method's signature to throw the derived exceptions

How to do it...

1. We will modify the `ReflectiveOperationExceptionExample` class developed in the *Catching multiple exception types to improve type checking* recipe. Modify the `main` method to call the `deleteFile` method in the try block, as shown in the following code:

```
public class ReflectiveOperationExceptionExample {

    public static void main(String[] args) {
        try {
            deleteFile(Paths.get(new URI("file:///tmp.txt")));
    }
    catch (URISyntaxException ex) {
            ex.printStackTrace();
```

```
        }
        catch (IOException ex) {
                ex.printStackTrace();
        }
    }
```

2. Add the `deleteFile` method, shown as follows:

```
    private static void deleteFile(Path path) throws
    NoSuchFileException, DirectoryNotEmptyException {
            try {
                Files.delete(path);
        }
        catch (IOException ex) {
                if(path.toFile().isDirectory()) {
                    throw new DirectoryNotEmptyException(null);

        }
        else {

                    throw new NoSuchFileException(null);
        }
        }
        }
    }
```

3. Execute the application using a file that does not exist. The output should be as follows:

java.nio.file.NoSuchFileException

  at packt.ReflectiveOperationExceptionExample.deleteFile(ReflectiveOperationE xceptionExample.java:33)

  at packt.ReflectiveOperationExceptionExample.main(ReflectiveOperationExcept ionExample.java:16)

How it works...

The `main` method called and handled exceptions generated by the `deleteFile` call. The method declared that it can throw a `NoSuchFileException` and a `DirectoryNotEmptyException`. Notice that the base class, `IOException`, was used to catch exceptions. Within the catch block, a test was made to determine what caused the exception, using the `File` class' `isDirectory` method. Once the root cause of the exception was determined, the appropriate exception was thrown. The use of the `Files` class is detailed in *Chapter 4, Managing Files and Directories*.

By specifying precisely which exceptions can be thrown by the method, we can be clear about what callers of the method can expect. In addition, it prevents the inadvertent throwing of other `IOException` derived exceptions from the method. The drawback of this example is that if another exception, such as a `FileSystemException`, is the root cause, then we will have missed it. It will be caught in the `deleteFile` method, since it is derived from the `IOException`. However, we have failed to handle it in the method or pass it to the calling method.

See also

The previous three recipes provide additional coverage of exception handling in Java 7.

Using the diamond operator for constructor type inference

The use of the diamond operator simplifies the use of generics when creating an object. It avoids unchecked warnings in a program, and it reduces generic verbosity by not requiring explicit duplicate specification of parameter types. Instead, the compiler infers the type. Dynamically-typed languages do this all the time. While Java is statically typed, the use of the diamond operator allows more inferences than before. There is no difference in the resulting compiled code.

The compiler will infer the parameter types for the constructors. This is an example of the convention over configuration (http://en.wikipedia.org/wiki/Convention_over_configuration). By letting the compiler infer the parameter type (convention), we avoid explicit specification (configuration) of the object. Java also uses annotations in many areas to affect this approach. Type inference is now available, whereas it was only available for methods before.

Getting ready

To use the diamond operator:

1. Create a generic declaration of an object.
2. Use the diamond operator, `<>`, to specify the type inference that is to be used.

How to do it...

1. Create a simple Java application with a `main` method. Add the following code example to the `main` method to see how they work. For example, to declare a `java.util.List` of strings, we can use the following:

```
List<String> list = new ArrayList<>();
```

2. The identifier, `list`, is declared as a list of strings. The diamond operator, `<>`, is used to infer the `List` type as `String`. No warnings are generated for this code.

How it works...

When an object is created without specifying the data type, it is called a raw type. For example, the following uses a raw type when instantiating the identifier, `list`:

```
List<String> list = new ArrayList();   // Uses raw type
```

When the code is compiled, the following warnings are generated:

Note: packt\Bin.java uses unchecked or unsafe operations.

Note: Recompile with -Xlint:unchecked for details.

An unchecked warning is generated. It is generally desirable to eliminate unchecked warnings in an application. When the **–Xlint:unchecked** is used we get the following:

packt\Bin.java:26: warning: [unchecked] unchecked conversion

    List<String> arrayList = new ArrayList();

                       ^

 required: List<String>

 found: ArrayList

1 warning

Before Java 7, we could address this warning by explicitly using a parameter type as follows:

```
List<String> list = new ArrayList<String>();
```

With Java 7, the diamond operator makes this shorter and simpler. This operator becomes even more useful with more complex data types, such as, a `List` of `Map` objects as follows:

```
List<Map<String, List<String>> stringList = new ArrayList<>();
```

There's more...

There are several other aspects of type inference that should be discussed:

- Using the diamond operator when the type is not obvious
- Suppressing unchecked warnings
- Understanding erasure

Using the diamond operator when the type is not obvious

Type inference is supported in Java 7 and later, only if the parameter type for the constructor is obvious. For example, if we use the diamond operator without specifying a type for the identifier shown as follows, we will get a series of warnings:

```
List arrayList = new ArrayList<>();
arrayList.add("First");
arrayList.add("Second");
```

Compiling the program with **–Xlint:unchecked**, results in the following warnings:

... packt\Bin.java:29: warning: [unchecked] unchecked call to add(E) as a member of the raw type ArrayList

    arrayList.add("First");

 where E is a type-variable:

  E extends Object declared in class ArrayList

... \packt\Bin.java:30: warning: [unchecked] unchecked call to add(E) as a member of the raw type ArrayList

    arrayList.add("Second");

 where E is a type-variable:

  E extends Object declared in class ArrayList

2 warnings

These warnings will go away if the data type is specified as follows:

```
            List<String> arrayList = new ArrayList<>();
```

Suppressing unchecked warnings

While not necessarily desirable, it is possible to use the `@SuppressWarnings` annotation to suppress unchecked exceptions generated by the failure to use the diamond operator. The following is an example of this:

```
@SuppressWarnings("unchecked")
    List<String> arrayList = new ArrayList();
```

Understanding erasure

Erasure occurs when generics are used. The data type used in the declaration is not available at run-time. This language design decision was made when Java 1.5 introduced generics, to make the code backwards compatible.

Consider the following three methods. They differ only in the declaration of the `arrayList` variable:

```java
    private static void useRawType() {
        List<String> arrayList = new ArrayList();
        arrayList.add("First");
        arrayList.add("Second");
        System.out.println(arrayList.get(0));
    }

    private static void useExplicitType() {
        List<String> arrayList = new ArrayList<String>();
        arrayList.add("First");
        arrayList.add("Second");
        System.out.println(arrayList.get(0));
}

    private static void useImplicitType() {
        List<String> arrayList = new ArrayList<>();
        arrayList.add("First");
        arrayList.add("Second");
        System.out.println(arrayList.get(0));
}
```

When these methods are compiled, the type information available at compile-time is lost. If we examine the compiled bytecode for these three methods, we will find that there is no difference between them.

Using the following command will display the byte codes for the program:

`javap -v -p packt/Bin`

The generated code is identical for these three methods. The code for the `useImplicitType` is shown as follows. It is identical to the other two methods;

```
    private static void useImplicitType();
      flags: ACC_PRIVATE, ACC_STATIC
      Code:
        stack=3, locals=1, args_size=0
           0: new            #5          // class java/util/
    ArrayList
```

```
        3: dup
        4: invokespecial  #6          // Method java/util/
ArrayList."<in
it>":()V
        7: astore_0
        8: aload_0
        9: ldc             #7          // String First
       11: invokevirtual  #8          // Method java/util/
ArrayList.add:
(Ljava/lang/Object;)Z
       14: pop
       15: aload_0
       16: ldc             #9          // String Second
       18: invokevirtual  #8          // Method java/util/
ArrayList.add:
(Ljava/lang/Object;)Z
       21: pop
       22: getstatic       #10         // Field java/lang/
System.out:Ljav
a/io/PrintStream;
       25: aload_0
       26: iconst_0
       27: invokevirtual  #11         // Method java/util/
ArrayList.get:
(I)Ljava/lang/Object;
       30: checkcast       #12         // class java/lang/
String
       33: invokevirtual  #13         // Method java/io/
PrintStream.prin
tln:(Ljava/lang/String;)V
       36: return
```

Using the @SafeVarargs annotation

The `@SafeVarargs` and `@SuppressWarnings` annotations can be used to deal with various warnings that are normally harmless. The `@SuppressWarnings` annotation, as its name implies, will suppress specific types of warnings.

The `@SafeVarargs` annotation, introduced in Java 7, is used to designate certain methods and constructors that use a variable number of arguments as safe. Methods can be passed with a variable number of arguments. These arguments may be generics. If they are, then it may be desirable to suppress harmless warnings using the `@SafeVarargs` annotation.

The `@SafeVarargs` annotation is used with constructors and methods. To use the `@SafeVarargs` annotation, the following steps need to be followed:

1. Create a method or constructor that uses a variable number of generic parameters.
2. Add the `@SafeVarargs` annotation before the method declaration.

In Java 7, mandatory compiler warnings are generated with generic variable argument methods or constructors. The use of the `@SafeVarargs` annotation suppresses warnings, when these methods or constructors are deemed to be harmless.

How to do it...

1. To demonstrate the `@SafeVarargs` annotation, create an application with a method called `displayElements` as follows. The method displays information about each parameter and its value:

```
package packt;

import java.util.ArrayList;

public class SafeVargExample {
    public static void main(String[] args) {
    }

    @SafeVarargs
    public static <T> void displayElements(T... array) {
        for (T element : array) {
            System.out.println(element.getClass().getName() + ": "
+ element);
        }
    }
}
```

The method uses a variable number of generic parameters. Java implements a variable number of arguments as an array of objects, which only hold reifiable types. A **reifiable** type is discussed in the *How it works* section.

2. Add the following code in the `main` method to test the method:

```
ArrayList<Integer> a1 = new ArrayList<>();
a1.add(new Integer(1));
a1.add(2);
ArrayList<Float> a2 = new ArrayList<>();
a2.add(new Float(3.0));
a2.add(new Float(4.0));
displayElements(a1, a2, 12);
```

3. Execute the application. The output should appear as follows:

   java.util.ArrayList: [1, 2]

   java.util.ArrayList: [3.0, 4.0]

   java.lang.Integer: 12

4. Notice the use of the diamond operator, `<>`, in the declaration of the `java.util.ArrayList`. This operator is new to Java 7, and is discussed in the recipe: *Using the diamond operator for constructor type inference*.

How it works...

In Java, a method or constructor with a variable number of arguments is created using the `...` notation as used in the `displayElements` method. In this case, the element type is a generic.

The basic problem is the inability of generics and arrays to play well together. When generics were added to the Java language in 1.5, they were implemented to make them backwards compatible with earlier code. This meant that they were implemented using erasure. That is, any type of information that was available at compile-time was removed at run-time. This data is referred to as **non-reifiable**.

Arrays are reified. Information about an array's element type is retained and can be used at run-time. Note that it is not possible to declare an array of generics. It is possible to create a simple array of strings as follows:

```
String arr[] = {"First", "Second"};
```

However, we cannot create an array of generics, such as the following:

```
List<String> list1 = new ArrayList<String>();
list1.add("a");
List<String> list2 = new ArrayList<String>();
list2.add("b");
List<String> arr[] = {list1, list2}
```

This code will generate the following error message:

Cannot create a generic array of List<String>

A method that uses a variable number of arguments is implemented as an array of objects. It can only deal with reifiable types. When a method using a variable number of arguments is invoked, an array is created to hold these parameters.

Since we used a method with variable number of generic arguments, a run-time problem can occur known as **heap pollution**. Heap pollution occurs when a variable of a parameterized type is assigned a different type than that used to define it. At run-time, this will manifest itself as an unchecked warning. At run-time, it will result in a `java.lang.ClassCastException`. Use the `@SafeVarargs` annotation to designate a method as one that avoids heap pollution.

Methods that use a variable number of generic arguments will result in a compile-time warning. However, not all methods that use a variable number of generic arguments will result in a run-time exception. The `@SafeVarargs` is used to mark the safe methods as safe. If it is possible for a run-time exception to occur, then the annotation should not be used. This is further explored in the next section.

Notice that if the `@SafeVarargs` annotation was not used then the following warnings will be generated:

warning: [unchecked] unchecked generic array creation for varargs parameter of type ArrayList<? extends INT#1>[]

warning: [unchecked] Possible heap pollution from parameterized vararg type T

The first warning is applied against the `displayElements` invocation and the second warning is applied against the actual method. There is nothing wrong with the code, so suppression of these warnings is perfectly acceptable.

We could use the `@SuppressWarnings("unchecked")` annotation instead to suppress the warning at the declaration of the method, but warnings are still generated with their usage. Using `@SafeVarargs` suppresses warnings at both places.

There's more...

Also of interest is:

- The use of `@SafeVarargs` annotation in the Java core libraries
- An example of heap pollution

The use of @SafeVarargs annotation in Java core libraries

JDK 1.7 libraries have incorporated the `@SafeVarargs` annotation. These include the following:

- `public static <T> List<T> java.util.Arrays.asList(T... a)`
- `public static <T> boolean java.util.Collections.`
  `addAll(Collection<? super T> c, T... elements)`

- public static <E extends Enum<E>> java.util.EnumSet<E> EnumSet.
  of(E first, E... rest)
- protected final void javax.swing.SwingWorker.publish(V...
  chunks)

These methods were tagged with the @SafeVarargs annotation to indicate that they will not cause heap pollution. These methods are considered to be safe.

An example of heap pollution

Some methods should not be marked as safe, as illustrated with the following code adapted from the javadoc description of the @SafeVarargs annotation (http://download. oracle.com/javase/7/docs/api/index.html under the java.lang.SafeVarargs annotation documentation).

Add the following method to your code:

```
@SafeVarargs // Not actually safe!
static void merge(List<String>... stringLists) {
    Object[] array = stringLists;
    List<Integer> tmpList = Arrays.asList(42);
    array[0] = tmpList; // Semantically invalid, but compiles
without warnings
    String element = stringLists[0].get(0); // runtime
ClassCastException
}
```

Test the method with the following code:

```
List<String> list1 = new ArrayList<>();
list1.add("One");
list1.add("Two");
list1.add("Three");
List<String> list2 = new ArrayList<>();
list2.add("Four");
list2.add("Five");
list2.add("Six");
merge(list1,list2);
```

Execute the program. You should get the following error message:

Exception in thread "main" java.lang.ClassCastException: java.lang.Integer cannot be cast to java.lang.String

A list of strings was passed to the method and assigned to the identifier `stringList`. Next, an array of objects was declared and assigned to the same object referenced by `stringList`. At this point, the `stringList` and `array` referenced the same object, a `java.util.List` of strings. The following illustrates the configuration of the memory at this point:

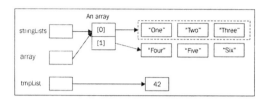

With the following assignment:

        `array[0] = tmpList`

The first element of the array is reassigned to `tmpList`. This reassignment is illustrated in the following figure:

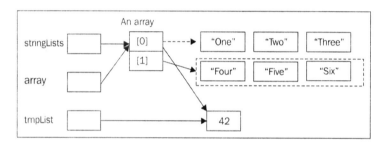

At this point, we have effectively assigned an `Integer` object to a `String` reference variable. It has been assigned to the first element of the array referenced by both `stringLists` and `array`. The dashed line shows the old reference, which has been replaced with the line. When an attempt is made at run-time to assign this `Integer` object to a `String` reference variable, the `ClassCastException` occurs.

This method results in heap pollution and should not be annotated with `@SafeVarargs` as it is not safe. The assignment of `tmpList` to the first element of the array is permitted, since we are simply assigning a `List<Integer>` object to an `Object` reference variable. This is an example of **upcasting**, which is legal in Java.

See also

The previous recipe *Using the diamond operator for constructor type inference* explains an improvement in the use of generics.

2

Locating Files and Directories Using Paths

In this chapter, we will cover the following:

- ▶ Creating a Path object
- ▶ Interoperability between java.io.File and java.nio.file.Files
- ▶ Converting a relative path into an absolute path
- ▶ Removing redundancies by normalizing a path
- ▶ Combining paths using path resolution
- ▶ Creating a path between two locations
- ▶ Converting between path types
- ▶ Determining whether two paths are equivalent
- ▶ Managing symbolic links

Introduction

A filesystem is a way of organizing data on a computer. Normally, it consists of one or more top-level directories, each of which contains a hierarchy of files. The top-level directory is frequently referred to as the root. In addition, the filesystem is stored on a media, which is referred to as the file store.

Java 7 introduces a number of new classes and interfaces to make working with filesystems easier and more efficient. These have largely supplemented older classes found in the `java.io` package.

In this and subsequent chapters, we will demonstrate how a filesystem can be managed using the directory structure, as shown in the following diagram:

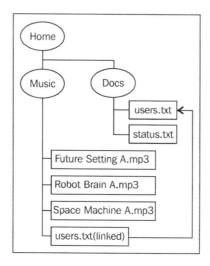

The ovals represent a directory/folder, while rectangles represent files. Unix-based systems and Windows systems differ in their support of a root node. Unix systems support a single root node, while Windows systems permit more than one root node. The location of a directory or file is described using a path. The elements, directories and files of the path are separated by either a forward or backward slash. In Unix, a forward slash is used. In Windows, a backward slash is used.

The music files were obtained from `http://freepd.com/70s%20Sci%20Fi/`. The `status.txt` is intended to hold simple status information, while the `users.txt` is assumed to hold a list of users. The `users.txt` file in the music directory is a symbolic link to the actual file in the `docs` directory as reflected with the red line. These files will be used in various examples throughout this chapter. Of course, you can use any file or file structure that you wish.

Symbolic links are more common in Unix-based platforms. To create a symbolic link for the `users.txt` file in the music directory, use the following command in the command console: `mklink users.txt c:\home\docs\users.txt`. This requires administrator privileges to execute.

This chapter is concerned with the management of paths as represented by the `java.nio.file.Path` class. A `Path` object is used extensively by classes in the `java.nio` package and is composed of several parts that are as follows:

- A root which is the base of the path, such as a C drive
- A separator used to separate the names that make up directories and files of the path
- The names of the intermediate directories
- A terminal element, which can be a file or directory

These are discussed and illustrated in the *Understanding paths* recipe. The following are the classes dealing with files and directories:

- `java.nio.file.Paths` contains static methods for the creation of a `Path` object
- `java.nio.file.Path` interface contains numerous methods for working with paths
- `java.nio.file.FileSystems` is the primary class used to access a filesystem
- `java.nio.file.FileSystem` represents a filesystem, such as the /on a UNIX system or the C drive on a Windows platform
- `java.nio.file.FileStore` represents the actual storage device and provides device-specific information
- `java.nio.file.attribute.FileStoreAttributeView` provides access to file information

The last two classes are discussed in more depth in later chapters. To gain access to a file or directory, we will typically use the `FileSystems` class' `getDefault` method to retrieve a reference to the filesystem accessible by the JVM. To get access to a specific drive, we can use the `getFileSystem` method with a **Uniform Resource Identifier** (**URI**) object representing the drive or directory of interest.

The `FileSystems` class provides techniques to create or access a filesystem. In this chapter, we are interested in how the class supports the creation of `Path` objects. Once we have reference to a file system object, we can obtain a `Path` object using any one of several methods:

- `getPath`: This uses a system-dependent path to obtain a `Path` object. The `Path` object is used to locate and access the file.
- `getPathMatcher`: This creates a `PathMatcher`. It performs various matching type operations on a file and is covered in the *Getting filesystem information* recipe in *Chapter 5*.
- `getRootDirectories`: This is used to obtain a list of root directories. This method is illustrated in the *Getting filesystem information* recipe in *Chapter 5*.

The creation and general use of `Path` objects is introduced in the *Understanding paths* recipe. This knowledge is used in subsequent recipes and other chapters, so be sure to understand the basic processes covered in this recipe.

You can still use the older `java.io` package elements. A path representing a `java.io.File` object can be created using the `File` class's `toPath` method. This is discussed in the *Interoperability between java.io.File and java.nio.file.Files* recipe and can be useful when maintaining older code.

Paths can be either relative or absolute. These types of paths and techniques for dealing with them are discussed in the *Working with relative and absolute paths* recipe.

Paths can contain redundancies and extraneous elements. Removal of these elements is called **normalization**. The *Removing redundancies in a path by normalizing the path* recipe examines the techniques available to simplify these types of paths.

Paths can be combined to form a new composite path. This is known as resolving a path and is addressed in the *Combining paths using path resolution* recipe. This technique can be useful for creating new paths, where parts of the path are available from different sources.

When a reference is needed for a file, that path is sometimes relative to the current location or some other location. The *Creating a path between two locations* recipe illustrates the creation of such a path. The process is called **relativizing**.

Not only are there relative and absolute paths, but there are also other ways of representing a path such as with a `java.net.URI` object. When a `Path` object is created, it is not necessary that the actual path exists. For example, the `Path` may be created to create a new filesystem element. The *Converting between path types* recipe looks at methods used to convert between these different types of paths.

Paths are system-dependent. That is, a path on one system such as UNIX is different from one found on a Windows system. Comparing two paths found on the same platform may or may not be the same. This is examined in the *Determining whether two paths are equivalent* recipe.

Creating a Path object

A path to a directory or file is needed to identify that resource. The focus of this recipe is on how to obtain a `Path` object for typical file and directory operations. Paths are used for most of the recipes in this and many of the subsequent chapters that deal with files and directories.

There are several methods that create or return a `Path` object. Here, we will examine those methods used to create a `Path` object and how to use its methods to further our understanding of the path concept as used in Java.

Getting ready

In order to create a `Path` object, we need to use either one of the following:

- The `FileSystem` class' `getPath` method
- The `Paths` class' `get` method

We will use the `getPath` method first. The `get` method is explained in the *There's more* section of this recipe.

How to do it...

1. Create a console application with a `main` method. In the `main` method, add the following code sequence that creates a `Path` object for the file `status.txt`. We will use several `Path` class' methods to examine the path created as follows:

```
Path path = FileSystems.getDefault().getPath("/home/docs/
status.txt");
System.out.println();
System.out.printf("toString: %s\n", path.toString());
System.out.printf("getFileName: %s\n", path.getFileName());
System.out.printf("getRoot: %s\n", path.getRoot());
System.out.printf("getNameCount: %d\n", path.getNameCount());
for(int index=0; index<path.getNameCount(); index++) {
System.out.printf("getName(%d): %s\n", index, path.
getName(index));
}
System.out.printf("subpath(0,2): %s\n", path.subpath(0, 2));
System.out.printf("getParent: %s\n", path.getParent());
System.out.println(path.isAbsolute());
}
```

2. Notice the use of the forward slashes in the `path` string. This approach will work on any platform. However, on Windows you can also use back slashes shown as follows:

```
Path path = FileSystems.getDefault().getPath("\\home\\
docs\\status.txt");
```

3. While either approach will work for a Windows platform, the use of forward slashes is more portable.

4. Execute the program. Your output should appear as follows:

toString: \home\docs\status.txt

getFileName: status.txt

**getRoot: **

getNameCount: 3

getName(0): home

getName(1): docs

getName(2): status.txt

subpath(0,2): home\docs

getParent: \home\docs

false

How it works...

The `Path` object was created using invocation chaining, starting with the `FileSystems` class' `getDefault` method. This returns a `FileSystem` object representing the filesystem available to the JVM. The `FileSystem` object normally refers to the working directory of the current user. Next, the `getPath` method was executed using a string representing the file of interest.

The rest of the code used various methods to display information about the path. As detailed in the introduction of this chapter, we can display information about the parts of the path using methods of the `Path` class. The `toString` method is executed against the path to illustrate what you get by default.

The `getFileName` returned the file name of the `Path` object, and the `getRoot` returned the root. The `getNameCount` method returned the number of intermediate directories plus one for the filename. The for loop listed the elements of the path. In this case, there were two directories and one file giving a count of three. The three elements make up the path.

While a simple for loop was used to display these names, we could have also used the `iterator` method to list these names, as shown in the following code:

```
        Iterator iterator = path.iterator();
    while(iterator.hasNext()) {
            System.out.println(iterator.next());
    }
```

The `Path` object may consist of other paths. Subpaths can be retrieved using the `subpath` method. The method possesses two arguments. The first represents an initial index and the second argument specifies the last index exclusively. In this example, the first argument was set to 0 indicating that the root level directory was to be retrieved. The last index was set to 2, which means only the top two directories were listed.

The `getParent` method in this case also returned the identical path. However, notice that it began with the backslash. This represents the path from the top level element following each element except the last one.

There's more...

There are several issues that bear further consideration:

- ▶ Using the `Paths` class' `get` method
- ▶ The meaning of the parent path

Using the Paths class' get method

The `Paths` class' `get` method can also be used to create a `Path` object. This method uses a variable number of `String` arguments to construct a path. In the following code sequence, a `path` is created starting at the root of the current filesystem:

```
try {
    path = Paths.get("/home", "docs", "users.txt");
    System.out.printf("Absolute path: %s", path.
toAbsolutePath());
}
catch (InvalidPathException ex) {
    System.out.printf("Bad path: [%s] at position %s",
        ex.getInput(), ex.getIndex());
}
```

The output using the `toAbsolutePath` method shows the path constructed. Notice the **E** element. The code was executed on a Windows system where the current drive was the **E** drive. The `toAbsolutePath` method is discussed in the *Working with relative and absolute paths* recipe.

Absolute path: E:\home\docs\users.txt

If we do not use the forward slash in the path's `String`, then the path is created based on the current working directory. Remove the forward slash and execute the program. Your output should be similar to the following where, **currentDirectory**, is replaced with the one in use when the code is executed:

Absolute path: currentDirectory\home\docs\users.txt

A more flexible approach is to use the resolve method as discussed in the *Combining paths using path resolution* recipe.

The conversion of the input arguments to a path is system-dependent. If the characters used in the creation of the path are invalid for the filesystem, then a `java.nio.file.InvalidPathException` is thrown. For example, in most filesystems a null value is an illegal character. To illustrate this, add a back slash O to the `path` string as shown in the following code:

```
path = Paths.get("/home\0", "docs", "users.txt");
```

When executed, the output in part will appear as follows:

Bad path: [/home \docs\users.txt] at position 5

The `InvalidPathException` class' `getInput` method returns the concatenated string used for creating the path. The `getIndex` method returns the position of the offending character, which in this case is the null character.

The meaning of the parent path

The `getParent` method returns the parent path. However, the method does not access the filesystem. This means that for a given `Path` object, there may or may not be a parent.

Consider the following path declaration:

```
path = Paths.get("users.txt");
```

This refers to the `users.txt` file found in the current working directory. The `getNameCount` will return 1, and the `getParent` method will return null. In reality, the file exists in a directory structure and has a root and a parent. Thus, the results of this method may not be useful in some contexts.

The use of this method is roughly equivalent to the following use of the `subpath` method:

```
path = path.subpath(0,path.getNameCount()-1));
```

See also

The `toRealPath` method is discussed in the *Working with relative and absolute paths* recipe and in the *Removing redundancies in a path by normalizing the path* recipe.

Interoperability between java.io.File and java.nio.file.Files

Prior to the introduction of the `java.nio` package the classes and interfaces of the `java.io` package were the only ones available to Java developers for working with files and directories. While most of the capability of the `java.io` package has been supplemented by the newer packages, it is still possible to work with the older classes, in particular the `java.io.File` class. This recipe discusses how this can be accomplished.

Getting ready

To obtain a `Path` object using a `File` class, the following steps need to be followed:

1. Create a `java.io.File` object representing the file of interest
2. Apply the `toPath` method to it to obtain a `Path` object

How to do it...

1. Create a console application. Add the following main method where we create a `File` object and a `Path` object representing the same file. Next, we compare the two objects to determine whether they represent the same file or not:

```java
public static void main(String[] args) {
try {
        Path path =
Paths.get(new URI("file:///C:/home/docs/users.txt"));
        File file = new File("C:\\home\\docs\\users.txt");
        Path toPath = file.toPath();
System.out.println(toPath.equals(path));
}
catch (URISyntaxException e) {
System.out.println("Bad URI");
}
}
```

2. When you execute the application, the output will be true.

How it works...

Two `Path` objects were created. The first `Path` object was declared using the Paths class' `get` method. It created a `Path` object to the `users.txt` file using a `java.net.URI` object. The second `Path` object, `toPath`, was created from a `File` object using the `toPath` method. The Path's `equals` method was used to demonstrate that the paths are equivalent.

> Notice the use of the forward and backward slashes for the strings used to represent the file. The `URI` string uses forward slashes, which is operating system-independent. Whereas, the back slash is used for a Windows path.

See also

The creation of a `Path` object is illustrated in the *Understanding paths* recipe. Also, the creation of a `URI` object is discussed in the *Working with relative and absolute paths* recipe.

Converting a relative path into an absolute path

A path can be expressed either as an absolute path or a relative path. Both are common and are useful in different situations. The `Path` class and related classes support the creation of both absolute and relative paths.

A relative path is useful for specifying the location of a file or directory in relationship to the current directory location. Typically, a single dot or two dots are used to indicate the current directory or next higher level directory respectively. However, the use of a dot is not required when creating a relative path.

An absolute path starts at the root level and lists each directory separated by either forward slashes or backward slashes, depending on the operating system, until the desired directory or file is reached.

In this recipe, we will determine the path separator used for the current system and learn how to convert a relative path to an absolute path. This is useful when handling user input for filenames. Related to absolute and relative paths is the URI representation of a path. We will learn how to use the `Path` class' `toUri` method to return this representation for a given path.

Getting ready

The following methods are frequently used when dealing with absolute and relative paths:

- The `getSeparator` method determines the file separator
- The `subpath` method obtains a part or all parts/elements of a path
- The `toAbsolutePath` method obtains the absolute path for a relative path
- The `toUri` method obtains the URI representation of a path

How to do it...

1. We will address each of the previous methods one at a time. Start by creating a console application using the following `main` method:

```
public static void main(String[] args) {
        String separator  = FileSystems.getDefault().
getSeparator();
System.out.println("The separator is " + separator);
try {
            Path path = Paths.get(new URI("file:///C:/home/docs/
users.txt"));
System.out.println("subpath: " + path.subpath(0, 3));
path = Paths.get("/home", "docs", "users.txt");
System.out.println("Absolute path: " + path.toAbsolutePath());
System.out.println("URI: " + path.toUri());
}
catch (URISyntaxException ex) {
System.out.println("Bad URI");
}
catch (InvalidPathException  ex) {
System.out.println("Bad path: [" + ex.getInput() + "] at position
" + ex.getIndex());
}
}
```

2. Execute the program. On a Windows platform, the output should appear as follows:

**The separator is **

subpath: home\docs\users.txt

Absolute path: E:\home\docs\users.txt

URI: file:///E:/home/docs/users.txt

How it works...

The `getDefault` method returned a `FileSystem` object representing the filesystem currently accessible to the JVM. The `getSeparator` method is executed against this object, returning a backslash character indicating that the code was executed on a Windows machine.

A `Path` object was created for the `users.txt` file and the `subpath` method was executed against it. This method is discussed in more detail in the *Understanding paths* recipe. The `subpath` method always returns a relative path.

Next, a path was created using the `get` method. Since the forward slash was used with the first argument, the path started at the root of the current filesystem. In this example, the path provided is relative.

The URI representation of a path is related to absolute and relative paths. The `Path` class' `toUri` method returns this representation for a given path. A `URI` object is used to represent a resource on the Internet. In this case, it returned a string in the form of a URI scheme for files.

The absolute path can be obtained using the `Path` class' `toAbsolutePath` method. An absolute path contains the root element and all of the intermediate elements for the path. This can be useful when users are requested to enter the name of a file. For example, if the user is asked to supply a filename to save results, the filename can be added to an existing path representing a working directory. The absolute path can then be obtained and used as necessary.

There's more...

Bear in mind that the `toAbsolutePath` method works regardless of whether the path references a valid file or directory. The file used in the previous example does not need to exist. Consider the use of a bogus file as shown in the following code. The assumption is that the file, `bogusfile.txt`, does not exist in the specified directory:

```
Path path = Paths.get(new URI("file:///C:/home/docs/
bogusfile.txt"));
System.out.println("File exists: " + Files.exists(path));

path = Paths.get("/home", "docs", "bogusfile.txt");
System.out.println("File exists: " + Files.exists(path));
```

When the program is executed, the output will appear as follows:

**The separator is **

File exists: false

subpath: home\docs\bogusfile.txt

File exists: false

Absolute path: E:\home\docs\bogusfile.txt

URI: file:///E:/home/docs/bogusfile.txt

If we want to know whether this is a real path or not, we can use the `toRealPath` method as discussed in the _Removing redundancies in a path by normalizing the path_ recipe.

See also

Redundancies in a path can be removed using the `normalize` method as discussed in the _Removing redundancies in a path by normalizing the path_ recipe.

When symbolic links are used for files, then the path may not be the real path for the file. The `Path` class' `toRealPath` method will return the real absolute path for the file. This is demonstrated in the _Removing redundancies in a path by normalizing the path_ recipe.

Removing redundancies by normalizing a path

When the "." or ".." notation is used in defining a path, their use may introduce redundancies. That is, the path described may be simplified by removing or otherwise altering the path. This recipe discusses the use of the `normalize` method to affect this type of conversion. By simplifying a path, it avoids errors and can improve the performance of the application. The `toRealPath` method also performs normalization and is explained in the _There's more ..._ section of this recipe.

Getting ready

The basic steps used for removing redundancies in a path include the following:

- Identifying paths that may contain redundancies
- Using the `normalize` method to remove the redundancies

How to do it...

The directory structure from the introduction is duplicated here for convenience:

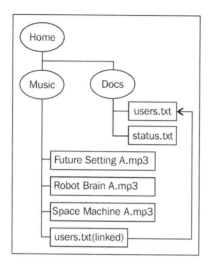

First consider the following paths:

```
/home/docs/../music/ Space Machine A.mp3
/home/./music/ Robot Brain A.mp3
```

These contain redundancies or extraneous parts. In the first example, the path starts at `home` and then goes down a directory level to `docs` directory. The `..` notation then leads back up to the `home` directory. This then proceeds down the `music` directory and to the `mp3` file. The `docs/..` element is extraneous.

In the second example, the path starts at `home` and then encounters a single period. This represents the current directory, that is, the `home` directory. Next, the path goes down the `music` directory and then encounters the `mp3` file. The `/.` is redundant and is not needed.

1. Create a new console application and add the following `main` method:

```
public static void main(String[] args) {
            Path path = Paths.get("/home/docs/../music/Space
Machine A.mp3");
System.out.println("Absolute path: " + path.toAbsolutePath());
System.out.println("URI: " + path.toUri());
System.out.println("Normalized Path: " + path.normalize());
System.out.println("Normalized URI: " + path.normalize().toUri());
System.out.println();
```

```
path = Paths.get("/home/./music/ Robot Brain A.mp3");
System.out.println("Absolute path: " + path.toAbsolutePath());
System.out.println("URI: " + path.toUri());
System.out.println("Normalized Path: " + path.normalize());
System.out.println("Normalized URI: " + path.normalize().toUri());
}
```

2. Execute the application. You should get the following output, though the root directory may differ depending on the configuration of your system:

Absolute path: E:\home\docs\..\music\Space Machine A.mp3

URI: file:///E:/home/docs/../music/Space%20Machine%20A.mp3

Normalized Path: \home\music\Space Machine A.mp3

Normalized URI: file:///E:/home/music/Space%20Machine%20A.mp3

Absolute path: E:\home\.\music\ Robot Brain A.mp3

URI: file:///E:/home/./music/%20Robot%20Brain%20A.mp3

Normalized Path: \home\music\ Robot Brain A.mp3

Normalized URI: file:///E:/home/music/%20Robot%20Brain%20A.mp3

How it works...

`Paths` class' `get` method was used to create two paths using the redundant extraneous paths discussed previously. The code that follows the `get` methods displayed the absolute path and the URI equivalent to illustrate the actual path created. Next, the `normalize` method was used and was then chained with the `toUri` method to further illustrate the normalization process. Notice that the redundancy and extraneous path elements are gone. The `toAbsolutePath` and `toUri` methods are discussed in the *Working with relative and absolute paths* recipe.

The `normalize` method does not check to see if the files or path are valid. The method simply performs a syntactic operation against the path. If a symbolic link was part of the original path, then the normalized path may no longer be valid. Symbolic links are discussed in the *Managing symbolic links* recipe.

There's more...

The `Path` class' `toRealPath` will return a path representing the actual path to the file. It does check to see if the path is valid and will return a `java.nio.file.NoSuchFileException` if the file does not exist.

Modify the previous example to use the `toRealPath` method with a non-existent file as shown in the following code:

```
try

            Path path = Paths.get("/home/docs/../music/
NonExistentFile.mp3");
    System.out.println("Absolute path: " + path.toAbsolutePath());
    System.out.println("Real path: " + path.toRealPath());

    }
    catch (IOException ex) {
    System.out.println("The file does not exist!");
    }
```

Execute the application. The result should contain the following output:

Absolute path: \\Richard-pc\e\home\docs\..\music\NonExistentFile.mp3

The file does not exist!

The `toRealPath` method normalizes the path. It also resolves any symbolic links, though there were none in this example.

See also

The creation of a `Path` object is discussed in the *Understanding paths* recipe. Symbolic links are discussed in the *Managing symbolic links* recipe.

Combining paths using path resolution

The `resolve` method is used to combine two paths, where one contains a root element and the other is a partial path. This is useful when creating paths that can vary, such as those used in the installation of an application. For example, there may be a default directory where an application is installed. However, the user may be able to select a different directory or drive. Using the `resolve` method to create a path allows the application to be configured independent of the actual installation directory.

Getting ready

The use of the `resolve` method involves two basic steps:

- Create a `Path` object that uses a root element
- Execute the `resolve` method against this path with a second partial path

A partial path is one where only a part of the full path is provided and does not contain a root element.

How to do it...

1. Create a new application. Add the following `main` method to it:

```
public static void main(String[] args) {
        Path rootPath = Paths.get("/home/docs");
        Path partialPath = Paths.get("users.txt");
        Path resolvedPath = rootPath.resolve(partialPath);
System.out.println("rootPath: " + rootPath);
System.out.println("partialPath: " + partialPath);
System.out.println("resolvedPath: " + resolvedPath);
System.out.println("Resolved absolute path: " + resolvedPath.
toAbsolutePath());
}
```

2. Execute the code. You should get the following output:

    rootPath: \home\docs

    partialPath: users.txt

    resolvedPath: \home\docs\users.txt

    Resolved absolute path: E:\home\docs\users.txt

How it works...

The following three paths were created:

- ▶ `\home\docs`: This is the root path
- ▶ `users.txt`: This is the partial path
- ▶ `\home\docs\users.txt`: This is the resulting resolved path

The resolved path was created by using the `partialPath` variable as an argument to the `resolve` method executed against the `rootPath` variable. These paths along with the absolute path of the `resolvedPath` were then displayed. The absolute path included the root directory, though this may differ on your system.

There's more...

The `resolve` methods are overloaded, one using a `String` argument and the second using a `Path` argument. The `resolve` method can also be misused. In addition, there is also an `overloadedresolveSibling` method that works similar to the `resolve` method except it removes the last element of the root path. These issues are addressed here.

Using a String argument with the resolve method

The `resolve` method is overloaded with one that accepts a `String` argument. The following statement will achieve the same results as in the previous example:

```
Path resolvedPath = rootPath.resolve("users.txt");
```

The path separator can also be used as follows:

```
Path resolvedPath = rootPath.resolve("backup/users.txt");
```

Using these statements with the earlier code results in the following output:

rootPath: \home\docs

partialPath: users.txt

resolvedPath: \home\docs\backup\users.txt

Resolved absolute path: E:\home\docs\backup\users.txt

Notice that the resolved path is not necessarily a valid path as the backup directory may or may not exist. The `toRealPath` method in the *Removing redundancies in a path by normalizing the path* recipe can be used to determine if it is valid or not.

Improper use of the resolve method

There are three uses of the `resolve` method that can result in unexpected behavior:

- Incorrect order of the root and partial paths
- Using a partial path twice
- Using the root path twice

If we reverse the order in which the `resolve` method is used, that is apply the root path to the partial path, only the root path is returned. This is illustrated with the following code:

```
Path resolvedPath = partialPath.resolve(rootPath);
```

When the code is executed, we get the following results:

rootPath: \home\docs

partialPath: users.txt

resolvedPath: \home\docs

Resolved absolute path: E:\home\docs

Only the root path is returned here. The partial path is not appended to the root path. Using the partial path twice as shown in the following code:

```
Path resolvedPath = partialPath.resolve(partialPath);
```

will result in the following output:

rootPath: \home\docs

partialPath: users.txt

resolvedPath: users.txt\users.txt

Resolved absolute path: currentWorkingDIrectory\users.txt\users.txt

Notice the resolved path is incorrect and that the absolute path uses the current working directory. Using the root path twice as shown below:

```
Path resolvedPath = rootPath.resolve(rootPath);
```

results in the same output as when using the paths in the reverse order:

rootPath: \home\docs

partialPath: users.txt

resolvedPath: \home\docs

Resolved absolute path: E:\home\docs

Whenever an absolute path is used as the argument of the `resolve` method, that absolute path is returned. If an empty path is used as an argument to the method, the root path is returned.

Using the resolveSibling

The `resolveSibling` method is overloaded taking either a `String` or a `Path` object. With the `resolve` method, the partial path is appended to the end of the root path. The `resolveSibling` method differs from the `resolve` method in that the last element of the root path is removed before the partial path is appended. Consider the following code sequence:

```
Path rootPath = Paths.get("/home/music/");

resolvedPath = rootPath.resolve("tmp/Robot Brain A.mp3");
System.out.println("rootPath: " + rootPath);
System.out.println("resolvedPath: " + resolvedPath);
System.out.println();

resolvedPath = rootPath.resolveSibling("tmp/Robot Brain A.mp3");
System.out.println("rootPath: " + rootPath);
System.out.println("resolvedPath: " + resolvedPath);
```

When executed we get the following output:

rootPath: \home\music

resolvedPath: \home\music\tmp\Robot Brain A.mp3

rootPath: \home\music

resolvedPath: \home\tmp\Robot Brain A.mp3

Notice the resolved path differs in the presence of the directory `music`. When the `resolve` method is used, the directory is present. It is absent when the `resolveSibling` method is used. If there is no parent path, or the argument of the method is an absolute path, then the argument passed to the method is returned. If the argument is empty then the parent is returned.

See also

The creation of a `Path` object is discussed in the *Understanding paths* recipe. Also, the `toRealPath` method is explained in the *Removing redundancies in a path by normalizing the path* recipe.

Creating a path between two locations

To relativize a path means to create a path based on two other paths such that the new path represents a way of navigating from one of the original paths to the other. This technique finds a relative path from one location to another. For example, the first path could represent an application default directory. The second path could represent a target directory. A relative path created from these directories could facilitate operations against the target.

Getting ready

To use the `relativize` method to create a new path from one path to another, we need to do the following:

1. Create a `Path` object that represents the first path.

2. Create a `Path` object that represents the second path.

3. Apply the `relativize` method against the first path using the second path as its argument.

How to do it...

1. Create a new console application and use the following `main` method. This method creates two `Path` objects, and shows the relative path between them as follows:

```
public static void main(String[] args) {
        Path firstPath;
        Path secondPath;
firstPath = Paths.get("music/Future Setting A.mp3");
secondPath = Paths.get("docs");
System.out.println("From firstPath to secondPath: " + firstPath.
relativize(secondPath));
System.out.println("From secondPath to firstPath: " + secondPath.
relativize(firstPath));
System.out.println();

firstPath = Paths.get("music/Future Setting A.mp3");
secondPath = Paths.get("music");
System.out.println("From firstPath to secondPath: " + firstPath.
relativize(secondPath));
System.out.println("From secondPath to firstPath: " + secondPath.
relativize(firstPath));
System.out.println();

firstPath = Paths.get("music/Future Setting A.mp3");
```

```
secondPath = Paths.get("docs/users.txt");
System.out.println("From firstPath to secondPath: " + firstPath.
relativize(secondPath));
System.out.println("From secondPath to firstPath: " + secondPath.
relativize(firstPath));
System.out.println();
}
```

2. Execute the application. Your results should be similar to the following:

From firstPath to secondPath: ..\..\docs

From secondPath to firstPath: ..\music\Future Setting A.mp3

From firstPath to secondPath: ..

From secondPath to firstPath: Future Setting A.mp3

From firstPath to secondPath: ..\..\docs\users.txt

From secondPath to firstPath: ..\..\music\Future Setting A.mp3

How it works...

In the first example, a relative path was created from the `Future Setting A.mp3` file to the `docs` directory. The `music` and `docs` directories are assumed to be siblings. The `. .` notation means to move up one directory. This chapter's introduction illustrated the assumed directory structure for this example.

The second example demonstrates creating a path from within the same directory. The path from `firstpath` to `secondPath` is actually a potential error. Depending on how this is used, we could end up in the directory above the `music` directory since the path returned is `. .` meaning to move up one directory level. The third example is similar to the first example except both of the paths contain file names.

The relative path created by this method may not be a valid path. This is illustrated by using the potentially non-existent `tmp` directory, shown as follows:

```
firstPath = Paths.get("music/Future Setting A.mp3");
secondPath = Paths.get("docs/tmp/users.txt");
System.out.println("From firstPath to secondPath: " + firstPath.
relativize(secondPath));
System.out.println("From secondPath to firstPath: " + secondPath.
relativize(firstPath));
```

The output should appear as follows:

From firstPath to secondPath: ..\..\docs\tmp\users.txt

From secondPath to firstPath: ..\..\..\music\Future Setting A.mp3

There's more...

There are three other cases that we need to consider:

- Both paths are equal
- One path contains a root
- Both paths contain a root

Both paths are equal

When both paths are equal, the `relativize` method will return an empty path as illustrated with the following code sequence:

```
firstPath = Paths.get("music/Future Setting A.mp3");
secondPath = Paths.get("music/Future Setting A.mp3");
System.out.println("From firstPath to secondPath: " + firstPath.
relativize(secondPath));
System.out.println("From secondPath to firstPath: " + secondPath.
relativize(firstPath));
System.out.println();
```

The output is as follows:

From firstPath to secondPath:

From secondPath to firstPath:

While this is not necessarily an error, note that it does not return a single dot which is frequently used to represent the current directory.

One path contains a root

If only one of the paths contains a root element, then it may not be possible to construct a relative path. Whether it is possible or not is system-dependent. In the following example, the first path contains the root element `c`:

```
firstPath = Paths.get("c:/music/Future Setting A.mp3");
secondPath = Paths.get("docs/users.txt");
System.out.println("From firstPath to secondPath: " + firstPath.
relativize(secondPath));
System.out.println("From secondPath to firstPath: " + secondPath.
relativize(firstPath));
System.out.println();
```

When this code sequence is executed on Windows 7, we get the following output:

Exception in thread "main" java.lang.IllegalArgumentException: 'other' is different type of Path

From firstPath to secondPath: ..

From secondPath to firstPath: Future Setting A.mp3

atsun.nio.fs.WindowsPath.relativize(WindowsPath.java:388)

atsun.nio.fs.WindowsPath.relativize(WindowsPath.java:44)

atpackt.RelativizePathExample.main(RelativizePathExample.java:25)

Java Result: 1

Notice the reference to **other** in the output. This refers to the argument of the `relativize` method.

Both paths contain a root

The ability of the `relativize` method to create a relative path when both paths contain a root element is also system-dependent. This situation is illustrated in the following example:

```
firstPath = Paths.get("c:/music/Future Setting A.mp3");
secondPath = Paths.get("c:/docs/users.txt");
System.out.println("From firstPath to secondPath: " + firstPath.
relativize(secondPath));
System.out.println("From secondPath to firstPath: " + secondPath.
relativize(firstPath));
System.out.println();
```

When executed on Windows 7, we get the following output:

From firstPath to secondPath: ..\..\docs\users.txt

From secondPath to firstPath: ..\..\music\Future Setting A.mp3

See also

The creation of a `Path` object is discussed in the *Understanding paths* recipe. Symbolic links results are system-dependent and are discussed in more depth in the *Managing symbolic links* recipe.

Converting between path types

The `Path` interface represents a path within a filesystem. This path may or may not be a valid path. There are times when we may want to use an alternative representation of a path. For example, a file can be loaded into most browsers using a URI for the file. The `toUri` method provides this representation of a path. In this recipe we will also see how to obtain an absolute path and a real path for a `Path` object.

Getting ready

There are three methods that provide alternative path representations:

- ▶ The `toUri` method returns the URI representation
- ▶ The `toAbsolutePath` method returns the absolute path
- ▶ The `toRealPath` method returns the real path

How to do it...

1. Create a new console application. Within the `main` method, we will use each of the previous methods. Add the following `main` method to the application:

```
public static void main(String[] args) {
try {
            Path path;
path = Paths.get("users.txt");
System.out.println("URI path: " + path.toUri());
System.out.println("Absolute path: " + path.toAbsolutePath());
System.out.println("Real path: " + path.toRealPath(LinkOption.
NOFOLLOW_LINKS));
}
catch (IOException ex) {
Logger.getLogger(ConvertingPathsExample.class.getName()).
log(Level.SEVERE, null, ex);
}
}
```

2. If not already present, add a `users.txt` file in the working directory of your application. Execute the program. Your output should be similar to the following, except the **...** in this output should reflect the location of the `users.txt` file:

URI path: file:///.../ConvertingPathsExample/users.txt

Absolute path...\ConvertingPathsExample\users.txt

Real path: ...\ConvertingPathsExample\users.txt

How it works...

A `users.txt` file was added to the working directory of the Java application. This file should contain a list of usernames. The `get` method returned a `Path` object representing this file. Each of the three methods were then executed against this object.

The `toUri` and `toAbsolutePath` methods returned paths as expected for that method type. The path returned is dependent on the application's working directory. The `toRealPath` method should have returned the same output as the `toAbsolutePath` method. This is to be expected, since the `users.txt` file was not created as a symbolic link. Had this been a symbolic link, then a different path representing the actual path to the file would have been displayed.

There's more...

Since it is possible that a `Path` object may not actually represent a file, the use of the `toRealPath` method may throw a `java.nio.file.NoSuchFileException` if the file does not exist. Use an invalid file name, shown as follows:

```
path = Paths.get("invalidFileName.txt");
```

The output should appear as follows:

URI path: file:///.../ConvertingPathsExample/invalidFileName.txt

Absolute path: ...\ConvertingPathsExample\invalidFileName.txt

Sep 11, 2011 6:40:40 PM packt.ConvertingPathsExample main

SEVERE: null

java.nio.file.NoSuchFileException: ...\ConvertingPathsExample\invalidFileName.txt

Notice that the `toUri` and `toAbsolutePath` work regardless of whether the specified file exists or not. In situations where we want to use these methods, we can test whether the file exists or not using the `Files` class' `exists` method. The previous code sequence has been modified to use the `exists` method shown as follows:

```
if(Files.exists(path)) {
        System.out.println("Real path: " + path.toRealPath(LinkOption.
NOFOLLOW_LINKS));
}
else {
        System.out.println("The file does not exist");
}
```

The `java.nio.fil.LinkOption` enumeration was added in Java 7. It is used to specify whether symbolic links should be followed or not.

When executed, the output should appear as follows:

URI path: file:///.../ConvertingPathsExample/invalidFileName.txt

Absolute path: ...\ConvertingPathsExample\invalidFileName.txt

The file does not exist

Determining whether two paths are equivalent

At times it may be necessary to compare paths. The `Path` class allows you to test the paths for equality using the `equals` method. You can also use the `compareTo` method to compare two paths lexicographically using an implementation of the `Comparable` interface. Finally, the `isSameFile` method can be used to determine if two `Path` objects will locate the same file.

Getting ready

In order to compare two paths, you must:

1. Create a `Path` object that represents the first path.
2. Create a `Path` object that represents the second path.
3. Apply either the `equals`, `compareTo`, or `isSameFile` methods to the paths as needed.

How to do it...

1. Create a new console application and add a `main` method. Declare three `Path` object variables such as `path1`, `path2` and `path3`. Set the first two to the same file and the third one to a different path. All the three files must exist. Follow this with calls to three comparison methods:

```
public class ComparingPathsExample {

    public static void main(String[] args) {
        Path path1 = null;
        Path path2 = null;
        Path path3 = null;

        path1 = Paths.get("/home/docs/users.txt");
        path2 = Paths.get("/home/docs/users.txt");
        path3 = Paths.get("/home/music/Future Setting A.mp3");

        testEquals(path1, path2);
        testEquals(path1, path3);

        testCompareTo(path1, path2);
        testCompareTo(path1, path3);

        testSameFile(path1, path2);
        testSameFile(path1, path3);
    }
```

2. Add three static methods as follows:

```
    private static void testEquals(Path path1, Path path2) {
        if (path1.equals(path2)) {
            System.out.printf("%s and %s are equal\n",
                    path1, path2);
    }
    else {
            System.out.printf("%s and %s are NOT equal\n",
                    path1, path2);
    }
    }

    private static void testCompareTo(Path path1, Path path2) {
        if (path1.compareTo(path2) == 0) {
            System.out.printf("%s and %s are identical\n",
                    path1, path2);
    }
```

```
    else {
                System.out.printf("%s and %s are NOT identical\n",
                        path1, path2);
    }
    }

        private static void testSameFile(Path path1, Path path2) {
            try {
                if (Files.isSameFile(path1, path2)) {
                    System.out.printf("%s and %s are the same file\n",
                            path1, path2);
    }
    else {
                System.out.printf("%s and %s are NOT the same
file\n",
                        path1, path2);
    }
    }
    catch (IOException e) {
                e.printStackTrace();
    }
    }
```

3. Execute the application. Your output should be similar to the following:

   \home\docs\users.txt and \home\docs\users.txt are equal

   \home\docs\users.txt and \home\music\Future Setting A.mp3 are **NOT** equal

   \home\docs\users.txt and \home\docs\users.txt are identical

   \home\docs\users.txt and \home\music\Future Setting A.mp3 are **NOT** identical

   \home\docs\users.txt and \home\docs\users.txt are the same file

   \home\docs\users.txt and \home\music\Future Setting A.mp3 are **NOT** the same file

How it works...

In the testEquals method, we determined whether the path objects were considered to be equal. The equals method will return true if they are equal. However, the definition of equality is system-dependent. Some filesystems will use the case, among other factors, to determine if the paths are equal.

The testCompareTo method used the compareTo method to compare the paths alphabetically. If the paths are identical, the method returns a zero. The method returns an integer less than zero if the path is less than the argument and a value greater than zero if the path follows the argument lexicographically.

The `testSameFile` method determines whether the paths locate the same file. The `Path` objects are first tested to see if they are the same object. If they are, the method will return true. If the `Path` objects are not equal, the method then determines whether the paths locate the same file. The method will return false if the `Path` objects were generated by different filesystem providers. A try block was used since the method may throw an `IOException`.

There's more...

The `equals` and `compareTo` methods will not successfully compare paths from different filesystems. However, as long as the files are on the same filesystem, the files in question do not have to exist and the filesystem is not accessed. The `isSameFile` method may require access to the files if the path objects being tested are not found to be equal. In this case, the files must exist otherwise the method will return false.

See also

The `Files` class' `exists` and `notExists` methods can be used to determine whether a file or directory exists or not. This is covered in the *Getting file and directory information* recipe in Chapter 3, *Obtaining File and Directory Information*.

Managing symbolic links

Symbolic links are used to create a reference to a file that actually exists in a different directory. In the introduction, a file hierarchy was detailed that listed the file, `users.txt`, twice; once in the `docs` directory and a second time in the `music` directory. The actual file is located in the `docs` directory. The `users.txt` file in the `music` directory is a symbolic link to the real file. To a user they appear to be different files. In reality, they are the same. Modification of either file results in the real file being changed.

From a programmer's perspective, we are often interested in knowing which files are symbolic links and which are not. In this recipe we will discuss the methods available in Java 7 to work with symbolic links. It is important to understand how a method behaves when used with a symbolic link.

Getting ready

While several methods may behave differently based on whether a `Path` object represents a symbolic link or not, in this chapter only the `toRealPath`, `exists`, and `notExists` methods take an optional `LinkOption` enumeration argument. This enumeration has only a single element: `NOFOLLOW_LINKS`. If the argument is not used then the methods default to following symbolic links.

How to do it...

1. Create a new console application. Use the following `main` method where we create several `Path` objects representing both the real and the symbolic `users.txt` file. The behavior of several of this chapter's `Path`-related methods is illustrated.

```
public static void main(String[] args) {
    Path path1 = null;
    Path path2 = null;

    path1 = Paths.get("/home/docs/users.txt");
    path2 = Paths.get("/home/music/users.txt");

    System.out.println(Files.isSymbolicLink(path1));
    System.out.println(Files.isSymbolicLink(path2));

    try {
        Path path = Paths.get("C:/home/./music/users.txt");
        System.out.println("Normalized: " + path.normalize());
        System.out.println("Absolute path: " + path.
toAbsolutePath());
        System.out.println("URI: " + path.toUri());
        System.out.println("toRealPath (Do not follow links):
" + path.toRealPath(LinkOption.NOFOLLOW_LINKS));
        System.out.println("toRealPath: " + path.
toRealPath());

        Path firstPath = Paths.get("/home/music/users.txt");
        Path secondPath = Paths.get("/docs/status.txt");
        System.out.println("From firstPath to secondPath: " +
firstPath.relativize(secondPath));
        System.out.println("From secondPath to firstPath: " +
secondPath.relativize(firstPath));
        System.out.println("exists (Do not follow links): " +
Files.exists(firstPath, LinkOption.NOFOLLOW_LINKS));
        System.out.println("exists: " + Files.
exists(firstPath));
        System.out.println("notExists (Do not follow links): "
+ Files.notExists(firstPath, LinkOption.NOFOLLOW_LINKS));
        System.out.println("notExists: " + Files.
notExists(firstPath));

    }
    catch (IOException ex) {
            Logger.getLogger(SymbolicLinkExample.class.getName()).
log(Level.SEVERE, null, ex);
```

```
        }
        catch (InvalidPathException ex) {
                System.out.println("Bad path: [" + ex.getInput() + "]
        at position " + ex.getIndex());
        }
        }
```

2. The behavior of these methods can differ based on the underlying operating system. When the code is executed on a Windows platform, we get the following output:

   false

   true

   Normalized: C:\home\music\users.txt

   Absolute path: C:\home\.\music\users.txt

   URI: file:///C:/home/./music/users.txt

   toRealPath (Do not follow links): C:\home\music\users.txt

   toRealPath: C:\home\docs\users.txt

   From firstPath to secondPath: ..\..\..\docs\status.txt

   From secondPath to firstPath: ..\..\home\music\users.txt

   exists (Do not follow links): true

   exists: true

   notExists (Do not follow links): false

   notExists: false

How it works...

The `path1` and `path2` objects were created which referenced the real file and the symbolic link respectively. The `Files` class' `isSymbolicLink` method was executed against these objects indicating which path referenced the real file.

The `Path` object was created using an extraneous dot notation. The result of the `normalize` method executed against the symbolic link returns a normalized path to the symbolic link. The use of the `toAbsolutePath` and `toUri` methods results in a path to the symbolic link and not the real file.

The `toRealPath` method possesses an optional `LinkOption` argument. We used this to obtain a path to the real file. This method is useful when you need the real path, which is often not returned by the other methods executed against a symbolic link.

The `firstPath` and `secondPath` objects were used to explore how the `relativize` method works with symbolic links. In these examples, the symbolic links were used. The last set of examples used the `exists` and `notExists` methods. The use of symbolic links did not affect the results of these methods.

See also

The use of symbolic files as they affect other filesystem methods is discussed in subsequent chapters.

3
Obtaining File and Directory Information

In this chapter, we will cover the following:

- ▸ Determining the file content type
- ▸ Obtaining a single attribute at a time using the getAttribute method
- ▸ Obtaining a map of file attributes
- ▸ Getting file and directory information
- ▸ Determining operating system support for attribute views
- ▸ Maintaining basic file attributes using the BasicFileAttributeView
- ▸ Maintaining POSIX file attributes using the PosixFileAttributeView
- ▸ Maintaining FAT table attributes using the DosFileAttributeView
- ▸ Maintaining file ownership attributes using the FileOwnerAttributeView
- ▸ Maintaining a file's ACL using the AclFileAttributeView
- ▸ Maintaining user-defined file attributes using the UserDefinedFileAttributeView

Introduction

Many applications need access to file and directory information. This information includes such attributes as whether the file can be executed or not, the size of the file, the owner of the file, and even its content type. In this chapter, we examine the various techniques available for obtaining information regarding a file or directory. We have organized the recipes according to the type of access desired.

There are five general approaches to obtaining file and directory information using the `java.nio.file.Files` class that are as follows:

- Obtaining a single attribute at a time using the `Files` class' specific methods, such as the `isDirectory` method. This is detailed in the *Getting file and directory information* recipe.

- Obtaining a single attribute at a time using the `Files` class' `getAttribute` method. This is detailed in the *Obtaining a single attribute at a time using the getAttribute method* recipe.

- Returning a map of attributes using the `readAttributes` method using a `String` to specify which attributes to return. This is explained in the *Obtaining a map of file attributes* recipe.

- Using the `readAttributes` method with a `BasicFileAttributes` derived class to return an attribute class for that set of attributes. This is detailed in the *Maintaining basic file attributes using the BasicFileAttributeView* recipe.

- Using the `getFileAttributes` method to return a view that provides access to a specific set of attributes. This is also detailed in the *Using the BasicFileAttributeView method to maintain basic file attributes* recipe. It is found in the *There's More...* section of the recipe.

Dynamic access to attributes is supported through several methods and allows the developer to specify an attribute using a `String`. The `Files` class' `getAttribute` method typifies this approach.

Java 7 introduces a number of interfaces that are based on a file view. A view is simply a way of organizing information about a file or directory. For example, the `AclFileAttributeView` provides methods related to the file's **Access Control List** (**ACL**). The `FileAttributeView` interface is the base interface for other interfaces that provide specific types of file information. Sub-interfaces found in the `java.nio.file.attribute` package include the following:

- `AclFileAttributeView`: This is used to maintain the file's ACL and ownership attributes

- `BasicFileAttributeView`: This is used to access basic information about a file and to set time-related attributes

- `DosFileAttributeView`: This is designed to be used with the legacy **Disk Operating System** (**DOS**) file attributes

- `FileOwnerAttributeView`: This is used to maintain the ownership of a file

- `PosixFileAttributeView`: This supports **Portable Operating System Interface** (**POSIX**) attributes

- `UserDefinedFileAttributeView`: This supports user-defined attributes for a file

The relationships between the views are shown as follows:

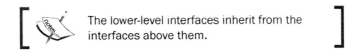

The lower-level interfaces inherit from the interfaces above them.

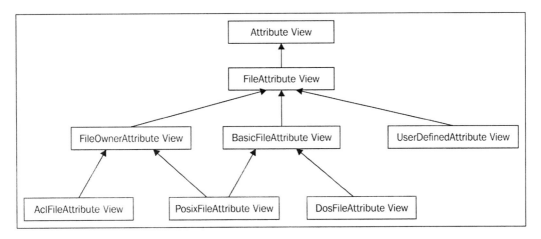

The `readAttributes` method's second parameter specifies the type of attributes to be returned. Three attribute interfaces are supported and their relationship is illustrated in the following figure. These interfaces provide a means of accessing their corresponding view interfaces:

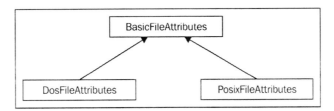

There is a recipe devoted to each of these views. The `FileStoreAttributeView` is not discussed here, but is covered in the *Getting FileStore information* recipe found in *Chapter 4, Managing Files and Directories*.

Files and the directory structure used for examples in this chapter are described in the introduction to *Chapter 2, Locating Files and Directories Using Paths*.

Determining the file content type

The type of a file can often be derived from its extension. However this can be misleading, and files with the same extension may contain different types of data. The `Files` class' `probeContentType` method is used to determine the content type of a file, if possible. This is useful when the application needs some indication of what is in a file in order to process it.

Getting ready

In order to determine the content type, the following steps need to be completed:

1. Obtain a `Path` object that represents the file.
2. Use the `Path` object as the argument to the `probeContentType` method.
3. Use the results to process the file.

How to do it...

1. Create a new console application. Add three different types of files to the /home/ docs directory. Use the following for the `main` method. While you may use any files that you choose, this example uses a text file, a Word document, and an executable file as follows:

   ```java
   public static void main(String[] args) throws Exception {
       displayContentType("/home/docs/users.txt");
       displayContentType("/home/docs/Chapter 2.doc");
       displayContentType("/home/docs/java.exe");
   }

   static void displayContentType(String pathText) throws
   Exception {
       Path path = Paths.get(pathText);
       String type = Files.probeContentType(path);
       System.out.println(type);
   }
   ```

2. Execute the application. Your output should appear as follows. The type returned is dependent on the actual files you used:

   text/plain

   application/msword

   application/x-msdownload

How it works...

A `java.nio.file.Path` variable was created and assigned to each of the three different files. The `Files` class' `probeContentPath` method was executed for each of these files. The result returned was a `String`, which was displayed for illustration purposes. The `probeContentType` method throws a `java.io.IOException` and we handle this by having the `displayConentType` method and the `main` method throw a base class exception. The `probeContentPath` method may also throw a `java.lang.SecurityException`, but you are not required to handle it.

In the files used for this example, the first file was a text file. The returned type was **text/plain**. The other two were a Word document and the executable `java.exe` file. The return types were **application/msword** and **application/x-msdownload** respectively.

There's more...

The result of the method is a `String` as defined by the **Multipurpose Internet Mail Extension (MIME): RFC 2045: Multipurpose Internet Mail Extensions (MIME) Part One: Format of Internet Message Bodies**. This permits the `String` to be parsed using the RFC 2045 grammar specifications. If the content type is not recognized, then null is returned.

A MIME type is composed of a type and a subtype with one or more optional parameters. The type is separated from the subtype using a forward slash. In the previous output, the text document type was text and its subtype was plain. The other two types were both of the type application, but had different subtypes. Subtypes that begin with x- are non-standard.

The implementation of the `probeContentType` method is system-dependent. The method will use a `java.nio.file.spi.FileTypeDetector` implementation to determine the content type. It may examine the filename or possibly access file attributes to determine the file content type. Most operating systems will maintain a list of file detectors. A detector from this list is loaded and used to determine the file type. The `FileTypeDetector` class is not extended, and it is not currently possible to determine which file detectors are available.

Obtaining a single attribute at a time using the getAttribute method

If you are interested in getting a single file attribute, and you know the name of the attribute, then the `Files` class' `getAttribute` method is simple and easy to use. It will return information about the file based upon a `String` representing the attribute. The first part of this recipe illustrates a simple use of the `getAttribute` method. Other available attributes are listed in the *There's More...* section of this recipe.

Getting ready

To obtain a single file attribute value:

1. Create a `Path` object representing the file of interest.
2. Use this object as the first argument of the `getAttribute` method.
3. Use a `String` containing the name of the attribute as the method's second argument.

How to do it...

1. Create a new console application and use the following `main` method. In this method we determine the size of the file as follows:

    ```
    public static void main(String[] args) {
        try {
            Path path = FileSystems.getDefault().getPath("/home/
    docs/users.txt");
            System.out.println(Files.getAttribute(path, "size"));
    }
    catch (IOException ex) {
            System.out.println("IOException");
    }
    }
    ```

2. The output will be as follows, and will depend upon the actual size of the file used:

    30

How it works...

A `Path` was created representing the `users.txt` file. This path was then used as the first argument of the `Files` class' `getAttribute` method. When the code was executed the size of the file was displayed.

There's more...

The `Files` class' `getAttribute` method possesses the following three arguments:

‣ A `Path` object representing the file
‣ A `String` containing the name of the attribute
‣ An optional `LinkOption` to use when dealing with symbolic files

The following table lists the valid attribute names that can be used with this method:

Attribute Name	Data Type
lastModifiedTime	FileTime
lastAccessTime	FileTime
creationTime	FileTime
size	long
isRegularFile	Boolean
isDirectory	Boolean
isSymbolicLink	Boolean
isOther	Boolean
fileKey	Object

If an invalid name is used then a runtime error occurs. This is the primary weakness of this approach. For example, if the name is misspelled, we will get a runtime error. This approach is shown as follows, where the attribute specified has an extra s at the end of the attribute String:

```
System.out.println(Files.getAttribute(path, "sizes"));
```

When the application is executed, you should get results similar to the following:

Exception in thread "main" java.lang.IllegalArgumentException: 'sizes' not recognized

   at sun.nio.fs.AbstractBasicFileAttributeView$AttributesBuilder.<init>(AbstractBasicFile AttributeView.java:102)

   at sun.nio.fs.AbstractBasicFileAttributeView$AttributesBuilder.create(AbstractBasicFile AttributeView.java:112)

   at sun.nio.fs.AbstractBasicFileAttributeView.readAttributes(AbstractBasicFileAttributeV iew.java:166)

   at sun.nio.fs.AbstractFileSystemProvider.readAttributes(AbstractFileSystemProvider. java:92)

   at java.nio.file.Files.readAttributes(Files.java:1896)

   at java.nio.file.Files.getAttribute(Files.java:1801)

   at packt.SingleAttributeExample.main(SingleAttributeExample.java:15)

Java Result: 1

A list of file attributes can be obtained as described in the *Obtaining a map of file attributes* recipe. This can be used to avoid using an invalid name.

Obtaining a map of file attributes

An alternative way of accessing file attributes is to use the `Files` class' `readAttributes` method. There are two overloaded versions of this method, and they differ in their second argument and their return data types. In this recipe, we will explore the version that returns a `java.util.Map` object as it allows more flexibility in what attributes it can return. The second version of the method is discussed in a series of recipes, each devoted to a specific class of attributes.

Getting ready

To obtain a list of attributes in the form of a `Map` object, the following steps need to be done:

1. Create a `Path` object representing a file.
2. Apply the static `readAttributes` method against the `Files` class.
3. Specify the value of its arguments:

   - The `Path` object representing the file of interest
   - A `String` argument representing the attributes to be returned
   - An optional third argument specifying whether symbolic links should be followed or not

How to do it...

1. Create a new console application. Use the following `main` method:

```
public static void main(String[] args) throws Exception {
        Path path = Paths.getPath("/home/docs/users.txt");
        try {
            Map<String, Object> attrsMap = Files.
readAttributes(path, "*");
            Set<String> keys = attrsMap.keySet();

            for(String attribute : keys) {
                out.println(attribute + ": "
                        + Files.getAttribute(path, attribute));
}
}
}
```

2. Execute the application. Your output should appear similar to the following:

lastModifiedTime: 2011-09-06T01:26:56.501665Z

fileKey: null

isDirectory: false

lastAccessTime: 2011-09-06T21:14:11.214057Z

isOther: false

isSymbolicLink: false

isRegularFile: true

creationTime: 2011-09-06T21:14:11.214057Z

size: 30

How it works...

The example used the `users.txt` file in the `docs` directory. A `Map` object with a key type of `String` and a value type of `Object` was declared and then assigned a value from the `readAttributes` method. A `java.util.Set` object was created using the `Map` interface's `keySet` method. This gives us access to both the keys and the values of the `Map`. In the for each loop, each member of the set was used as an argument to the `getAttribute` method. This corresponding attribute and its value were displayed for the file. The `getAttribute` method is explained in the *Obtaining a single attribute at a time using the getAttribute method* recipe.

In this example, we used the string literal, `"*"`, as the second argument. This value instructs the method to return all available attributes of the file. As we will see shortly, other string values can be used to get different results.

The `readAttributes` method is an atomic filesystem operation. By default, symbolic links are followed. To direct the method to not follow symbolic links, use the `java.nio.file` package's `LinkOption.NOFOLLOW_LINKS` enumeration constant, shown as follows:

```
        Map<String, Object> attrsMap = Files.readAttributes(path,
    "*", LinkOption.NOFOLLOW_LINKS);
```

There's more...

The interesting aspect of this method is its second argument. The syntax for the `String` argument consists of an optional `viewName` and a colon followed by an attribute list. A `viewName` is typically one of the following:

- acl
- basic

- owner
- user
- dos
- posix

Each of these `viewNames` corresponds to the name of a view interface.

The attribute list is a comma delimited list of attributes. The attribute list may contain zero or more elements. If an invalid element name is used, it is ignored. Using an asterisk will return all of the attributes associated with that `viewName`. If a `viewName` is not included, then all of the basic file attributes are returned as illustrated earlier.

Using the basic view as an example, the following table illustrates how we can be selective about which attributes we return:

String	Attributes returned
`"*"`	All of the basic file attributes
`"basic:*"`	All of the basic file attributes
`"basic:isDirectory,lastAccessTime"`	Only the `isDirectory` and `lastAccessTime` attributes
`"isDirectory,lastAccessTime"`	Only the `isDirectory` and `lastAccessTime` attributes
`" "`	None - a `java.lang.IllegalArgumentException` is generated

The attribute `String` is used in the same way with views other than basic.

> There cannot be any embedded spaces in the attribute `String`. For example, the `String`, `"basic:isDirectory, lastAccessTime"`, where there is a blank after the comma will result in an `IllegalArgumentException`.

Getting file and directory information

It is frequently necessary to retrieve basic information about a file or directory. This recipe examines how the `java.nio.file.Files` class provides the direct support. These methods provide only partial access to file and directory information and are typified by methods such as the `isRegularFile` method. A list of such methods are found in the *There's more...* section of this recipe.

Getting ready

To use the methods of the `Files` class to display information is easy since most, if not all, of these methods are static. This means that the methods can easily be executed against the `Files` class name. To use this technique:

1. Create a `Path` object representing a file or directory.
2. Use the `Path` object as an argument to the appropriate `Files` class' method.

How to do it...

1. To demonstrate how to obtain file attributes, we will develop a method to display the attributes of a file. Create a new console application that contains the following `main` method. In the method, we create a reference to a file and then call a `displayFileAttribute` method. It uses several methods to display information about the path as follows:

```
public static void main(String[] args) throws Exception {
    Path path = FileSystems.getDefault().getPath("/home/docs/
users.txt");
    displayFileAttributes(path);
}

    private static void displayFileAttributes(Path path) throws
Exception {
    String format =
            "Exists: %s %n"
        + "notExists: %s %n"
        + "Directory: %s %n"
        + "Regular: %s %n"
        + "Executable: %s %n"
        + "Readable: %s %n"
        + "Writable: %s %n"
        + "Hidden: %s %n"
        + "Symbolic: %s %n"
        + "Last Modified Date: %s %n"
        + "Size: %s %n";

    System.out.printf(format,
            Files.exists(path, LinkOption.NOFOLLOW_LINKS),
            Files.notExists(path, LinkOption.NOFOLLOW_LINKS),
            Files.isDirectory(path, LinkOption.NOFOLLOW_
LINKS),
```

```
                              Files.isRegularFile(path, LinkOption.NOFOLLOW_
         LINKS),
                              Files.isExecutable(path),
                              Files.isReadable(path),
                              Files.isWritable(path),
                              Files.isHidden(path),
                              Files.isSymbolicLink(path),
                              Files.getLastModifiedTime(path, LinkOption.
         NOFOLLOW_LINKS),
                              Files.size(path));
         }
```

2. Execute the program. Your output should appear as follows:

Exists: true

notExists: false

Directory: false

Regular: true

Executable: true

Readable: true

Writable: true

Hidden: false

Symbolic: false

Last Modified Date: 2011-10-20T03:18:20.338139Z

Size: 29

How it works...

A `Path` to the `users.txt` file was created. This `Path` object was then passed to the `displayFileAttribute` method, which displayed many of the attributes of the file. The methods that return these attributes are summarized in the following table:

Method	Description
exists	Returns true if the files exist
notExists	Returns true if the file does not exist
isDirectory	Returns true if the Path represents a directory
isRegularFile	Returns true if the Path represents a regular file
isExecutable	Returns true if the file can be executed
isReadable	Returns true if the file can be read

Method	Description
isWritable	Returns true if the file can be written to
isHidden	Returns true if the file is hidden and not visible to the unprivileged user
isSymbolicLink	Returns true if the file is a symbolic link
getLastModifiedTime	Returns the last time the file was modified
size	Returns the size of the file

Several of these methods possess a second argument that specifies how to handle symbolic links. When LinkOption.NOFOLLOW_LINKS is present, then symbolic links are not followed. The second argument is optional. If it is left out then symbolic links are not followed. Symbolic links are discussed in the *Managing symbolic links* recipe of *Chapter 2, Locating Files and Directories Using Paths*.

There's more...

The following table summarizes the exceptions thrown, and whether the method is non-atomic. Methods that may throw a SecurityException will do so if the calling thread is not permitted to read the file.

 When a method is said to be **non-atomic**, it means that other filesystem operations may execute concurrently with that method. Non-atomic operations can result in inconsistent results. That is, it is possible that concurrent operations against the method's target may result in possible modification of the state of the file while these methods are executing. This should be considered when using these methods.

The results of these methods marked as outdated are not necessarily valid upon their return. That is, there is no guarantee that any subsequent access will succeed as the file may have been deleted or otherwise modified.

Methods designated as **Cannot be determined** indicate that false may be returned if it is not possible to otherwise ascertain the results. For example, the exists method will return false if it cannot determine whether the file exists. It may exist, but the method was not able to determine definitively if it exists or not:

Method	SecurityException	IOException	Non-atomic	Outdated	Cannot be determined
exists	Yes			Yes	Yes
notExists	Yes			Yes	Yes
isDirectory	Yes				Yes

Method	SecurityException	IOException	Non-atomic	Outdated	Cannot be determined
isRegularFile	Yes				Yes
isExecutable	Yes		Yes	Yes	Yes
isReadable	Yes		Yes	Yes	Yes
isWritable	Yes		Yes	Yes	Yes
isHidden	Yes	Yes			
isSymbolicLink	Yes				Yes
getLastModifiedTime	Yes	Yes			
size	Yes	Yes			

Note that the `notExists` method is not the inverse of the `exists` method. With the use of either method, it may not be possible to determine if the file exists or not. When this is the case, both methods will return `false`.

The `isRegularFile` determines if the file is a regular file. Both the `isDirectory`, `isSymbolicLink`, and the `isRegularFile` methods may return `false` if:

 ▸ It is not one of those types
 ▸ If the file does not exist or
 ▸ If it is not possible to determine whether it is a file or a directory

For these methods, their corresponding methods in the `BasicFileAttributes` interface may provide better results. These methods are covered in the *Maintaining basic file attributes using the BasicFileAttributeView* recipe.

The `isExecutable` method checks to see if the file exists and if the JVM has access rights to execute the file. If the file is a directory, then the method determines whether the JVM has sufficient privileges to search the directory. It will return `false` if:

 ▸ The file does not exist
 ▸ The file is not executable
 ▸ If it is not possible to determine whether it is executable

The meaning of hidden is system-dependent. On UNIX systems, a file is hidden if its name begins with a period. On Windows, a file is hidden if the DOS hidden attribute is set.

Determining operating system support for attribute views

An operating system may not support all the attribute views found in Java. There are three basic techniques for determining which views are supported. Knowing which views are supported allows the developer to avoid exceptions that can occur when trying to use a view that is not supported.

Getting ready

The three techniques include using:

- The `java.nio.file.FileSystem` class' `supportedFileAttributeViews` method to return a set of all views supported.

- The `java.nio.file.FileStore` class' `supportsFileAttributeView` method with a class argument. If that class is supported, the method will return `true`.

- The `FileStore` class' `supportsFileAttributeView` method with a `String` argument. If the class represented by that `String` is supported, the method will return `true`.

The first approach is the simplest and will be illustrated first.

How to do it...

1. Create a new console application with the following `main` method. In this method, we will display all views supported on the current system as follows:

```
public static void main(String[] args)

    Path path = Paths.get("C:/home/docs/users.txt");
    FileSystem fileSystem = path.getFileSystem();
    Set<String> supportedViews = fileSystem.
supportedFileAttributeViews();
    for(String view : supportedViews) {
        System.out.println(view);
}
}
```

2. When the application is executed on a Windows 7 system, you should get the following output:

   acl

   basic

   owner

   user

   dos

3. When the application is executed under Ubuntu, version 10.10, you should get the following output:

   basic

   owner

   user

   unix

   dos

   posix

Notice that the **acl** view is not supported and a **unix** and **posix** view are supported. There is not a `UnixFileAttributeView` available as part of the Java 7 release. However, this interface can be found as part of the JSR203-backport project.

How it works...

A `Path` object was created for the `users.txt` file. The filesystem for this `Path` was obtained next using the `getFileSystem` method. The `FileSystem` class possesses the `supportedFileAttributeViews` method, which returns a set of strings representing the views supported. A for each loop was then used to display each string value.

There's more...

There are two other methods that we can use to determine which views are supported:

  ▶ Using the `supportsFileAttributeView` method with a class argument
  ▶ Using the `supportsFileAttributeView` method with a `String` argument

These two techniques are very similar. They both allow you to test for a specific view.

Using the supportsFileAttributeView method with a class argument

The overloaded `supportsFileAttributeView` method accepts a class object representing the view in question. Add the following code to the previous example's `main` method. In this code, we determine which of the several views are supported:

```
try {
    FileStore fileStore = Files.getFileStore(path);
    System.out.println("FileAttributeView supported: " +
fileStore.supportsFileAttributeView(
            FileAttributeView.class));
    System.out.println("BasicFileAttributeView supported: " +
fileStore.supportsFileAttributeView(
            BasicFileAttributeView.class));
    System.out.println("FileOwnerAttributeView supported: " +
fileStore.supportsFileAttributeView(
            FileOwnerAttributeView.class));
    System.out.println("AclFileAttributeView supported: " +
fileStore.supportsFileAttributeView(
            AclFileAttributeView.class));
    System.out.println("PosixFileAttributeView supported: " +
fileStore.supportsFileAttributeView(
            PosixFileAttributeView.class));
    System.out.println("UserDefinedFileAttributeView
supported: " + fileStore.supportsFileAttributeView(
            UserDefinedFileAttributeView.class));
    System.out.println("DosFileAttributeView supported: " +
fileStore.supportsFileAttributeView(
            DosFileAttributeView.class));
}
catch (IOException ex) {
    System.out.println("Attribute view not supported");
}
```

When executed on a Windows 7 machine, you should get the following output:

FileAttributeView supported: false

BasicFileAttributeView supported: true

FileOwnerAttributeView supported: true

AclFileAttributeView supported: true

PosixFileAttributeView supported: false

UserDefinedFileAttributeView supported: true

DosFileAttributeView supported: true

Using the supportsFileAttributeView method with a String argument

The overloaded supportsFileAttributeView method that accepts a String object works in a similar fashion. Add the following code to the try block of the main method:

```
            System.out.println("FileAttributeView supported: " +
    fileStore.supportsFileAttributeView(
                    "file"));
            System.out.println("BasicFileAttributeView supported: " +
    fileStore.supportsFileAttributeView(
                    "basic"));
            System.out.println("FileOwnerAttributeView supported: " +
    fileStore.supportsFileAttributeView(
                    "owner"));
            System.out.println("AclFileAttributeView supported: " +
    fileStore.supportsFileAttributeView(
                    "acl"));
            System.out.println("PosixFileAttributeView supported: " +
    fileStore.supportsFileAttributeView(
                    "posix"));
            System.out.println("UserDefinedFileAttributeView
    supported: " + fileStore.supportsFileAttributeView(
                    "user"));
            System.out.println("DosFileAttributeView supported: " +
    fileStore.supportsFileAttributeView(
                    "dos"));
```

When executed on a Windows 7 platform, you should get the following output:

FileAttributeView supported: false

BasicFileAttributeView supported: true

FileOwnerAttributeView supported: true

AclFileAttributeView supported: true

PosixFileAttributeView supported: false

UserDefinedFileAttributeView supported: true

DosFileAttributeView supported: true

Maintaining basic file attributes using the BasicFileAttributeView

The `java.nio.file.attribute.BasicFileAttributeView` provides a series of methods that obtain basic information about a file such as its creation time and size. The view possesses a `readAttributes` method, which returns a `BasicFileAttributes` object. The `BasicFileAttributes` interface possesses several methods for accessing file attributes. This view provides an alternative means of obtaining file information than that supported by the `Files` class. The results of this method may be more reliable at times than those of the `Files` class.

Getting ready

There are two approaches for obtaining a `BasicFileAttributes` object. The first approach is to use the `readAttributes` method that uses the `BasicFileAttributes.class` as the second argument. The second approach uses the `getFileAttributeView` method and is explored in the *There's more...* section of this recipe.

The `Files` class' `readAttributes` method is easiest to use:

1. Use a `Path` object representing the file of interest as the first argument.
2. Use `BasicFileAttributes.class` as the second argument.
3. Use the returned `BasicFileAttributes` object methods to access the file attributes.

This basic approach is used for the other views illustrated in this chapter. Only the attribute view class differs.

How to do it...

1. Create a new console application. Use the following `main` method. In the method, we create a `BasicFileAttributes` object and use its methods to display information about a file:

    ```
    public static void main(String[] args) {
        Path path
    = FileSystems.getDefault().getPath("/home/docs/users.txt");
        try {
            BasicFileAttributes attributes = Files.
    readAttributes(path, BasicFileAttributes.class);

            System.out.println("Creation Time: " + attributes.
    creationTime());
    ```

```
                System.out.println("Last Accessed Time: " +
        attributes.lastAccessTime());
                System.out.println("Last Modified Time: " +
        attributes.lastModifiedTime());
                System.out.println("File Key: " + attributes.
        fileKey());
                System.out.println("Directory: " + attributes.
        isDirectory());
                System.out.println("Other Type of File: " +
        attributes.isOther());
                System.out.println("Regular File: " + attributes.
        isRegularFile());
                System.out.println("Symbolic File: " + attributes.
        isSymbolicLink());
                System.out.println("Size: " + attributes.size());
        }
        catch (IOException ex) {
        System.out.println("Attribute error");
        }
        }
```

2. Execute the application. Your output should be similar to the following:

Creation Time: 2011-09-06T21:14:11.214057Z

Last Accessed Time: 2011-09-06T21:14:11.214057Z

Last Modified Time: 2011-09-06T01:26:56.501665Z

File Key: null

Directory: false

Other Type of File: false

Regular File: true

Symbolic File: false

Size: 30

How it works...

First, we created a `Path` object representing the `users.txt` file. Next, we obtained a `BasicFileAttributes` object using the `Files` class' `readAttributes` method. The first argument of the method is a `Path` object. The second argument specifies the type of object that we want returned. In this case, it was a `BasicFileAttributes.class` object.

This was followed by a series of print statements that display specific attribute information about the file. The `readAttributes` method retrieves all of the basic file attributes for a file. Since it can throw an `IOException`, the code sequence was enclosed in a try block.

Most of the `BasicFileAttributes` interface methods are easy to follow, but a few require further explanation. First, if the `isOther` method returns `true`, it means that the file is not a regular file, directory, or a symbolic link. Additionally, although the file size is in bytes, due to issues such as file compression and implementation of sparse files, the actual size may be different. If the file is not a regular file, then the meaning of the return value is system-dependent.

The `fileKey` method returns an object that uniquely identifies that file. In UNIX, the device id or inode is used for this purpose. The file key will not necessarily be unique if the filesystem and its files are changed. They can be compared using the `equals` method, and can be used in collections. Again, the assumption is that the filesystem has not changed in a way that affects the file key. The comparison of two files is covered in the *Determining whether two paths are equivalent* recipe in *Chapter 2, Locating Files and Directories Using Paths*.

There's more...

An alternative approach to getting an object is to use the `Files` class' `getFileAttributeView` method. It returns an `AttributeView` derived `object` based on its second parameter. To get an instance of a `BasicFileAttributeView` object:

1. Use a `Path` object representing the file of interest as the first argument.

2. Use the `BasicFileAttributeView` as the second argument.

   Instead of using the following statement:

   ```
   BasicFileAttributes attributes = Files.readAttributes(path,
   BasicFileAttributes.class);
   ```

   We can replace it with the following code sequence:

   ```
   BasicFileAttributeView view = Files.getFileAttributeView(path,
   BasicFileAttributeView.class);
   BasicFileAttributes attributes = view.readAttributes();
   ```

   A `BasicFileAttributeView` object is returned using the `getFileAttributeView` method. The `readAttributes` method then returns the `BasicFileAttributes` object. This approach is longer, but we now have access to three additional methods, which are shown as follows:

   - `name`: This returns the name of the attribute view

   - `readAttributes`: This returns a `BasicFileAttributes` object

   - `setTimes`: This is used to set the file's time attributes

3. We then use the `name` method shown as follows:

   ```
   System.out.println("Name: " + view.name());
   ```

This results in the following output:

Name: basic

However, this does not provide us with much useful information. The `setTimes` method is illustrated in the *Setting time related attributes of a file or directory* recipe in *Chapter 4, Managing Files and Directories*.

Maintaining POSIX file attributes using the PosixFileAttributeView

Many operating systems support the **Portable Operating System Interface** (**POSIX**) standard. This provides a more portable way of writing applications that can be ported across operating systems. Java 7 supports access to file attributes using the `java.nio.file.attribute.PosixFileAttributeView` interface.

Not all operating systems support the POSIX standard. The *Determining operating system support for attribute views* recipe illustrates how to determine whether a specific operating system supports POSIX or not.

Getting ready

In order to obtain POSIX attributes for a file or directory, we need to do the following:

1. Create a `Path` object representing the file or directory of interest.
2. Obtain an instance of the `PosixFileAttributeView` interface using the `getFileAttributeView` method.
3. Use the `readAttributes` method to obtain a set of attributes.

How to do it...

1. Create a new console application. Use the `main` method that follows. In this method, we obtain attributes for the `users.txt` file as follows:

```
public static void main(String[] args) throws Exception {
        Path path = Paths.get("home/docs/users.txt");
        FileSystem fileSystem = path.getFileSystem();
        PosixFileAttributeView view = Files.
getFileAttributeView(path, PosixFileAttributeView.class);

        PosixFileAttributes attributes = view.
readAttributes();
        System.out.println("Group: " + attributes.group());
```

```
            System.out.println("Owner: " + attributes.owner().
getName());

            Set<PosixFilePermission> permissions = attributes.
permissions();
            for(PosixFilePermission permission : permissions) {
                System.out.print(permission.name() + " ");
}
}
```

2. Execute the application. Your output should appear as follows. The owner names will probably be different. In this case, it is **richard**:

Group: richard

Owner: richard

OWNER_READ OWNER_WRITE OTHERS_READ GROUP_READ

How it works...

A `Path` object was created for the `users.txt` file. This was used as the first argument of the `Files` class' `getFileAttributeView` method. The second argument was `PosixFileAttributeView.class`. A `PosixFileAttributeView` object was returned.

Next, an instance of the `PosixFileAttributes` interface was obtained using the `readAttributes` method. The `group` and `getName` methods were used to display the group and owner of the file. The permissions methods returned a set of `PosixFilePermission` enumerations. These enumerations represent the permissions assigned to the file.

There's more...

The `PosixFileAttributes` interface extends the `java.nio.file.attribute.BasicFileAttributes` interface, and thus has access to all of its methods. The `PosixFileAttributeView` interface extends the `java.nio.file.attribute.FileOwnerAttributeView` and `BasicFileAttributeView` interfaces and inherits their methods also.

The `PosixFileAttributeView` interface has a `setGroup` method that can be used to configure the group owner of the file. The permissions of the file can be maintained using the `setPermissions` method. Maintaining file permissions is discussed in the *Managing POSIX attributes* recipe in *Chapter 4, Managing Files and Directories*.

See also

The *Maintaining basic file attributes using the BasicFileAttributeView* recipe details the attributes available through this view. The *Maintaining file ownership attributes using the FileOwnerAttributeView* recipe discusses ownership issues. To determine whether POSIX is supported by an operating system, look at the *Determining operating system support for attribute views* recipe.

Maintaining FAT table attributes using the DosFileAttributeView

The `java.nio.file.attribute.DosFileAttributeView` is concerned with the older **Disk Operating System** (**DOS**) files. It has limited value on most computers today. However, this is the only interface that can be used to determine if a file is marked for archive or is a system file.

Getting ready

To use the `DosFileAttributeView` interface:

1. Use the `Files` class' `getFileAttributeView` method to obtain an instance of a `DosFileAttributeView`.

2. Use the view's `readAttributes` method to return an instance of `DosFileAttributes`.

3. Use the `DosFileAttributes` class' methods to obtain file information.

This view supports the following four methods:

▶   `isArchive`: which is concerned with whether the file needs to be backed up or not

▶   `isHidden`: returns `true` if the file is not visible to users

▶   `isReadOnly`: returns `true` if the file can only be read

▶   `isSystem`: returns `true` if the file is part of the operating system

How to do it...

1. Create a new console application and add the following `main` method. In this method, we create an instance of the `DosFileAttributes` and then use its methods to display information about the file:

    ```
    public static void main(String[] args) {
        Path path = FileSystems.getDefault().getPath("/home/docs/
    users.txt");
    ```

```
        try {
            DosFileAttributeView view = Files.
    getFileAttributeView(path, DosFileAttributeView.class);
            DosFileAttributes attributes = view.readAttributes();

            System.out.println("isArchive: " + attributes.
    isArchive());
            System.out.println("isHidden: " + attributes.
    isHidden());
            System.out.println("isReadOnly: " + attributes.
    isReadOnly());
            System.out.println("isSystem: " + attributes.
    isSystem());

        }
        catch (IOException ex) {
            ex.printStackTrace();
        }
    }
```

2. Execute the program. Your output should appear as follows:

isArchive: true

isHidden: false

isReadOnly: false

isSystem: false

How it works...

A `Path` object representing the `users.txt` file was created. This object was used as an argument to the `Files` class' `getFileAttributeView` method along with `DosFileAttributeView.class`. An instance of the `DosFileAttributeView` interface was returned. This was used to create an instance of the `DosFileAttributes` interface, which was used with the four methods of the interface.

The `DosFileAttributeView` extends the `BasicFileAttributes` interface, and thus inherits all of its attributes as detailed in the *Maintaining basic file attributes using the BasicFileAttributeView* recipe.

See also

See the *Maintaining basic file attributes using the BasicFileAttributeView* recipe for more information about its methods.

Maintaining file ownership attributes using the FileOwnerAttributeView

If we are only interested in accessing information about the owners of a file or directory, then the `java.nio.file.attribute.FileOwnerAttributeView` interface provides methods for retrieving and setting this type of information. The setting of file ownership is covered in the *Setting file and directory owner* recipe of *Chapter 4, Managing Files and Directories*.

Getting ready

To retrieve the owner of a file:

1. Obtain an instance of the `FileOwnerAttributeView` interface.

2. Use its `getOwner` method to return a `UserPrincipal` object representing the owner.

How to do it...

1. Create a new console application. Add the following `main` method to it. In this method, we will determine the owner of the `users.txt` file as follows:

```
public static void main(String[] args) {
    Path path = Paths.get("C:/home/docs/users.txt");
    try {
        FileOwnerAttributeView view = Files.
getFileAttributeView(path, FileOwnerAttributeView.class);
        UserPrincipal userPrincipal = view.getOwner();
        System.out.println(userPrincipal.getName());
}
catch (IOException e) {
        e.printStackTrace();
}
}
```

2. Execute the application. Your output should be similar to the following, except the PC and usernames should be different.

Richard-PC\Richard

How it works...

A `Path` object was created for the `users.txt` file. Next, the `Files` class' `getFileAttributeView` method was called using the `Path` object as the first argument. The second argument was `FileOwnerAttributeView.class`, which results in a `FileOwnerAttributeView` object for the file being returned.

The view's `getOwner` method was then invoked to return a `UserPrincipal` object. Its `getName` method returns the name of the user, which was then displayed.

See also

See the *Maintaining basic file attributes using the BasicFileAttributeView* recipe for more information about its methods.

Maintaining a file's ACL using the AclFileAttributeView

The `java.nio.file.attribute.AclFileAttributeView` interface provides access to ACL attributes of a file or directory. These attributes include the user principal, the type of attribute, and flags and permissions for the file. The ability to use this interface allows the user to determine what permissions are available and to modify these attributes.

Getting ready

To determine the attributes of a file or directory:

1. Create a `Path` object representing that file or directory.
2. Use this `Path` object as the first argument of the `Files` class' `getFileAttributeView` method.
3. Use `AclFileAttributeView.class` as its second argument.
4. Use the `AclFileAttributeView` object, which was returned to access the list of ACL entries for that file or directory.

How to do it...

1. Create a new console application. In the `main` method, we will examine the ACL attributes of the `users.txt` file. The `getFileAttributeView` method is used to obtain a view and access the ACL entry list. Two helper methods are used to support this example: `displayPermissions` and `displayEntryFlags`. Use the following `main` method:

```
public static void main(String[] args) {
    Path path = Paths.get("C:/home/docs/users.txt");
    try {
        AclFileAttributeView view = Files.
getFileAttributeView(path, AclFileAttributeView.class);
        List<AclEntry> aclEntryList = view.getAcl();
        for (AclEntry entry : aclEntryList) {
            System.out.println("User Principal Name: " +
entry.principal().getName());
            System.out.println("ACL Entry Type: " + entry.
type());
            displayEntryFlags(entry.flags());
            displayPermissions(entry.permissions());
            System.out.println();
        }
    }
    catch (IOException e) {
        e.printStackTrace();
    }
}
```

2. Create the method `displayPermissions` to display the list of permissions for the file as follows:

```
private static void displayPermissions(Set<AclEntryPermission>
permissionSet) {
    if (permissionSet.isEmpty()) {
        System.out.println("No Permissions present");
    }
    else {
        System.out.println("Permissions");
        for (AclEntryPermission permission : permissionSet) {
            System.out.print(permission.name() + " ");
        }
        System.out.println();
    }
}
```

3. Create the method `displayEntryFlags` method to display the list of ACL flags for the file as follows:

```
    private static void displayEntryFlags(Set<AclEntryFlag>
flagSet) {
        if (flagSet.isEmpty()) {
            System.out.println("No ACL Entry Flags present");
}
else {
            System.out.println("ACL Entry Flags");
            for (AclEntryFlag flag : flagSet) {
                System.out.print(flag.name() + " ");
}
            System.out.println();
}
}
```

4. Execute the application. You should get an output similar to the following:

User Principal Name: BUILTIN\Administrators

ACL Entry Type: ALLOW

No ACL Entry Flags present

Permissions

WRITE_ATTRIBUTES EXECUTE DELETE READ_ATTRIBUTES WRITE_DATA READ_ ACL READ_DATA WRITE_OWNER READ_NAMED_ATTRS WRITE_ACL APPEND_DATA SYNCHRONIZE DELETE_CHILD WRITE_NAMED_ATTRS

User Principal Name: NT AUTHORITY\SYSTEM

ACL Entry Type: ALLOW

No ACL Entry Flags present

Permissions

WRITE_ATTRIBUTES EXECUTE DELETE READ_ATTRIBUTES WRITE_DATA READ_ ACL READ_DATA WRITE_OWNER READ_NAMED_ATTRS WRITE_ACL APPEND_DATA SYNCHRONIZE DELETE_CHILD WRITE_NAMED_ATTRS

User Principal Name: BUILTIN\Users

ACL Entry Type: ALLOW

No ACL Entry Flags present

Permissions

READ_DATA READ_NAMED_ATTRS EXECUTE SYNCHRONIZE READ_ATTRIBUTES READ_ACL

User Principal Name: NT AUTHORITY\Authenticated Users

ACL Entry Type: ALLOW

No ACL Entry Flags present

Permissions

READ_DATA READ_NAMED_ATTRS WRITE_ATTRIBUTES EXECUTE DELETE APPEND_DATA SYNCHRONIZE READ_ATTRIBUTES WRITE_NAMED_ATTRS WRITE_ DATA READ_ACL

How it works...

A `Path` was created to the `users.txt` file. This was then used along with the `AclFileAttributeView.class` parameter as the arguments to the `getFileAttributeView` method. This returned an instance of the `AclFileAttributeView`.

The `AclFileAttributeView` interface has three methods: `name`, `getAcl`, and `setAcl`. For this example, only the `getAcl` method was used, which returned a list of `AclEntry` elements. Each entry represents a specific ACL for the file.

A for each loop was used to iterate through the list. The user principal's name and the entry type were displayed. Next the `displayEntryFlags` and `displayPermissions` methods were invoked to display more information about the entries.

These two methods are similar in construction. A check was made to determine if there are any elements in the sets and the appropriate messages were displayed. Next, each element of the sets was displayed on a single line to conserve vertical space on the output.

There's more...

The `AclFileAttributeView` is derived from the `java.nio.file.attribute.FileOwnerAttributeView` interface. This provides access to the `getOwner` and `setOwner` methods. These methods either return or set a `UserPrincipal` object respectively for the file or directory.

There are three `AclFileAttributeView` methods:

▶ The `getAcl` method, which returns a list of ACL entries as illustrated previously

▶ The `setAcl` method, which allows us to add a new attribute to the file

▶ The `name` method, which simply returns **acl**

The `getAcl` method will return a list of `AclEntrys`. One of the elements of an entry is a `java.nio.file.attribute.UserPrincipal` object. As we saw in the earlier example, this represents the users who have access to the file. An alternate technique to access a user is to use the `java.nio.file.attribute.UserPrincipalLookupService` class. An instance of this class can be obtained using the `FileSystem` class' `getUserPrincipalLookupService` method, shown as follows:

```
try {
        UserPrincipalLookupService lookupService = FileSystems.
getDefault().getUserPrincipalLookupService();
        GroupPrincipal groupPrincipal = lookupService.lookupPrinci
palByGroupName("Administrators");
        UserPrincipal userPrincipal = lookupService.lookupPrincipa
lByName("Richard");
        System.out.println(groupPrincipal.getName());
        System.out.println(userPrincipal.getName());
}
        catch (IOException e) {
        e.printStackTrace();
}
```

There are two methods available to the service that can look for the users either by username or by group name. In the previous code we used the `Administrators` group and the user `Richard`.

Add this code to the previous example and change the names to reflect groups and users on your system. When the code executes, you should receive output similar to the following:

BUILTIN\Administrators

Richard-PC\Richard

However, note that the `UserPrincipal` and `java.nio.file.attribute.GroupPrincipal` objects' methods provide little more information than the names of the users. User or group names may or may not be case-sensitive depending on the operating system. If an invalid name is used, a `java.nio.file.attribute.UserPrincipalNotFoundException` is thrown.

See also

Managing file ownership and permissions is discussed in *Chapter 4, Managing Files and Directories*, in the *Setting file and directory owner* recipe. Also covered in *Chapter 4* is the setting of ACL attributes as illustrated in the *Managing ACL file permissions* recipe.

Maintaining user-defined file attributes using the UserDefinedFileAttributeView

The `java.nio.file.attribute.UserDefinedFileAttributeView` interface permits the attachment of a non-standard attribute to a file or directory. These types of attributes are sometimes called **extended** attributes. Typically, a user-defined attribute stores metadata about a file. This data is not necessarily understood or used by the filesystem.

These attributes are stored as a name/value pair. The name is a `String` and the value is stored as a `ByteBuffer` object. The size of this buffer should not exceed `Integer.MAX_VALUE`.

Getting ready

A user-defined attribute must first be attached to a file. This is accomplished by:

1. Obtaining an instance of a `UserDefinedFileAttributeView` object
2. Creating an attribute in the form of a `String` name and a `ByteBuffer` value
3. Using the `write` method to attach the attribute to a file

The process of reading a user-defined attribute is illustrated in the *There's more...* section of this recipe.

How to do it...

1. Create a new console application. In the `main` method, we will create a user-defined attribute called `publishable` and attach it to the `users.txt` file. Use the following `main` method:

```
public static void main(String[] args) {
    Path path = Paths.get("C:/home/docs/users.txt");
    try {
        UserDefinedFileAttributeView view = Files.
getFileAttributeView(path, UserDefinedFileAttributeView.class);
        view.write("publishable", Charset.defaultCharset().
encode("true"));
        System.out.println("Publishable set");

}
catch (IOException e) {
        e.printStackTrace();
}
}
```

2. Execute the application. Your output should appear as follows:

Publishable set

How it works...

First, we created a `Path` object representing the `users.txt` file. We then used the `Files` class' `getFileAttributeView` method using the `Path` object, and `UserDefinedFileAttributeView.class` for the second argument. This returns an instance of the `UserDefinedFileAttributeView` for the file.

Using this object, we execute the `write` method against it using the attribute `publishable`, and created a `java.nio.ByteBuffer` object containing the attribute value `true`. The `java.nio.Charset` class' `defaultCharset` method returns a `Charset` object that uses the locale and character set used by the underlying operating system. The `encode` method took the `String` and returned a `ByteBuffer` for the attribute value. We then displayed a simple message indicating the successful completion of the process.

There's more...

The `read` method is used to read an attribute. To get a user-defined attribute associated with a file, the following steps need to be followed:

1. Obtain an instance of a `UserDefinedFileAttributeView` object.
2. Create a `String` for the attribute name.
3. Allocate a `ByteBuffer` to hold the value.
4. Use the `read` method to get the attribute value.

The following code sequence accomplishes this task for the previously attached `publishable` attribute:

```
String name = "publishable";
ByteBuffer buffer = ByteBuffer.allocate(view.size(name));
view.read(name, buffer);
buffer.flip();
String value = Charset.defaultCharset().decode(buffer).
toString();
System.out.println(value);
```

A `String` for the attribute name was created first. Next, a `ByteBuffer` was created to hold the attribute value to be retrieved. The `allocate` method allocates space as specified by the `UserDefinedFileAttributeView` interface's `size` method. This method determines the size of the attached attribute and returns the size.

The `read` method is then executed against the `view` object. The buffer is populated with the attribute value. The `flip` method resets the buffer. The buffer is converted to a `String` object using the `decode` method, which uses the operating system's default character set.

Replace the user-defined attribute `write` sequence in the `main` method with this `read` sequence. When the application is executed, you should get an output similar to the following:

true

There is also a `delete` method that is used to remove a user-defined attribute from a file or directory. In addition, note that the use of a `UserDefinedFileAttributeView` object requires a runtime permission of `accessUserDefinedAttributes`.

4
Managing Files and Directories

In this chapter, we will cover the following:

- ▶ Creating files and directories
- ▶ Controlling how a file is copied
- ▶ Managing temporary files and directories
- ▶ Setting time-related attributes of a file or directory
- ▶ Managing file ownership
- ▶ Managing ACL file permissions
- ▶ Managing POSIX attributes
- ▶ Moving a file or directory
- ▶ Deleting files and directories
- ▶ Managing symbolic links

Introduction

It is often necessary to perform file manipulations such as creating files, manipulating their attributes and contents, or removing them from the filesystem. The addition of the `java.lang.object.Files` class in Java 7 simplifies this process. This class relies heavily on the use of the new `java.nio.file.Path` interface, which is discussed in depth in *Chapter 2, Locating Files and Directories Using Paths*. The methods of the class are all static in nature, and generally assign the actual file manipulation operations to the underlying filesystem.

Many of the operations described in this chapter are atomic in nature, such as those used to create and delete files or directories. Atomic operations will either execute successfully to completion or fail and result in an effective cancellation of the operation. During execution, they are not interrupted from the standpoint of a filesystem. Other concurrent file operations will not impact the operation.

> To execute many of the examples in this chapter, the application needs to run as administrator. To run an application as administrator under Windows, right-click on the **Command Prompt** menu and choose **Run as administrator**. Then navigate to the appropriate directory and execute using the `java.exe` command. To run as administrator on a UNIX system, use the `sudo` command in a terminal window followed by the `java` command.

Basic file management is covered in this chapter. The methods required for the creation of files and directories are covered in the *Creating Files and Directories* recipe. This recipe focuses on normal files. The creation of temporary files and directories is covered in the *Managing temporary files and directories* recipe, and the creation of linked files is covered in the *Managing symbolic links* recipe.

The options available for copying files and directories are found in the *Controlling how a file is copied* recipe. The techniques illustrated there provide a powerful way of dealing with file replication. Moving and deleting files and directories are covered in the *Moving a file or directory* and *Deleting files and directories* recipes, respectively.

The *Setting time-related attributes of a file or directory* recipe illustrates how to assign time attributes to a file. Related to this effort are other attributes, such as file ownership and permissions. File ownership is addressed in the *Managing file ownership* recipe. File permissions are discussed in two recipes: *Managing ACL file permissions* and *Managing POSIX file permissions*.

Creating files and directories

The process of creating new files and directories is greatly simplified in Java 7. The methods implemented by the `Files` class are relatively intuitive and easy to incorporate into your code. In this recipe, we will cover how to create new files and directories using the `createFile` and `createDirectory` methods.

Getting ready

In our example, we are going to use several different methods to create a `Path` object that represents a file or directory. We will do the following:

1. Create a `Path` object.

2. Create a directory using the `Files` class' `createDirectory` method.

3. Create a file using the `Files` class' `createFile` method.

The `FileSystem` class' `getPath` method can be used to create a `Path` object as can the `Paths` class' `get` method. The `Paths` class' static `get` method returns an instance of a `Path` based on a string sequence or a `URI` object. The `FileSystem` class' `getPath` method also returns a `Path` object, but only uses a string sequence to identify the file.

How to do it...

1. Create a console application with a `main` method. In the `main` method, add the following code that creates a `Path` object for the directory `/home/test` in the C directory. Within a try block, invoke the `createDirectory` method with your `Path` object as the parameter. This method will throw an `IOException` if the path is invalid. Next, create a `Path` object for the file `newFile.txt` using the `createFile` method on this `Path` object, again catching the `IOException` as follows:

```
try {
        Path testDirectoryPath  = Paths.get("C:/home/test");
        Path testDirectory = Files.createDirectory(testDirecto
ryPath);
        System.out.println("Directory created successfully!");
        Path newFilePath = FileSystems.getDefault().
getPath("C:/home/test/newFile.txt");
        Path testFile = Files.createFile(newFilePath);
        System.out.println("File created successfully!");
}
catch (IOException ex) {
        ex.printStackTrace();
}
```

2. Execute the program. Your output should appear as follows:

Directory created successfully!

File created successfully!

3. Verify that the new file and directory exists in your filesystem. Next, add a catch block prior to the `IOException` after both methods, and catch a `FileAlreadyExistsException`:

```
}
catch (FileAlreadyExistsException a) {
        System.out.println("File or directory already
exists!");
}
catch (IOException ex) {
        ex.printStackTrace();
}
```

4. When you execute the program again, your output should appear as follows:

File or directory already exists!

How it works...

The first `Path` object was created and then used by the `createDirectory` method to create a new directory. After the second `Path` object was created, the `createFile` method was used to create a file within the directory, which had just been created. It is important to note that the `Path` object used in the file creation could not be instantiated before the directory was created, because it would have referenced an invalid path. This would have resulted in an `IOException`.

When the `createDirectory` method is invoked, the system is directed to check for the existence of the directory first, and if it does not exist, create it. The `createFile` method works in a similar fashion. The method fails if the file already exists. We saw this when we caught the `FileAlreadyExistsException`. Had we not caught that exception, an `IOException` would have been thrown. Either way, the existing file would not be overwritten.

There's more...

The `createFile` and `createDirectory` methods are atomic in nature. The `createDirectories` method is available to create directories as discussed next. All three methods provide the option to pass file attribute parameters for more specific file creation.

Using the createDirectories method to create a hierarchy of directories

The `createDirectories` method is used to create a directory and potentially other intermediate directories. In this example, we build upon the previous directory structure by adding a `subtest` and a `subsubtest` directory to the `test` directory. Comment out the previous code that created the directory and file and add the following code sequence:

```
        Path directoriesPath = Paths.get("C:/home/test/subtest/
    subsubtest");
        Path testDirectory = Files.createDirectories(directoriesP
    ath);
```

Verify that the operation succeeded by examining the resulting directory structure.

See also

Creating temporary files and directories is covered in the *Managing temporary files and directories* recipe. The creation of symbolic files is illustrated in the *Managing symbolic links* recipe.

Controlling how a file is copied

The process of copying files is also simplified in Java 7, and allows for control over the manner in which they are copied. The `Files` class' copy method supports this operation and is overloaded providing three techniques for copying which differ by their source or destination.

Getting ready

In our example, we are going to create a new file and then copy it to another target file. This process involves:

1. Creating a new file using the `createFile` method.
2. Creating a path for the destination file.
3. Copying the file using the `copy` method.

How to do it...

1. Create a console application with a `main` method. In the `main` method, add the following code sequence to create a new file. Specify two `Path` objects, one for your initial file and one for the location where it will be copied. Then add the `copy` method to copy that file to the destination location as follows:

```
        Path newFile = FileSystems.getDefault().getPath("C:/home/
docs/newFile.txt");
        Path copiedFile = FileSystems.getDefault().getPath("C:/
home/docs/copiedFile.txt");
        try {
            Files.createFile(newFile);
            System.out.println("File created successfully!");
            Files.copy(newFile, copiedFile);
            System.out.println("File copied successfully!");
}
catch (IOException e) {
            System.out.println("IO Exception.");
}
```

2. Execute the program. Your output should appear as follows:

   File created successfully!

   File copied successfully!

How it works...

The `createFile` method created your initial file, and the `copy` method copied that file to the location specified by the `copiedFile` variable. If you were to attempt to run that code sequence twice in a row, you would have encountered an `IOException`, because the `copy` method will not, by default, replace an existing file. The `copy` method is overloaded. Use the copy method with the `java.lang.enum.StandardCopyOption` enumeration value of `REPLACE_EXISTING` to allow the file to be replaced, as shown below.

The three enumeration values for `StandardCopyOption` are listed in the following table:

Value	Meaning
ATOMIC_MOVE	Perform the copy operation atomically
COPY_ATTRIBUTES	Copy the source file attributes to the destination file
REPLACE_EXISTING	Replace the existing file if it already exists

Replace the `copy` method call in the previous example with the following:

```
    Files.copy(newFile, copiedFile, StandardCopyOption.REPLACE_
EXISTING);
```

When the code executes, the file should be replaced. Another example of the use of the copy options is found in the *There's more...* section of the *Moving a file and directory* recipe.

There's more...

If the source file and the destination file are the same, then the method completes, but no copy actually occurs. The `copy` method is not atomic in nature.

There are two other overloaded `copy` methods. One copies a `java.io.InputStream` to a file and the other copies a file to a `java.io.OutputStream`. In this section, we will examine, in more depth, the processes of:

- ▶ Copying a symbolic link file
- ▶ Copying a directory
- ▶ Copying an input stream to a file
- ▶ Copying a file to an output stream

Copying a symbolic link file

When a symbolic link file is copied, the target of the symbolic link is copied. To illustrate this, create a symbolic link file called `users.txt` in the `music` directory to the `users.txt` file in the `docs` directory. This can be done either by using the process described in the *Managing symbolic links* recipe in *Chapter 2, Locating Files and Directories Using Paths*, or using the methods illustrated in the *Managing symbolic links* recipe in this chapter.

Use the following code sequence to perform the copy operation:

```
        Path originalLinkedFile = FileSystems.getDefault().
getPath("C:/home/music/users.txt");
        Path newLinkedFile = FileSystems.getDefault().getPath("C:/
home/music/users2.txt");
        try {
            Files.copy(originalLinkedFile, newLinkedFile);
            System.out.println("Symbolic link file copied
successfully!");
        }
catch (IOException e) {
            System.out.println("IO Exception.");
        }
```

Execute the code. You should get the following output:

Symbolic link file copied successfully!

Examine the resulting `music` directory structure. The `user2.txt` file has been added and is not connected to either the linked file or the original target file. Modification of the `user2.txt` does not affect the contents of the other two files.

Copying a directory

When a directory is copied, an empty directory is created. The files in the original directory are not copied. The following code sequence illustrates this process:

```
        Path originalDirectory = FileSystems.getDefault().getPath("C:/
home/docs");
        Path newDirectory = FileSystems.getDefault().getPath("C:/home/
tmp");
        try {
            Files.copy(originalDirectory, newDirectory);
            System.out.println("Directory copied successfully!");
        }
catch (IOException e) {
            e.printStackTrace();
        }
```

When this sequence is executed, you should get the following output:

Directory copied successfully!

Examine the `tmp` directory. It should be empty as any files in the source directory are not copied.

Copying an input stream to a file

The `copy` method has a convenient overloaded version that permits the creation of a new file based on the input from an `InputStream`. The first argument of this method differs from the original `copy` method, in that it is an instance of an `InputStream`.

The following example uses this method to copy the `jdk7.java.net` website to a file:

```
        Path newFile = FileSystems.getDefault().getPath("C:/home/docs/
    java7WebSite.html");
        URI url = URI.create("http://jdk7.java.net/");
        try (InputStream inputStream = url.toURL().openStream())

            Files.copy(inputStream, newFile);
            System.out.println("Site copied successfully!");
    }
    catch (MalformedURLException ex) {
            ex.printStackTrace();
    }
    catch (IOException ex) {
            ex.printStackTrace();
    }
```

When the code executes, you should get the following output:

Site copied successfully!

A `java.lang.Object.URI` object was created to represent the website. Using the `URI` object instead of a `java.lang.Object.URL` object immediately avoids having to create a separate try-catch block to handle the `MalformedURLException` exception.

The `URL` class' `openStream` method returns an `InputStream` which is used as the first parameter of the `copy` method. Notice the use of the try-with-resource block. This try block is new to Java 7 and is illustrated in the *Using the try-with-resource block to improve exception handling code* recipe in *Chapter 1, Java Language Improvements*.

The `copy` method was then executed. The new file can now be opened with a browser or otherwise can be processed as needed. Notice that the method returns a long value representing the number of bytes written.

Copying a file to an output stream

The third overloaded version of the `copy` method will open a file and write its contents to an `OutputStream`. This can be useful when the content of a file needs to be copied to a non-file object such as a `PipedOutputStream`. It can also be useful when communicating to other threads or writing to an array of bytes as illustrated here. In this example, the content of the `users.txt` file is copied to an instance of a `ByteArrayOutputStream`. Its `toByteArray` method is then used to populate an array as follows:

```
        Path sourceFile = FileSystems.getDefault().getPath("C:/home/
docs/users.txt");
        try (ByteArrayOutputStream outputStream = new
ByteArrayOutputStream()) {
            Files.copy(sourceFile, outputStream);
            byte arr[] = outputStream.toByteArray();
            System.out.println("The contents of " + sourceFile.
getFileName());
            for(byte data : arr) {
                System.out.print((char)data);
}

            System.out.println();

}
catch (IOException ex) {
            ex.printStackTrace();

}
```

Execute this sequence. The output will depend on the contents of your file, but should be similar to the following:

The contents of users.txt

Bob

Jennifer

Sally

Tom

Ted

Notice the use of the try-with-resources block that handles the opening and closing of the file. It is always a good idea to close the `OutputStream` when the copy operation is complete or exceptions occur. The try-with-resources block handles this nicely. The method may block until the operation is complete in certain situations. Much of its behavior is implementation-specific. Also, the output stream may need to be flushed since it implements the `Flushable` interface. Notice that the method returns a long value representing the number of bytes written.

See the *Managing symbolic links* recipe for more details on working with symbolic links.

Managing temporary files and directories

The process of creating temporary files and directories can be an essential part of many applications. Temporary files may be used for intermediate data or as a temporary store to be cleaned up later. The process of managing temporary files and directories can be accomplished simply via the `Files` class. In this recipe, we will cover how to create temporary files and directories using the `createTempDirectory` and `createTempFile` methods.

Getting ready

In our example, we are going to create a temporary directory and then create a temporary file within the directory as follows:

1. Create `Path` objects representing the temporary file and directory.
2. Create a temporary directory using the `createTempDirectory` method.
3. Create a temporary file using the `createTempFile` method.

How to do it...

1. Create a console application with a `main` method. In the `main` method, create a `Path` object `rootDirectory` using the `getPath` method. Invoke the `createTempDirectory` method using `rootDirectory` as the first argument, and an empty string as the second argument. Then use the `toString` method to convert the returning `Path` object `dirPath` to a `String` and print it to the screen. Next, add the `createTempFile` method using `dirPath` as the first argument with empty strings as the second and third arguments. Use the `toString` method again to print out this resulting path as follows:

```
try {
        Path rootDirectory = FileSystems.getDefault().
getPath("C:/home/docs");
        Path tempDirectory = Files.createTempDirectory(rootDir
ectory, "");
        System.out.println("Temporary directory created
successfully!");

        String dirPath = tempDirectory.toString();
        System.out.println(dirPath);
        Path tempFile = Files.createTempFile(tempDirectory,"",
"");
```

```
                System.out.println("Temporary file created
        successfully!");

                String filePath = tempFile.toString();
                System.out.println(filePath);
        }
        catch (IOException e) {
                System.out.println("IO Exception.");
        }
```

2. This code sequence will result in an output similar to the following:

Temporary directory created successfully!

C:\home\docs\7087436262102989339

Temporary file created successfully!

C:\home\docs\7087436262102989339\3473887367961760381

How it works...

The `createTempDirectory` method creates an empty directory and returns a `Path` object representing the location of this new directory. Likewise, the `createTempFile` method creates an empty file and returns a `Path` object representing this new file. In our previous example, we used the `toString` method to see the path where our directory and file were created. The previous numeric directory and filenames are assigned by the system and are platform-specific.

This `createTempDirectory` method requires at least two parameters, namely, the `Path` object directing the location for the new directory, and a `String` variable specifying the directory prefix. In our previous example, we left the prefix blank. However, if we had wanted to specify text to precede the filename assigned by the system, the second variable could have been populated with this prefix string.

The `createTempFile` method works in a similar manner as the `createTempDirectory` method, and had we wanted to assign a prefix to our temporary file, we could have used the second parameter to specify the string. The third parameter of this method could have also been used to specify a suffix, or file type, for our file, such as `.txt`.

It is important to note that, although in our example we specified the `Path` in which we wanted our directory and file created, there is another version of each method in which the initial argument, the `Path` object, could be omitted, and the directory and/or file would be created in the system's default temporary directory. Additionally, these methods do not check for the file or directory's existence before creating them, and will overwrite any existing file or directory with the same temporary, system-assigned name.

There's more...

File attribute names can also be passed to the overloaded `createTempDirectory` or `createTempFile` methods. These attributes are optional, but can be used to specify how the temporary files will be handled, such as whether the file should be deleted upon closing. The creation of a file attribute is described in the *There's more...* section of the *Managing POSIX file permissions* recipe.

The `createTempDirectory` and the `createTempFile` methods are intended to have a limited existence. If it is desirable to delete these files or directories automatically, a shutdown hook or the `java.io.File` class' `deleteOnExit` method can be used. These two techniques will result in the deletion of the element when the application or the JVM terminates.

Setting time-related attributes of a file or directory

The timestamp for a file can be critical for some applications. For example, the order in which operations execute may be dependent on the time a file was last updated. There are three dates supported by the `BasicFileAttributeView`:

- The last modified time
- The last access time
- The creation time

They can be set using the `BasicFileAttributeView` interface's `setTimes` method. As we will see in the *There's more...* section, the `Files` class can be used to set or get only the last modified time.

Getting ready

In order to set the times using the `setTimes` method. We need to do the following:

1. Obtain a `Path` object, which represents the file of interest.
2. Obtain a `BasicFileAttributeView` object.
3. Create `FileTime` objects for the times needed.
4. Use these `FileTime` objects as arguments of the `setTimes` method.

How to do it...

1. Create a new console application using the following `main` method. We will update the last modified time of our favorite file `users.txt` to the current time:

```
public static void main(String[] args) throws Exception {
        Path path = Paths.get("C:/home/docs/users.txt");
        BasicFileAttributeView view = Files.
getFileAttributeView(path, BasicFileAttributeView.class);
    FileTime lastModifedTime;
        FileTime lastAccessTime;
        FileTime createTime;

        BasicFileAttributes attributes = view.readAttributes();
        lastModifedTime = attributes.lastModifiedTime();
        createTime = attributes.creationTime();

        long currentTime = Calendar.getInstance().
getTimeInMillis();
        lastAccessTime = FileTime.fromMillis(currentTime);

        view.setTimes(lastModifedTime, lastAccessTime,
createTime);
        System.out.println(attributes.lastAccessTime());
}
```

2. Execute the application. Unless you have access to a time machine, or have otherwise manipulated your system's clock, your output should reflect a time later than the time shown as follows:

    2011-09-24T21:34:55.012Z

How it works...

A `Path` was first created for the `users.txt` file. Next, an instance of the `BasicFileAttributeView` interface was obtained using the `getFileAttributeView` method. A try block was used to catch any `IOExceptions` that might be thrown by the `readAttributes` or `setTimes` methods.

Within the try block, `FileTime` objects were created for each of the three types of time. The `lastModifedTime` and `createTime` times were not changed for the file. These were obtained using the corresponding methods of the `BasicFileAttributes` class, which was obtained using the `view` method.

The `currentTime` long variable was assigned the current time expressed in milliseconds. Its value was obtained using the `getTimeInMillis` method executed against an instance of the `Calendar` class. The three `FileTime` objects were then used as arguments to the `setTimes` method, effectively setting these time values.

There's more...

There is more to the use of the `FileTime` class than presented so far. In addition, the `Files` class provides alternative approaches for maintaining times. Here we will further explore the following:

- Understanding the `FileTime` class
- Using the `Files` class' `setLastModifiedTime` to maintain the last modified time
- Using the `Files` class' `setAttribute` method to set individual attributes

Understanding the FileTime class

The `java.nio.file.attribute.FileTime` class represents the time for use with several of the `java.nio` package methods. To create a `FileTime` object, we need to use either of the following two static `FileTime` methods:

- The `from` method, which accepts a long number representing a duration and a `TimeUnit` object representing a unit of time measurement
- The `fromMillis` method, which accepts a long argument representing the number of milliseconds based on the epoch

`TimeUnit` is an enumeration found in the `java.util.concurrent` package. It represents a time duration as defined in the following table. It is used in conjunction with another parameter whose combination represents a time duration:

Enumeration Value	Meaning
NANOSECONDS	One thousandth of a microsecond
MICROSECONDS	One thousandth of a millisecond
MILLISECONDS	One thousandth of a second
SECONDS	A second
MINUTES	Sixty seconds
HOURS	Sixty minutes
DAYS	Twenty four hours

The `from` method returns a `TimeUnit` object. Its value is computed by adding the first long argument, whose unit of measure is specified by the second `TimeUnit` argument, to the epoch.

The epoch is 1970-01-01T00:00:00Z, which is the base time used for specifying time on most computers. This base time represents midnight, **Coordinate Universal Time** on January 1, 1970.

For example, the `from` method can be used to present a point in time, which is 1000 days from the epoch using the following code sequence:

```
FileTime fileTime = FileTime.from(1000, TimeUnit.DAYS);
System.out.println(fileTime);
```

When executed you should get the following output:

1972-09-27T00:00:00Z

The `fromMillis` method is used to create a `FileTime` object, whose time is represented by adding its argument to the epoch where the argument is a long number representing a value in milliseconds. If we used the following `fromMillis` method instead of the `from` method as follows:

```
FileTime fileTime = FileTime.fromMillis(1000L*60*60*24*1000);
```

We will get the same results. Notice that the first argument is a long literal, which forces the result of the expression to be a long number. If we did not promote our results to be long values, we would have received an integer value, which would have resulted in overflow and an incorrect date. The first argument of either method can be negative.

 For more details regarding the use of time in Java, see
`http://www3.ntu.edu.sg/home/ehchua/programming/java/DateTimeCalendar.html`.

Using the Files class' setLastModifiedTime to maintain the last modified time

The `Files` class' `getLastModifiedTime` and `setLastModifiedTime` methods provide an alternative approach for setting the last modified attribute of a file. In the following code sequence, the `setLastModifiedTime` method uses the `lastModifedTime` object to set the time as follows:

```
Files.setLastModifiedTime(path, lastModifedTime);
```

The `Files` class' `getLastModifiedTime` returns a `FileTime` object. We could have this method to assign a value to the `lastModifedTime` variable as follows:

```
lastModifedTime = Files.getLastModifiedTime(path);
```

The method has an optional `LinkOption` argument that indicates whether symbolic links should be followed or not.

Using the Files class' setAttribute method to set individual attributes

The `setAttribute` method provides a flexible and dynamic approach for setting certain file attributes. To set the last modified time, we could have used the following code sequence:

```
            Files.setAttribute(path, "basic:lastAccessTime",
    lastAccessTime);
```

The *Obtaining a single attribute at a time using the getAttribute method* recipe in *Chapter 3, Obtaining File and Directory Information*, details the other attributes that can be set.

See also

The *Managing symbolic links* recipe discusses the use of symbolic links.

Managing file ownership

The owner of a file or directory can be modified after the file has been created. This is accomplished by using the `java.nio.file.attribute.FileOwnerAttributeView` interface's `setOwner` method, which can be useful when ownerships change and need to be controlled programmatically.

A `java.nio.file.attribute.UserPrincipal` object is used to represent a user. A `Path` object is used to represent a file or directory. Using these two objects with the `Files` class' `setOwner` method enables us to maintain file ownerships.

Getting ready

In order to change the owner of a file or directory:

1. Obtain a `Path` object, which represents the file or directory.
2. Use the `Path` as the argument to the `getFileAttributeView` method.
3. Create a `UserPrincipal` object representing the new owner.
4. Use the `FileOwnerAttributeView` interface's `setOwner` method to change the file's owner.

How to do it...

1. In this example, we will assume that the current owner of the `users.txt` file is `richard`. We will change the owner to a user called `jennifer`. To do this, create a new user on your system called `jennifer`. Create a new console application with the following `main` method. In the method, we will use the `FileOwnerAttributeView` and a `UserPrincipal` object to change the owner as follows:

```
public static void main(String[] args) throws Exception {
    Path path = Paths.get("C:/home/docs/users.txt");
    FileOwnerAttributeView view = Files.
getFileAttributeView(path, FileOwnerAttributeView.class);
    UserPrincipalLookupService lookupService = FileSystems.
getDefault().getUserPrincipalLookupService();
    UserPrincipal userPrincipal = lookupService.lookupPrincipa
lByName("jennifer");

    view.setOwner(userPrincipal);
    System.out.println("Owner: " + view.getOwner().getName());
}
```

2. In order to modify the ownership of a file, we must have appropriate privileges. The introduction to this chapter explains how to get administrator privileges. When the application is executed using Windows 7, the output should reflect the PC name and the file's owners shown as follows. The PC name is separated from the owner with a backslash:

Owner: Richard-PC\Richard

Owner: Richard-PC\Jennifer

How it works...

A `Path` was first created for the `users.txt` file. Next, an instance of the `FileOwnerAttributeView` interface was obtained using the `getFileAttributeView` method. Within the try block, a `UserPrincipalLookupService` object was created using the default `FileSystem` class' `getUserPrincipalLookupService` method. The `lookupPrincipalByName` method was passed the string `jennifer`, which returned a `UserPrincipal` object representing that user.

The last step was to pass the `UserPrincipal` object to the `setOwner` method. It then used the `getOwner` method to retrieve the current owner verifying the change.

Any interface derived from `FileOwnerAttributeView` can use the `getOwner` or `setOwner` methods. These include the `AclFileAttributeView` and `PosixFileAttributeView` interfaces. In addition, the `Files` class' `setOwner` method can also be used to change ownership of a file.

Using the Files class' setOwner method

The `Files` class' `setOwner` method works in the same way as the `FileOwnerAttributeView` interfaces' `setOwner` method. It differs in that it has two arguments, a `Path` object representing the file and a `UserPrincipal` object. The following sequence illustrates the process of setting the owner of the `users.txt` file to `jennifer`:

```
Path path = Paths.get("C:/home/docs/users.txt");
try {
        UserPrincipalLookupService lookupService = FileSystems.
getDefault().getUserPrincipalLookupService();

        UserPrincipal userPrincipal = lookupService.lookupPrincipa
lByName("jennifer");

        Files.setOwner(path, userPrincipal);
        System.out.println("Owner: " + view.getOwner().getName());
}
catch (IOException ex) {
        ex.printStackTrace();
}
```

Managing ACL file permissions

In this recipe, we will examine how ACL permissions can be set. The ability to set these permissions is important for many applications. For example, when we need to control who can modify or execute a file, we can affect this change programmatically. What we can change is indicated by the `AclEntryPermission` enumeration values listed later.

To set a new ACL permission for a file:

1. Create a `Path` object for the file whose attributes we want to change.
2. Obtain an `AclFileAttributeView` for that file.
3. Obtain a `UserPrincipal` object for the user.
4. Obtain a list of ACL entries currently assigned to the file.

5. Create a new `AclEntry.Builder` object holding the permission that we want to add.

6. Add the permission to the ACL list.

7. Use the `setAcl` method to replace the current ACL list with a new one.

How to do it...

1. Create a new console application with the following `main` method. In this method, we will initially simply display the current ACL list for the file `users.txt` as follows:

```
public static void main(String[] args) throws Exception {
    Path path = Paths.get("C:/home/docs/users.txt");
    AclFileAttributeView view = Files.
getFileAttributeView(path, AclFileAttributeView.class);
    List<AclEntry> aclEntryList = view.getAcl();
    displayAclEntries(aclEntryList);
}
```

2. To illustrate the process of adding and deleting ACL attributes, we will use a series of helper methods:

   - `displayAclEntries`: This displays the principal and entry type and then calls the other two helper methods
   - `displayEntryFlags`: This displays the entry flags if present
   - `displayPermissions`: This displays the entry permissions if any

3. Add the methods as shown in the following code to your application:

```
private static void displayAclEntries(List<AclEntry>
aclEntryList) {
    System.out.println("ACL Entry List size: " + aclEntryList.
size());
    for (AclEntry entry : aclEntryList) {
        System.out.println("User Principal Name: " + entry.
principal().getName());
        System.out.println("ACL Entry Type: " + entry.type());
        displayEntryFlags(entry.flags());
        displayPermissions(entry.permissions());
        System.out.println();
    }
}

private static void displayPermissions(Set<AclEntryPermission>
permissionSet) {
    if (permissionSet.isEmpty()) {
        System.out.println("No Permissions present");
```

```
        }
        else {
                System.out.println("Permissions");
                for (AclEntryPermission permission : permissionSet) {
                    System.out.print(permission.name() + " ");
        }
                System.out.println();
        }
        }


    private static void displayEntryFlags(Set<AclEntryFlag>
    flagSet) {
            if (flagSet.isEmpty()) {
                System.out.println("No ACL Entry Flags present");
        }
        else {
                System.out.println("ACL Entry Flags");
                for (AclEntryFlag flag : flagSet) {
                    System.out.print(flag.name() + " ");
        }
                System.out.println();
        }
        }
```

4. The ACL list contains the ACL entries for a file. When the `displayAclEntries` method is executed, it will display the number of entries as a convenience and then each entry will be separated by a blank line. The following illustrates a possible list for the `users.txt` file:

Owner: Richard-PC\Richard

ACL Entry List size: 4

User Principal Name: BUILTIN\Administrators

ACL Entry Type: ALLOW

No ACL Entry Flags present

Permissions

READ_DATA DELETE READ_NAMED_ATTRS READ_ATTRIBUTES WRITE_OWNER DELETE_CHILD WRITE_DATA APPEND_DATA SYNCHRONIZE EXECUTE WRITE_ATTRIBUTES WRITE_ACL WRITE_NAMED_ATTRS READ_ACL

User Principal Name: NT AUTHORITY\SYSTEM

ACL Entry Type: ALLOW

No ACL Entry Flags present

Permissions

READ_DATA DELETE READ_NAMED_ATTRS READ_ATTRIBUTES WRITE_OWNER DELETE_CHILD WRITE_DATA APPEND_DATA SYNCHRONIZE EXECUTE WRITE_ ATTRIBUTES WRITE_ACL WRITE_NAMED_ATTRS READ_ACL

User Principal Name: BUILTIN\Users

ACL Entry Type: ALLOW

No ACL Entry Flags present

Permissions

READ_DATA SYNCHRONIZE EXECUTE READ_NAMED_ATTRS READ_ATTRIBUTES READ_ACL

User Principal Name: NT AUTHORITY\Authenticated Users

ACL Entry Type: ALLOW

No ACL Entry Flags present

Permissions

APPEND_DATA READ_DATA DELETE SYNCHRONIZE EXECUTE READ_NAMED_ ATTRS READ_ATTRIBUTES WRITE_ATTRIBUTES WRITE_NAMED_ATTRS READ_ACL WRITE_DATA

5. Next, use the `UserPrincipalLookupService` class' `lookupService` method to return an instance of the `UserPrincipalLookupService` class. Use its `lookupPrincipalByName` method to return a `UserPrincipal` object based on a user's name. Add the following code after the `displayAclEntries` method is called:

```
        UserPrincipalLookupService lookupService =
FileSystems.getDefault().getUserPrincipalLookupService();
        UserPrincipal userPrincipal = lookupService.
lookupPrincipalByName("users");
```

6. Next, add the following code to create and set up an `AclEntry.Builder` object. This will be used to add `WRITE_ACL` and `DELETE` permissions for the user. Add the entry to the ACL list and use the `setAcl` method to attach it to the current file as follows:

```
        AclEntry.Builder builder = AclEntry.newBuilder();
        builder.setType(AclEntryType.ALLOW);
        builder.setPrincipal(userPrincipal);
        builder.setPermissions(
                AclEntryPermission.WRITE_ACL,
```

```
                          AclEntryPermission.DELETE);

              AclEntry entry = builder.build();
              aclEntryList.add(0, entry);
              view.setAcl(aclEntryList);
```

7. Execute the application. In order to modify some ACL attributes of a file, we must
   have the appropriate privileges. The introduction to this chapter gives the details of
   how to run the application as the administrator. Next, comment out the code that
   adds the ACL entry and verify that the ACL entry has been made. You should see the
   following entry added to the list:

   ACL Entry List size: 5

   User Principal Name: BUILTIN\Users

   ACL Entry Type: ALLOW

   No ACL Entry Flags present

   Permissions

   WRITE_ACL DELETE

How it works...

In the `main` method, we created the `Path` object, and then used it to obtain an instance of
the `java.nio.file.attribute.AclFileAttributeView` interface. The file represented
by the `Path` object was the `users.txt` file. The `AclFileAttributeView` object can be
used for several purposes. Here, we were only interested in using its `getAcl` method to return
a list of the ACL attributes associated with the file.

We displayed the list of current ACLs only to see what they were, and to eventually verify that
the attributes for the file have been changed. ACL attributes are associated with a user. In this
example, we created a `UserPrincipal` object that represented users.

A new ACL entry can be created using the `build` method of the `java.nio.file.`
`attribute.AclEntry.Builder` class. The static `newBuilder` method created an
instance of an `AclEntry.Builder` class. The `setPrincipal` method was executed to
set users as the principal for the attribute. The `setPermissions` method takes either a
set of `AclEntryPermission` objects or a variable number of `AclEntryPermission`
objects. In this example, we used a list consisting of two permissions separated by a comma:
`AclEntryPermission.WRITE_ACL` and `AclEntryPermission.DELETE`.

The `AclEntry.Builder` object was then added to the existing ACL for the file. The entry was
added at the beginning of the list. The last step was to use the `setAcl` method to replace the
old ACL list with this new one.

There's more...

To remove an ACL attribute, we need to obtain the current list and then identify the position of the attribute that we want to remove. We can use the `java.util.List` interface's `remove` method to remove that item. The `setAcl` method can then be used to replace the old list with the new one.

ACL attributes are explained in more detail in the **RFC 3530: Network File System (NFS) version 4 Protocol**. The following tables provide additional information and insight into the ACL permissions that are available. The enumeration `AclEntryType` has the following values:

Value	Meaning
ALARM	Results in an alarm being generated in a system-specific manner, when an attempt is made to access the attributes specified
ALLOW	Grants permissions
AUDIT	Logs the access requested in a system-dependent way, when an attempt is made to access the attributes specified
DENY	Denies access

The `AclEntryPermission` enumeration values are summarized in the table that follows:

Value	Meaning
APPEND_DATA	Ability to append data to a file
DELETE	Ability to delete the file
DELETE_CHILD	Ability to delete a file or directory within a directory
EXECUTE	Ability to execute a file
READ_ACL	Ability to read the ACL attribute
READ_ATTRIBUTES	Ability to read (non-ACL) file attributes
READ_DATA	Ability to read the data of the file
READ_NAMED_ATTRS	Ability to read the named attributes of a file
SYNCHRONIZE	Ability to access files locally at the server with synchronous reads and writes
WRITE_ACL	Ability to write the ACL attribute
WRITE_ATTRIBUTES	Ability to write (non-ACL) file attributes
WRITE_DATA	Ability to modify the file's data
WRITE_NAMED_ATTRS	Ability to write the named attributes of a file
WRITE_OWNER	Ability to change the owner

The `AclEntryFlag` enumeration is applied to directory entries. There are four values summarized as follows:

Value	Meaning
DIRECTORY_INHERIT	The ACL entry should be added to each new directory created
FILE_INHERIT	The ACL entry should be added to each new non-directory file created
INHERIT_ONLY	The ACL entry should be added to each new file or directory created
NO_PROPAGATE_INHERIT	The ACL entry should not be placed on the newly created directory, which is inheritable by subdirectories of the created directory

Currently, there are no flags associated with the `AclEntryType.AUDIT` or `AclEntryType.ALARM`.

Managing POSIX attributes

The POSIX attributes available include a group owner, a user owner, and a set of permissions. In this recipe, we will investigate how to maintain these attributes. The management of these attributes makes it easier to develop applications designed to execute on multiple operating systems. While the number of attributes is limited, they may be sufficient for many applications.

There are three approaches that can be used to manage POSIX attributes:

- The `java.nio.file.attribute.PosixFileAttributeView` interface
- The `Files` class' set/get POSIX file permission methods
- The `Files` class' `setAttribute` method

The approach used to gain access to the `PosixFileAttributes` object using the `PosixFileAttributeView` interface is detailed in the *Chapter 3* recipe *Using the PosixFileAttributeView to maintain POSIX file attributes*. Here, we will illustrate how to use the `PosixFileAttributeView` interface approach first, and demonstrate the last two approaches in the *There's more...* section of this recipe.

Getting ready

To maintain POSIX permission attributes for a file we need to:

1. Create a `Path` object representing the file or directory of interest.
2. Obtain a `PosixFileAttributes` object for that file.
3. Get a set of permissions for that file using the permissions method.

4. Modify the set of permissions.

5. Replace the permission using the `setPermissions` method.

How to do it...

1. We will create an application that obtains a `PosixFileAttributes` object and uses it to display the current permissions set for the `users.txt` file, and then add the `PosixFilePermission.OTHERS_WRITE` permission to the file. Create a new console application and add the following `main` method:

```
public static void main(String[] args) throws Exception {
    Path path = Paths.get("home/docs/users.txt");
    FileSystem fileSystem = path.getFileSystem();
    PosixFileAttributeView view = Files.
getFileAttributeView(path, PosixFileAttributeView.class);

    PosixFileAttributes attributes = view.readAttributes();
    Set<PosixFilePermission> permissions = attributes.
permissions();
    listPermissions(permissions);

    permissions.add(PosixFilePermission.OTHERS_WRITE);
    view.setPermissions(permissions);

    System.out.println();
    listPermissions(permissions);
}


    private static void listPermissions(Set<PosixFilePermission>
permissions) {
        System.out.print("Permissions: ");
        for (PosixFilePermission permission : permissions) {
            System.out.print(permission.name() + " ");
        }
        System.out.println();
    }
```

2. Execute the application on a system that supports POSIX. When executed under **Ubuntu 11.04** you should get results similar to the following:

Permissions: GROUP_READ OWNER_WRITE OTHERS_READ OWNER_READ

Permissions: GROUP_READ OWNER_WRITE OTHERS_WRITE OTHERS_READ OWNER_READ

How it works...

In the `main` method, we obtained a `Path` for the `users.txt` file and then used the `getFileAttributeView` method to get an instance of the `PosixFileAttributeView`. The `readAttributes` method was then used to obtain an instance of the `PosixFileAttributes` object representing the file's POSIX attributes.

The `listPermissions` method was used to list the permissions for the file. This method was executed once before and once after the new permission was added to the file. We did this simply to show the change in permissions.

The `PosixFilePermission.OTHERS_WRITE` permission was added to the permission set using the `add` method. The following table lists the `PosixFilePermission` enumeration values:

Value	Level	Permission Granted
GROUP_EXECUTE	Group	Execute and search
GROUP_READ		Read
GROUP_WRITE		Write
OTHERS_EXECUTE	Others	Execute and search
OTHERS_READ		Read
OTHERS_WRITE		Write
OWNER_EXECUTE	Owner	Execute and search
OWNER_READ		Read
OWNER_WRITE		Write

In this example, we added a `PosixFilePermission.OTHERS_WRITE` permission. In the next section, we will illustrate how to remove a permission.

There's more...

There are several other operations of interest including:

- ▶ Removing a file permission
- ▶ Modifying the POSIX ownership of a file
- ▶ Using the `Files` class' set/get POSIX file permission methods
- ▶ Using the `Files` class' `setAttribute` method
- ▶ Using the `PosixFilePermissions` class to create `PosixFilePermissions`

Removing a file permission

Removing a permission is simply a matter of:

▶ Obtaining a set of permissions for the file

▶ Using the `Set` interface's `remove` method to remove the permission

▶ Reassigning the set to the file

This is illustrated in the following code sequence, where the `PosixFilePermission.OTHERS_WRITE` permission is removed:

```
            Set<PosixFilePermission> permissions = attributes.
permissions();
            Permissions.remove(PosixFilePermission.OTHERS_WRITE);
            view.setPermissions(permissions);
```

Modifying the POSIX ownership of a file

The POSIX owners are specified at the group and user level. The `PosixFileAttributes` method's group and owner will return objects representing the group and user owners of the file. The `setGroup` and `setOwner` methods will set the corresponding memberships.

In the example that follows, the owners for the `users.txt` file are displayed and then changed. The `UserPrincipal` objects are created to support the `set` methods:

```
            Path path = Paths.get("home/docs/users.txt");
            try {
                FileSystem fileSystem = path.getFileSystem();
                PosixFileAttributeView view = Files.
getFileAttributeView(path, PosixFileAttributeView.class);

                PosixFileAttributes attributes = view.readAttributes();
                Set<PosixFilePermission> permissions = attributes.
permissions();

                System.out.println("Old Group: " + attributes.group().
getName());
                System.out.println("Old Owner: " + attributes.owner().
getName());
                System.out.println();

                UserPrincipalLookupService lookupService = FileSystems.
getDefault().getUserPrincipalLookupService();
                UserPrincipal userPrincipal = lookupService.lookupPrincipa
lByName("jennifer");
                GroupPrincipal groupPrincipal = lookupService.lookupPrinci
palByGroupName(("jennifer");
```

```
              view.setGroup(groupPrincipal);
              view.setOwner(userPrincipal);

              attributes = view.readAttributes();
              System.out.println("New Group: " + attributes.group().
    getName());
              System.out.println("New Owner: " + attributes.owner().
    getName());
              System.out.println();

    }
    catch (IOException ex) {
              ex.printStackTrace();
    }
```

When executed your output should appear as follows:

Setting owner for users.txt

Old Group: richard

Old Owner: richard

New Group: jennifer

New Owner: jennifer

You may need to execute the code as an administrator, as detailed in the introduction.

Using the Files class' set/get POSIX file permission methods

This approach uses the `Files` class' set `PosixFilePermissions` and
get `PosixFilePermissions` methods. The get `PosixFilePermissions` method returns
a set of `PosixFilePermissions` for the file specified by its first argument. Its second
argument is a `LinkOption`, which is used to determine how symbolic link files are handled.
Links are not normally followed, unless the `LinkOption.NOFOLLOW_LINKS` is used. We
could use the following code sequence to list the permissions associated with a file:

```
        Path path = Paths.get("home/docs/users.txt");
        try {
            Set<PosixFilePermission> permissions = Files.
    getPosixFilePermissions(path);
            System.out.print("Permissions: ");
            for (PosixFilePermission permission : permissions) {
                System.out.print(permission.name() + " ");
    }
```

```
        System.out.println();


}
catch (IOException ex) {
        ex.printStackTrace();
}
```

The `setPermissions` method takes a `Path` object representing the file and a set of `PosixFilePermission`. Instead of using the previous method:

```
        view.setPermissions(path, permissions);
```

We can use the `Files` class' `setPosixFilePermissions` method:

```
        Files.setPosixFilePermissions(path, permissions);
```

The use of the `Files` class simplifies the process by avoiding the creation of a `PosixFileAttributes` object.

Using the Files class' setAttribute method

The `Files` class' `getAttribute` method is detailed in the *Obtaining a single attribute at a time using the getAttribute method* recipe found in *Chapter 3*. The `setAttribute` method will set an attribute and has the following four arguments:

- ▸ A `Path` object representing the file
- ▸ A `String` containing the attribute to be set
- ▸ An object representing the value of the attribute
- ▸ An optional `LinkOption` value specifying how symbolic links are handled

The following illustrates adding the `PosixFilePermission.OTHERS_WRITE` permission to the `users.txt` file:

```
        Path path = Paths.get("home/docs/users.txt");
        try {
                Files.setAttribute(path, "posix:permission,
PosixFilePermission.OTHERS_WRITE);
}
catch (IOException ex) {
        ex.printStackTrace();
}
```

The `LinkOption` value was not used in this example.

Using the PosixFilePermissions class to create PosixFilePermissions

The `PosixFilePermissions` class possesses three methods:

- `asFileAttribute`, which returns a `FileAttribute` object that contains a set of `PosixFilePermissions`

- `fromString`, which also returns a set of `PosixFilePermissions` based on a `String` argument

- `toString`, which performs the inverse operation of the `fromString` method

All three methods are static. The first method returns a `FileAttribute` object, which can be used with the `createFile` or `createDirectory` method as discussed in the *Creating files and directories* recipe.

On Unix systems, file permissions are frequently expressed as a nine-character string. The string is grouped in three character groups. The first set represents permission of the user, the second represents permission of the group, and the last set represents the permission of all others. Each of the three character groups represent the read, write, or execute permissions granted for that set. An `r` in the first position grants read permission, a w in the second position indicates write permission, and an `x` in the last position grants execute permission. A - in any of these positions means that the permission is not set.

To illustrate these methods, execute the following code sequence:

```
Path path = Paths.get("home/docs/users.txt");
try {
    FileSystem fileSystem = path.getFileSystem();
    PosixFileAttributeView view = Files.
getFileAttributeView(path, PosixFileAttributeView.class);

    PosixFileAttributes attributes = view.readAttributes();
    Set<PosixFilePermission> permissions = attributes.
permissions();

    for(PosixFilePermission permission : permissions) {
        System.out.print(permission.toString() + ' ');
}
    System.out.println();

    FileAttribute<Set<PosixFilePermission>> fileAttributes =
PosixFilePermissions.asFileAttribute(permissions);
    Set<PosixFilePermission> fileAttributeSet =
fileAttributes.value();
    for (PosixFilePermission posixFilePermission :
fileAttributeSet) {
```

```
            System.out.print(posixFilePermission.toString() + ' ');
    }

        System.out.println();
        System.out.println(PosixFilePermissions.
  toString(permissions));
        permissions = PosixFilePermissions.fromString("rw-rw-r--");
        for(PosixFilePermission permission : permissions) {
            System.out.print(permission.toString() + ' ');
    }

        System.out.println();


    }
    catch (IOException ex) {
    }
```

Your output should be similar to the following:

OTHERS_READ OWNER_READ GROUP_READ OWNER_WRITE

OTHERS_READ OWNER_READ OWNER_WRITE GROUP_READ

rw-r--r--

OWNER_READ OWNER_WRITE GROUP_READ GROUP_WRITE OTHERS_READ

The first section of the code obtains a set of permissions for the users.txt file as detailed earlier in this recipe. The permissions were then displayed. Next, the asFileAttribute method was executed to return the FileAttribute for the file. The value method was used to obtain a set of the attributes, which were then displayed. The two sets of permissions were displayed but in a different order.

Next, the toString method was used to display this same set of permissions as a string. Notice each character reflects a permission granted for the users.txt file.

The last code segment created a new set of permissions using the fromString method. These permissions were then displayed to verify the conversion.

Moving a file and a directory

Moving a file or directory can be useful when reorganizing the structure of a user space. This operation is supported by the Files class' move method. When moving a file or directory there are several factors to consider. These include whether the symbolic link files are present, whether the move should replace existing files, and whether the move should be atomic.

A move may result in the renaming of the resource if the move occurs on the same file store. The use of this method will sometimes use the `Path` interface's `resolveSibling` method. This method will replace the last part of a path with its argument. This is useful when renaming files. The `resolveSibling` method is detailed in the *There's more...* section of the *Combining paths using path resolution* recipe in *Chapter 2, Locating Files and Directories Using Paths.*

Getting ready

In order to move a file or directory:

1. Obtain a `Path` object, which represents the file or directory to move.

2. Obtain a `Path` object, which represents the destination of the move.

3. Determine the copy options to control the move.

4. Execute the `move` method.

How to do it...

1. Create a new console application using the following `main` method. We will move the `users.txt` file to the `music` directory:

```
public static void main(String[] args) throws Exception {
    Path sourceFile = Paths.get("C:/home/docs/users.txt");
    Path destinationFile = Paths.get
        ("C:/home/music/users.txt");
    Files.move(sourceFile, destinationFile);
}
```

2. Execute the application. Examine the contents of the `docs` and `music` directories. The `users.txt` file should be absent from the `docs` directory, but present in the `music` directory.

How it works...

The `move` method used these two `Path` objects and did not use a third optional argument. This argument is used to determine how the copy operation works. When it is not used, the file copy operation defaults to a simple copy.

The `StandardCopyOption` enumeration implements the `CopyOption` interface and defines the types of copy operation supported. The `CopyOption` interface is used with the `Files` class' `copy` and `move` methods. The following table lists these options. These options are explained in more detail in the *There's more...* section:

Value	Meaning
`ATOMIC_MOVE`	The move operation is atomic in nature
`COPY_ATTRIBUTES`	The source file attributes are copied to the new file
`REPLACE_EXISTING`	The destination file is replaced if it exists

If the destination file already exists, then the `FileAlreadyExistsException` exception is thrown. However, if the `CopyOption.REPLACE_EXISTING` is used as the third argument of the `move` method, the exception is not thrown. When the source is a symbolic link, the link is copied and not the target of the link.

There's more...

There are several variations and issues that need to be covered. These include:

- Trivial uses of the `move` method
- The meaning of the `StandardCopyOption` enumeration values
- Using the `resolveSibling` method with the `move` method to affect a rename operation
- Moving a directory

Trivial uses of the move method

If the source file and the destination files are the same, the method will not have any effect. The following code sequence will have no effect:

```
Path sourceFile = ...;
Files.move(sourceFile, sourceFile);
```

No exception will be thrown and the file will not be moved.

The meaning of the StandardCopyOption enumeration values

The `StandardCopyOption` enumeration values require a bit more explanation. A value of the `StandardCopyOption.REPLACE_EXISTING` will replace the existing file if present. If the file is a symbolic link, then only the symbolic link file is replaced, not its target.

A value of `StandardCopyOption.COPY_ATTRIBUTES` will copy all of the attributes of the file. A value of `StandardCopyOption.ATOMIC_MOVE` specifies that the move operation is to be performed in an atomic fashion. All other enumeration values are ignored. However, if the destination file already exists, then either the file will be replaced or an `IOException` will be thrown. The result is implementation-dependent. If the move cannot be performed in an atomic fashion, then an `AtomicMoveNotSupportedException` is thrown. An atomic move may fail due to differences in the file store of the source and destination files.

If the following code sequence is executed on Windows 7:

```
Path sourceFile = Paths.get("C:/home/docs/users.txt");
Path destinationFile = Paths.get("C:/home/music/users.
  txt");
Files.move(sourceFile, destinationFile,
StandardCopyOption.ATOMIC_MOVE);
```

Then an `AccessDeniedException` exception is thrown if the destination file already exists. If the file does not exist, its execution will result in the following error message:

java.nio.file.AtomicMoveNotSupportedException: C:\home\docs\users.txt -> E:\home\music\users.txt: The system cannot move the file to a different disk drive

Using the resolveSibling method with the move method to affect a rename operation

The `resolveSibling` method will replace the last part of a path with a different string. This can be used to affect a rename operation when using the `move` method. In the following sequence, the `users.txt` file is effectively renamed:

```
Path sourceFile = Paths.get("C:/home/docs/users.txt");
Files.move(sourceFile, sourceFile.resolveSibling(sourceFile.
getFileName()+".bak"));
```

The file has been renamed to `users.txt.bak`. Notice that the source file path was used twice. To rename the file and replace its extension, we can use an explicit name as follows:

```
Files.move(sourceFile, sourceFile.resolveSibling("users.bak"));
```

A more sophisticated approach might use the following sequence:

```
Path sourceFile = Paths.get("C:/home/docs/users.txt");
String newFileName = sourceFile.getFileName().toString();
newFileName = newFileName.substring(0, newFileName.indexOf('.'))
+ ".bak";
Files.move(sourceFile, sourceFile.resolveSibling(newFileName));
```

The `substring` method returned a new filename starting with the first character and ending with the character immediately preceding the period.

Moving a directory

When a directory is moved on the same file store, then the directory and subdirectories are moved. The following will move the `docs` directory, its files, and its subdirectories to the `music` directory as follows:

```
Path sourceFile = Paths.get("C:/home/docs");
Path destinationFile = Paths.get("C:/home/music/docs");
Files.move(sourceFile, destinationFile);
```

However, executing this code sequence, where the `docs` directory is to be moved to a similar file structure on the `E` drive will result in a `DirectoryNotEmptyException` exception:

```
Path sourceFile = Paths.get("C:/home/docs");
Path destinationFile = Paths.get("E:/home/music/docs");
Files.move(sourceFile, destinationFile);
```

Moving a directory across file stores will result in an exception if the directory is not empty. If the `docs` directory had been empty in the previous example, the `move` method would have executed successfully. If you need to move a non-empty directory across file stores, then this will normally involve a copy operation followed by a delete operation.

Deleting files or directories

Deleting files or directories when they are no longer needed is a common operation. It will save space on a system and result in a cleaner filesystem. There are two methods of the `Files` class that can be used to delete a file or directory: `delete` and `deleteIfExists`. They both take a `Path` object as their argument and may throw an `IOException`.

Getting ready

To delete a file or directory, the following needs to be done:

1. Obtain a `Path` object, which represents the file or directory.
2. Use either the `delete` or `deleteIfExists` methods to delete the element.

How to do it...

1. Create a new console application and use the following `main` method:
```
public static void main(String[] args) throws Exception {
        Path sourceFile = Paths.get("C:/home/docs/users.txt");
        Files.delete(sourceFile);
}
```

2. Execute the application. If the `users.txt` file existed in the directory when the program ran, it should not be there after the program executes. If the file did not exist, then your program output should appear similar to the following:

java.nio.file.NoSuchFileException: C:\home\docs\users.txt

How it works...

This method is simple to use. We created a `Path` object representing the `users.txt` method. We then used it as an argument to the `delete` method. Since `delete` method may throw an `IOException`, the code was enclosed in a try-catch block.

To avoid an exception that would be thrown if the file did not exist, we could have used the `deleteIfExists` method instead. Replace the `delete` method invocation with the following:

```
Files.deleteIfExists(sourceFile);
```

Make sure that the file does not exist and then execute this code. The program should terminate normally without any exceptions being thrown.

There's more...

If we try to delete a directory, the directory must first be empty. If the directory is not empty, then a `DirectoryNotEmptyException` exception will be thrown. Execute the following code sequence in lieu of the previous example:

```
Path sourceFile = Paths.get("C:/home/docs");
Files.delete(sourceFile);
```

Assuming that the `docs` directory is not empty, the application should throw a `DirectoryNotEmptyException` exception.

The definition of an empty directory is dependent on the filesystem implementation. On some systems where the directory only contains special files or symbolic links, the directory may be considered to be empty.

If a directory is not empty and needs to be deleted, then it will be necessary to delete its entries first using the `walkFileTree` method as illustrated in the *Using the SimpleFileVisitor class to traverse file systems* recipe in *Chapter 5, Managing File Systems*.

 If the file to be deleted is a symbolic link, only the link is deleted, not the target of the link. Also, it may not be possible to delete a file if the file is open or in use by other applications.

Managing symbolic links

Symbolic links are files, which are not real files, but rather links to or points to the real file typically called the target file. These are useful when it is desirable to have a file appearing to be in more than one directory without actually having to duplicate the file. This saves space and keeps all of the updates isolated to a single file.

The `Files` class possesses the following three methods for working with symbolic links:

- The `createSymbolicLink` method, which creates a symbolic link to a target file that may not exist
- The `createLink` method creates a hard link to an existing file
- The `readSymbolicLink` retrieves a `Path` to the target file

Links are typically transparent to the users of the file. Any access to the symbolic link is redirected to the referenced file. Hard links are similar to symbolic links, but have more restrictions. These types of links are discussed in more detail in the *There's more...* section of this recipe.

Getting ready

In order to create a symbolic link to a file:

1. Obtain a `Path` object, which represents the link.
2. Obtain a `Path` object, which represents the target file.
3. Use these paths as the argument to the `createSymbolicLink` method.

How to do it...

1. Create a new console application. Add the following `main` method to the application. In this application, we will create a symbolic link in the `music` directory to the actual `users.txt` file in the `docs` directory.

   ```
   public static void main(String[] args) throws Exception {
           Path targetFile = Paths.get("C:/home/docs/users.txt");
           Path linkFile = Paths.get("C:/home/music/users.txt");
           Files.createSymbolicLink(linkFile, targetFile);
   }
   ```

2. Execute the application. If the application does not have sufficient privileges, then an exception will be thrown. An example of this when executed on Windows 7 is shown as follows:

   java.nio.file.FileSystemException: C:\home\music\users.txt: A required privilege is not held by the client.

3. Verify that a new file called `users.txt` exists in the `music` directory. Check the properties of the file to verify that it is a symbolic link. On Windows 7, right-click on the filename and select **Properties**. Next, select the **Shortcut** tab. It should appear as shown in the following screenshot:

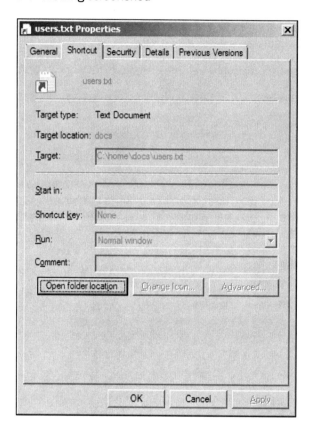

Notice that the target specified is the `users.txt` file in the `docs` directory.

How it works...

We created two `Path` objects. The first represented the target file in the `docs` directory. The second represented the link file to be created in the `music` directory. Next, we used the `createSymbolicLink` method to actually create the symbolic link. The entire code sequence was enclosed in a try block to catch any `IOExceptions` that may be thrown.

The third argument of the `createSymbolicLink` method can be one or more `FileAttribute` values. These are intended to be used to set attributes of the link file when it is created. However, it is currently not fully supported. Future versions of Java will enhance this capability. A `FileAttribute` can be created as detailed in the *There's more...* section of the *Managing POSIX file permissions* recipe.

There's more...

Here we will look more carefully at the following issues:

- Creating a hard link
- Creating a symbolic link to a directory
- Determining the target of a link file

Creating a hard link

Hard links have more restrictions placed upon them as opposed to symbolic links. These restrictions include the following:

- The target must exist. If not, an exception is thrown.
- A hard link cannot be made to a directory.
- Hard links can only be established within a single filesystem.

Hard links behave like a regular file. There are no overt properties of the file that indicate that it is a link file, as opposed to a symbolic link file which has a shortcut tab. All of the attributes of the hard link are identical to that of the target file.

Hard links are not used as frequently as soft links. `Path` class methods work with hard links and do not require any special considerations. A hard link is created using the `createLink` method. It accepts two arguments: a `Path` object for the link file and for the target file. In the following example, we create a hard link in the `music` directory instead of a symbolic link:

```
try {
    Path targetFile = Paths.get("C:/home/docs/users.txt");
    Path linkFile = Paths.get("C:/home/music/users.txt");
    Files.createLink(linkFile, targetFile);
}
catch (IOException ex) {
    ex.printStackTrace();
}
```

Execute the application. If you examine the properties of the link file, you observe that it is not displayed as a symbolic link. However, modifying the contents of either file will cause the other file to be modified also. They are effectively one and the same.

Creating a symbolic link to a directory

Creating a symbolic link to a directory uses the same methods as it did for files. In the following example, a new directory `tmp` is created, which is a symbolic link to the `docs` directory:

```
try {
    Path targetFile = Paths.get("C:/home/docs");
    Path linkFile = Paths.get("C:/home/tmp");
    Files.createSymbolicLink(linkFile, targetFile);
}
catch (IOException ex) {
    ex.printStackTrace();
}
```

All of the files in the `tmp` directory are effectively the symbolic links to the corresponding files in the `docs` directory.

Determining the target of a link file

The `isSymbolicLink` method, as discussed in the *Managing symbolic links* recipe in Chapter 2, *Locating Files and Directories Using Paths* determines whether a file is a symbolic link or not. The `readSymbolicLink` method accepts a `Path` object representing the link file and returns a `Path` object representing the target of the link.

The following code sequence illustrates this, where the `users.txt` file in the `music` directory is a symbolic link:

```
try {
    Path targetFile = Paths.get("C:/home/docs/users.txt");
    Path linkFile = Paths.get("C:/home/music/users.txt");
    System.out.println("Target file is: " + Files.
readSymbolicLink(linkFile));
}
catch (IOException ex) {
    ex.printStackTrace();
}
```

However, if the `users.txt` link file is a hard link, as created with the `createLink` method, we get the following exception when the code is executed:

java.nio.file.NotLinkException: The file or directory is not a reparse point.

A reparse point is an **NTFS** filesystem object that associates specific data to an application with a file or directory. A filesystem filter can be associated with the reparse point type. When the filesystem opens the file, it will pass this information to the filesystem filter for processing. This approach is a way of extending the functionality of the filesystem.

5

Managing Filesystems

In this chapter, we will cover the following:

- ▶ Getting FileStore information
- ▶ Getting FileSystem information
- ▶ Using the SimpleFileVisitor class to traverse filesystems
- ▶ Deleting a directory using the SimpleFileVisitor class
- ▶ Copying a directory using the SimpleFileVisitor class
- ▶ Processing the contents of a directory by using the DirectoryStream interface as explained in the *Filtering a directory using globbing* recipe
- ▶ Writing your own directory filter
- ▶ Monitoring file events using WatchEvents
- ▶ Understanding the ZIP filesystem provider

Introduction

A **filesystem** is one or more top-level root directories containing a hierarchy of files. A filesystem is supported by a file store that is the provider for the storage of the files. This chapter is concerned with obtaining information about these entities and typical filesystem tasks, such as determining the contents of a directory or monitoring filesystem events.

A file store represents a unit of storage. For example, it might represent a device, such as a C drive, a partition of a drive, or a volume. The `java.nio.file.FileStore` class supports file stores and provides several methods to this end. The *Getting FileStore information* recipe covers how to obtain basic information about a specific file store.

A filesystem supports access to a hierarchy of directories and files. It is represented in Java 7 with the `java.nio.file.FileSystem` class. Obtaining general information about a filesystem is covered in the *Getting FileSystem information* recipe. This includes how to obtain a list of root directories for a filesystem and the underlying file stores.

Traversing a directory hierarchy is useful for many applications. The *Using the SimpleFileVisitor class to traverse filesystems* recipe details the basic approach. This approach is used in the *Deleting a directory using the SimpleFileVisitor class* and *Copying a directory using the SimpleFileVisitor class* recipes.

When an operation is restricted to a single directory, the `java.nio.file.DirectoryStream` interface provides a convenient technique for examining each element in the directory as a `java.nio.file.Path` object. It is very easy to use a for each loop to process these paths. This approach is explored in the *Using the DirectoryStream interface to process the contents of a directory* recipe.

Sometimes we don't need the entire contents of a directory, but rather a subset of its elements. Java 7 provides a few approaches to filtering the contents of a directory as described in the *Filtering a directory using globbing* and *Writing your own directory filter* recipes. **Globbing** is a pattern-matching technique that is similar to regular expressions but is easier to use.

In the *Monitoring file events using WatchEvents* recipe we learn how Java 7 supports the detection of file creation, modification, and deletion within a directory by external processes. This can be very useful when it is necessary to know when changes to a directory are made.

With Java 7, it is now possible to treat the contents of a ZIP file as a filesystem. This makes it easier to manage the contents of a ZIP file and to manipulate the files contained within the ZIP file. This technique is demonstrated in the *Understanding the zip filesystem provider* recipe.

Getting FileStore information

Each filesystem supports a file storage mechanism. This may be a device, such as a C drive, a partition of a drive, a volume, or some other way of organizing a filesystem's space. The `java.nio.file.FileStore` class represents one of these storage divisions. This recipe details the methods available to obtain information about the file store.

Getting ready

To obtain and use a `FileStore` object:

1. Obtain an instance of the `java.nio.file.FileSystem` in use.
2. Use the `FileSystem` class' `getFileStores` method to return the available file stores.

How to do it...

1. Create a new console application. In the `main` method, we will use several methods of the `FileStore` class to demonstrate the support provided by this class. Let's start by adding the first part of the `main` method, where we display an initial header and get a `FileSystem` object. Also, define a `long` variable called `kiloByte`:

```
static final long kiloByte = 1024;

    public static void main(String[] args) throws IOException {
        String format = "%-16s %-20s %-8s %-8s %12s %12s %12s\n";
        System.out.printf(format,"Name", "Filesystem", "Type",
                "Readonly", "Size(KB)", "Used(KB)",
                "Available(KB)");
        FileSystem fileSystem = FileSystems.getDefault();

}
```

2. Next, we need to use the `getFileStores` method to retrieve the available file stores and then display them. In the first part of the block, we use several `FileStore` methods to get relevant information. In the last part, we display the information as follows:

```
        for (FileStore fileStore : fileSystem.getFileStores()) {
            try {
                long totalSpace = fileStore.getTotalSpace() /
kiloByte;
                long usedSpace = (fileStore.getTotalSpace() -
                        fileStore.getUnallocatedSpace()) /
kiloByte;
                long usableSpace = fileStore.getUsableSpace() /
kiloByte;
                String name = fileStore.name();
                String type = fileStore.type();
                boolean readOnly = fileStore.isReadOnly();

                NumberFormat numberFormat = NumberFormat.
getInstance();
                System.out.printf(format,
                        name, fileStore, type, readOnly,
                        numberFormat.format(totalSpace),
                        numberFormat.format(usedSpace),
                        numberFormat.format(usableSpace));
        }
        catch (IOException ex) {
                ex.printStackTrace();
        }
        }
```

3. Execute the application. Your output will differ from the following, but should reflect the drives on your system:

Name	Filesystem	Type	Readonly	Size(KB)	Used(KB)	Available(KB)
HP	HP (C:)	NTFS	false	301,531,984	163,041,420	138,490,564
FACTORY_IMAGE	FACTORY_IMAGE (D:)	NTFS	false	11,036,652	9,488,108	1,548,544
HP_PAVILION	HP_PAVILION (E:)	NTFS	false	312,568,640	66,489,184	246,079,456
TOSHIBA	TOSHIBA (H:)	FAT32	false	15,618,080	3,160,768	12,457,312

How it works...

A format string was created to simplify the display of the file store information. This string was used in both of the `printf` methods. Using the same string twice ensures consistent spacing of the output. A simple title was displayed using this string.

A `FileSystem` object was obtained using the `FileSystems` class' `getDefault` method. The `getFileStores` method was executed against this object to obtain a list of `FileStore` objects.

Within the loop, a try block was used to catch exceptions that might have been thrown. Several methods were invoked as detailed in the following table. An instance of the `NumberFormat` class was created to format file store size information. The last `printf` method displayed the file store information for each file store:

Method	Meaning
`getTotalSpace`	The total space available on the file store in bytes
`getUnallocatedSpace`	The number of unallocated bytes
`getUsableSpace`	The number of usable bytes available to the JVM
`name`	An implementation-specific string representing the file store name
`type`	An implementation-specific string representing the file store type
`isReadOnly`	If the method returns `true`, then attempts to create a file or open a file for writing will result in an `IOException` being thrown

The values returned by the `getUnallocatedSpace` or `getUsableSpace` methods can change if an external operation uses or releases space on the file store.

See also

The attribute views as supported by a `FileStore` are determined using one of the two `supportsFileAttributeView` methods. These are illustrated in the *There's more...* section of the *Determining operating system support for attribute views* recipe in *Chapter 3, Obtaining File and Directory Information*.

Getting Filesystem information

A filesystem is composed of a hierarchy of directories and files. There is a limited amount of information regarding a filesystem that is normally useful. For example, we may want to know whether the filesystem is read-only or who the provider is. In this recipe we will examine the methods available to retrieve filesystem attributes.

Getting ready

To access the method of a filesystem we need to:

1. Obtain a reference to a `java.nio.file.FileSystem` object.
2. Use the methods of this object to access filesystem information.

How to do it...

1. Create a new console application. Add the following code to the `main` method of the application. This sequence displays several `fileSystem` attributes, including the filesystem provider, file open status, whether the file is available to be read-only, the root directories, and the names of the file stores:

```
FileSystem fileSystem = FileSystems.getDefault();
FileSystemProvider provider = fileSystem.provider();

System.out.println("Provider: " + provider.toString());
System.out.println("Open: " + fileSystem.isOpen());
System.out.println("Read Only: " + fileSystem.isReadOnly());

Iterable<Path> rootDirectories = fileSystem.getRootDirectories();
System.out.println();
System.out.println("Root Directories");
```

```
        for (Path path : rootDirectories) {
            System.out.println(path);
    }


        Iterable<FileStore> fileStores = fileSystem.
getFileStores();
        System.out.println();
        System.out.println("File Stores");
        for (FileStore fileStore : fileStores) {
            System.out.println(fileStore.name());

    }
```

2. Execute the application. Your output will depend upon the configuration of your system. However, it should mimic the output that follows:

Provider: sun.nio.fs.WindowsFileSystemProvider@7b60e796

Open: true

Read Only: false

Root Directories

C:

D:

E:

F:

G:

H:

I:

J:

K:

L:

File Stores

HP

FACTORY_IMAGE

HP_PAVILION

TOSHIBA

The `getDefault` method returned the default filesystem used by the JVM. Next, several methods were invoked against this object:

- The `provider` method returned the provider, that is, implementer of the filesystem. In this case, it was a Windows filesystem provider that came bundled with the JVM.

- The `isOpen` method indicated that the filesystem is open and ready for use.

- The `isReadOnly` method returned `false`, meaning that we can read and write to the system.

- We used the `getRootDirectories` method to create an `Iterable` object that permitted us to list each root directory.

- The `getFileStores` method returned another `Iterable` object, which was used to display the names of the file stores.

While we do not normally need to close a filesystem, the `close` method can be used to close the filesystem. Any subsequent methods executed against the filesystem will result in a `ClosedFileSystemException` being thrown. Any open channels, directory streams, and watch services associated with the filesystem will also be closed. Note that the default filesystem cannot be closed.

The `FileSystems` class' `getFileSystem` method can be used to access a specific filesystem. In addition, the overloaded `newFileSystem` method will create new filesystems. The `close` method can be used with these instances.

Filesystems are thread-safe. However, if one thread attempts to close the filesystem while another thread is accessing the `filesystem` object, the close operation may be blocked until the access is complete.

Using the SimpleFileVisitor class to traverse filesystems

When working with directory systems, a common need is to traverse the filesystem examining each subdirectory within a file hierarchy. This task has been made easy with the `java.nio.file.SimpleFileVisitor` class. This class implements methods that execute before and after a directory is visited. In addition, callback methods are invoked for each instance a file is visited in a directory and if an exception occurs.

The `SimpleFileVisitor` class or a derived class is used in conjunction with the `java.nio.file.Files` class' `walkFileTree` method. It performs a depth first traversal, starting at a specific root directory.

Getting ready

To traverse a directory we need to:

1. Create a `Path` object representing the root directory.

2. Create an instance of a class derived from `SimpleFileVisitor`.

3. Use these objects as arguments to the `Files` class' `walkFileTree` method.

How to do it...

1. Create a new console application and use the following `main` method. Here, we will traverse the `home` directory and list each of its elements as follows:

```
public static void main(String[] args) {
        try {
                Path path = Paths.get("/home");
                ListFiles listFiles = new ListFiles();
                Files.walkFileTree(path, listFiles);
        }
catch (IOException ex) {
                ex.printStackTrace();
        }
        }
```

2. Add the following `ListFiles` class to your project. It illustrates the use of each of the `SimpleFileVisitor` methods:

```
class ListFiles extends SimpleFileVisitor<Path> {
    private final int indentionAmount = 3;
    private int indentionLevel;

    public ListFiles() {
        indentionLevel = 0;
    }

    private void indent() {
        for(int i=0 ; i<indentionLevel; i++) { {
            System.out.print(' ');
```

```
        }
    }

        @Override
        public FileVisitResult visitFile(Path file,
    BasicFileAttributes attributes) {
            indent();
            System.out.println("Visiting file:" + file.getFileName());
            return FileVisitResult.CONTINUE;
        }

        @Override
        public FileVisitResult postVisitDirectory(Path directory,
    IOException e) throws IOException {
            indentionLevel -= indentionAmount;
            indent();
            System.out.println("Finished with the directory: " +
    directory.getFileName());
            return FileVisitResult.CONTINUE;
        }

        @Override
        public FileVisitResult preVisitDirectory(Path directory,
    BasicFileAttributes attributes) throws IOException {
            indent();
            System.out.println("About to traverse the directory: " +
    directory.getFileName());
            indentionLevel += indentionAmount;
            return FileVisitResult.CONTINUE;
        }

        @Override
        public FileVisitResult visitFileFailed(Path file, IOException
    exc) throws IOException {
            System.out.println("A file traversal error ocurred");
            return super.visitFileFailed(file, exc);
        }
    }
```

3. Execute the application. Depending on the structure of your home directory, you may get results different from the following:

About to traverse the directory: home

  About to traverse the directory: docs

    Visiting file:users.bak

Visiting file:users.txt

Finished with the directory: docs

About to traverse the directory: music

Visiting file:Future Setting A.mp3

Visiting file:Robot Brain A.mp3

Visiting file:Space Machine A.mp3

Finished with the directory: music

Finished with the directory: home

Examine the `backup` directory to verify that it was created successfully.

How it works...

In the `main` method, we created a `Path` object for the `home` directory. Next, an instance of the `ListFiles` class was created. These objects were used as the arguments of the `walkFileTree` method. This method affected the traversal of the `home` directory and invoked the methods of the `ListFiles` class as required.

The `walkFileTree` method started at a root directory, and performed a depth first traversal of the directory hierarchy. Before a directory was traversed, the `preVisitDirectory` method was invoked. Next, each element of the directory was processed. If it was a file, then the `visitFile` method was invoked. Once all of the elements of the directory had been processed, the `postVisitDirectory` method was invoked. If an exception had occurred, then the `visitFileFailed` method would have been invoked.

Private helper methods were added, which made the output more readable. The `indentionAmount` variable controlled the depth of each indention. The `indentionLevel` variable was incremented and decremented as each subdirectory was visited. The `indent` method preformed the actual indention.

There's more...

There are two overloaded `walkFileTree` methods. One takes a `Path` and a `FileVisitor` object, which was illustrated previously. It will not follow links and will visit all levels of the directory. The second method takes two additional arguments: one that specifies the number of directory levels to be visited and a second one to configure the traversal. Currently, the only configuration option available is `FileVisitOption.FOLLOW_LINKS`, which directs the method to follow symbolic links.

Symbolic links are not followed by default. If they are followed when specified by an argument of the `walkFileTree` method, then care is taken to detect circular links. If a circular link is detected, it is treated as an error condition.

The number of levels of directories to visit is controlled by an integer argument. A value of 0 will result in only the top-level directory being visited. A value of `Integer.MAX_VALUE` means that all of the levels will be visited. A value of two means only the first two directory levels are traversed.

The traversal will terminate when one of the following conditions occurs:

- All files have been traversed
- A `visit` method returns `FileVisitResult.TERMINATE`
- A `visit` method terminates with an `IOException`, or other exception is propagated back

Any unsuccessful action will generally result in the `visitFileFailed` method being invoked and an `IOException` being thrown.

When a file is encountered, and if it is not a directory, then an attempt is made to read its `BasicFileAttributes`. If successful, the attribute is passed to the `visitFile` method. If unsuccessful, the `visitFileFailed` method is invoked, and it will throw an `IOException` unless it is dealt with.

If the file is a directory and the directory can be opened, then the `preVisitDirectory` is invoked and the elements of the directory and their descendants are visited.

If the file is a directory and the directory could not be opened, the `visitFileFailed` method is invoked and it will throw an `IOException`. However, the depth-first search will continue with the next sibling.

The following table summarizes the traversal process.

Element encountered	Can be opened	Fails to open
File	`visitFile` is invoked	`visitFileFailed` is invoked
Directory	`preVisitDirectory` is called Directory elements are processed `postVisitDirectory` is invoked	`visitFileFailed` is invoked

For convenience, the enumeration constants for the enumeration `FileVisitResult` are listed as follows:

Value	Meaning
CONTINUE	Continue the traversal
SKIP_SIBLINGS	Continue without visiting the siblings of this file or directory
SKIP_SUBTREE	Continue without visiting the entries in this directory
TERMINATE	Terminate

See also

The *Deleting a directory using the SimpleFileVisitor class* and *Copying a directory using the SimpleFileVisitor class* recipes utilize the approach described in this recipe to delete and copy a directory respectively.

Deleting a directory using the SimpleFileVisitor class

The ability to delete a directory is a requirement of some applications. This can be achieved using the `walkFileTree` method and a `java.nio.file.SimpleFileVisitor` derived class. This recipe builds on the foundation provided in the *Using the SimpleFileVisitor class to traverse filesystems* recipe.

Getting ready

To delete a directory, we need to:

1. Create a `Path` object representing the root directory.

2. Create an instance of a class derived from `SimpleFileVisitor` as follows:

    ❑ Override the `visitFile` method to delete the file

    ❑ Override the `postVisitDirectory` method to delete the directory

3. Use these objects as arguments to the `Files` class' `walkFileTree` method.

How to do it...

1. Create a new console application. Here, we will delete the `home` directory and all of its elements. Add the following code to the `main` method:

```
try {
        Files.walkFileTree(Paths.get("/home"), new
DeleteDirectory());
}
catch (IOException ex) {
        ex.printStackTrace();
}
```

2. The `DeleteDirectory` class is shown as follows. As each file and directory is deleted, a message is displayed to that effect:

```
public class DeleteDirectory extends SimpleFileVisitor<Path> {
    @Override
    public FileVisitResult visitFile(Path file,
BasicFileAttributes attributes)
            throws IOException {
        System.out.println("Deleting " + file.getFileName());
        Files.delete(file);
        return FileVisitResult.CONTINUE;
    }


    @Override
    public FileVisitResult postVisitDirectory(Path directory,
IOException exception)
            throws IOException {
        if (exception == null) {
            System.out.println("Deleting " + directory.
getFileName());
            Files.delete(directory);
            return FileVisitResult.CONTINUE;
    }
    else {
            throw exception;
    }
    }
    }
```

3. Back up the `home` directory and then execute the application. You should get the following output depending on the actual directory structure:

Deleting users.bak

Deleting users.txt

Deleting docs

Deleting Future Setting A.mp3

Deleting Robot Brain A.mp3

Deleting Space Machine A.mp3

Deleting music

Deleting home

Verify that the directory was deleted.

How it works...

In the `main` method, we created a `Path` object representing the `home` directory. Next, we created an instance of the `DeleteDirectory` class. These two objects were used as arguments to the `walkFileTree` method, which started the traversal process.

When a file is encountered, the `visitFile` method was executed. In this method, we displayed a message indicating that the file was being deleted, and then used the `Files` class' `delete` method to delete the file. When a directory was encountered, the `postVisitDirectory` method was invoked. A test was made to ensure that no errors had occurred, and then a message was displayed indicating that the directory was being deleted followed by the invocation of the `delete` method for that directory. Both of the methods returned `FileVisitResult.CONTINUE`, which continues the deletion process.

See also

The *Using the SimpleFileVisitor class to traverse filesystems* recipe provides more detail on the use of the `walkFileTree` method and the `SimpleFileVisitor` class. The *Copying a directory using the SimpleFileVisitor class* recipe also provides a variation of the use of this approach.

Copying a directory using the SimpleFileVisitor class

The ability to copy a directory is a requirement of some applications. This can be achieved using the `walkFileTree` method and a `java.nio.file.SimpleFileVisitor` derived class. This recipe builds on the foundation provided in the *Using the SimpleFileVisitor class to traverse filesystems* recipe.

Getting ready

To delete a directory, we need to:

1. Create a `Path` object representing the root directory.

2. Create an instance of a class derived from the `SimpleFileVisitor` as follows:

   ❏ Override the `visitFile` method to copy the file

   ❏ Override the `preVisitDirectory` method to copy the directory

3. Use these objects as arguments to the `Files` class' `walkFileTree` method.

How to do it...

1. Create a new console application. Here, we will copy the `home` directory and all of its elements to a `backup` directory. Add the following code to the `main` method:

```
try {
    Path source = Paths.get("/home");
    Path target = Paths.get("/backup");
    Files.walkFileTree(source,
    EnumSet.of(FileVisitOption.FOLLOW_LINKS),
            Integer.MAX_VALUE,
            new CopyDirectory(source, target));
}
catch (IOException ex) {
        ex.printStackTrace();
}
```

2. The `CopyDirectory` class is shown as follows. As each file and directory is deleted, a message is displayed to that effect:

```
public class CopyDirectory extends SimpleFileVisitor<Path> {
    private Path source;
    private Path target;

    public CopyDirectory(Path source, Path target) {
        this.source = source;
        this.target = target;
    }

    @Override
    public FileVisitResult visitFile(Path file,
BasicFileAttributes attributes) throws IOException {
        System.out.println("Copying " + source.relativize(file));
        Files.copy(file, target.resolve(source.relativize(file)));
        return FileVisitResult.CONTINUE;
```

```
        }
        @Override
        public FileVisitResult preVisitDirectory(Path directory,
    BasicFileAttributes attributes) throws IOException {
            Path targetDirectory = target.resolve(source.
    relativize(directory));
            try {
                System.out.println("Copying " + source.
    relativize(directory));
                Files.copy(directory, targetDirectory);
        }
        catch (FileAlreadyExistsException e) {
                if (!Files.isDirectory(targetDirectory)) {
                    throw e;
        }
        }

            return FileVisitResult.CONTINUE;
        }
        }
```

3. Execute the application. The exact output is dependent on the source file structure you used, but should be similar to the following:

Copying

Copying docs

Copying docs\users.bak

Copying docs\users.txt

Copying music

Copying music\Future Setting A.mp3

Copying music\Robot Brain A.mp3

Copying music\Space Machine A.mp3

How it works...

In the `main` method, we created `Path` objects for the `home` and `backup` directories. We used these objects to create a `CopyDirectory` object. We used a two-argument `CopyDirectory` constructor, so that its methods would have direct access to the two paths.

The `walkFileTree` method was invoked with the source `Path`. It was also passed as the second argument, an `EnumSet`, which specified that symbolic links were not to be followed. This argument required a set of options. The `EnumSet` class' static method created the set.

The third argument of the `walkFileTree` method was a value indicating how many levels to follow. We passed a value of `Integer.MAX_VALUE`, which results in all of the levels of the home directory being copied. The last argument was an instance of the `CopyDirectory` object.

When a file was encountered during the traversal, the `CopyDirectory` class' `visitFile` method was invoked. A message was displayed indicating that the file was being copied, followed by the use of the `copy` method to copy the source file to the target directory. The `relativize` method was used to obtain a relative path to the source, which was used as the argument of the `resolve` method. The result is a `Path` object representing the target directory with the source filename. These methods are discussed in the *Combining paths using path resolution* and *Creating a path between two locations* recipes in *Chapter 2, Locating Files and Directories Using Paths*.

When a directory was encountered during the traversal, the `preVisitDirectory` method was invoked. It works the same way as the `visitFile` method, except we copied a directory instead of a file. Both of the methods returned `FileVisitResult.CONTINUE`, which continues the copying process. It is still necessary to copy the individual files of a directory, since the `copy` method only copies a single file.

Notice that the `CopyDirectory` class extended the `SimpleFileVisitor` class using `Path` as the generic value. The `walkFileTree` method requires an object that implements the `Path` interface. Thus we had to use `Path` or an interface that extended `Path`.

See also

The *Using the SimpleFileVisitor class to traverse filesystems* recipe provides more detail on the use of the `walkFileTree` method and the `SimpleFileVisitor` class. The *Deleting a directory using the SimpleFileVisitor class* recipe also provides a variation on the use of this approach.

Processing the contents of a directory by using the DirectoryStream interface

Determining the contents of a directory is a fairly common requirement. There are several approaches to doing this. In this recipe, we will examine the use of the `java.nio.file.DirectoryStream` interface in support of this task.

A directory will consist of files or subdirectories. These files may be regular files or possibly linked or hidden. The `DirectoryStream` interface will return all of these element types. We will use the `java.nio.file.Files` class' `newDirectoryStream` method to obtain a `DirectoryStream` object. There are three overloaded versions of this method. The simplest use of the method is illustrated first. The versions used to filter the contents of the directory are shown in the *Filtering a directory using globbing* recipe and the *Writing your own directory filter* recipe.

Getting ready

In order to use the `DirectoryStream`, we need to:

1. Obtain an instance of a `DirectoryStream` object.

2. Iterate through the `DirectoryStream` to process its elements.

How to do it...

1. Create a new console application and add the following `main` method. We create a new `DirectoryStream` object and then use a for each loop to iterate through the directory elements as follows:

```
public static void main(String[] args) {
    Path directory = Paths.get("/home");
    try (DirectoryStream<Path> directoryStream = Files.
newDirectoryStream(directory)) {
        for (Path file : directoryStream) {
            System.out.println(file.getFileName());
}
}
catch (IOException | DirectoryIteratorException ex) {
        ex.printStackTrace();
}
}
```

2. Execute the application. Your output should reflect the contents of your home directory and should be similar to the following:

   docs

   music

How it works...

A `Path` object was created for the home directory. This object was used with the `newDirectoryStream` method, which returned a `DirectoryStream` object for the directory. The `DirectoryStream` interface extends the `Iterable` interface. This allowed the `DirectoryStream` object to be used with a for each statement, which simply printed the name of each element of the home directory. In this case, there were only two subdirectories: `docs` and `music`.

Notice the use of the try-with-resource block. This is new to Java 7 and is discussed in the *Using the try-with-resource block to improve exception handling code* recipe found in *Chapter 1, Java Language Improvements*. This guarantees that the directory stream will be closed. If this type of try block was not used, then it is important to close the stream after it is no longer needed.

The `Iterable` object used is not a general-purpose `iterator`. It differs in several important aspects as follows:

- It only supports a single `Iterator`
- The `hasNext` method performs a read-ahead of at least one element
- It does not support the `remove` method

The `DirectoryStream` interface has a single method, `iterator`, which returns an `Iterator` type object. The first time the method is invoked, an `Iterator` object is returned. Subsequent invocation of the method will throw an `IllegalStateException`.

The `hasNext` method will read ahead by at least one element. If the method returns `true`, then the next invocation of its next method is guaranteed to return an element. The order of the elements returned is not specified. Also, many operating systems have links to themselves and/or their parent as represented by a " . " or " . . " in many shells. These entries are not returned.

The `iterator` returned is sometimes referred to as **weakly consistent**. This means that while the `iterator` is thread-safe, any updates to the directory after the `iterator` has returned will not result in a change to the `iterator`.

There's more...

There are two overloaded `newDirectoryStream` methods, which allow the results of the method to be filtered either by a globbing pattern or a `DirectoryStream.Filter` object. A **globbing pattern** is a string containing a series of characters that define a pattern. The pattern is used to determine which directory elements to return. A `DirectoryStream.Filter` interface has a single method, `accept`, which returns a Boolean value indicating whether the directory element should be returned or not.

See also

The *Filtering a directory using globbing* recipe illustrates the use of the globbing pattern. The *Writing your own directory filter* recipe shows how to create and use a `DirectoryStream.Filter` object to filter the contents of a directory.

Filtering a directory using globbing

A globbing pattern is similar to a regular expression but it is simpler. Like a regular expression it can be used to match specific character sequences. We can use globbing in conjunction with the `newDirectoryStream` method to filter the contents of a directory. The use of this method is demonstrated in the *Using the DirectoryStream interface to process the contents of a directory* recipe.

Getting ready

To use this technique we need to:

1. Create a globbing string that meets our filtering requirements.
2. Create a `java.nio.file.Path` object for the directory of interest.
3. Use these two objects as arguments to the `newDirectoryStream` method.

How to do it...

1. Create a new console application and use the following `main` method. In this example, we will list only those directory elements that start with `java` and end with `.exe`. We will use the Java 7 `bin` directory. The `globbing` string uses the special character, `*` to represent zero or more characters as follows:

```
Path directory = Paths.get("C:/Program Files/Java/
jdk1.7.0/bin");
    try (DirectoryStream<Path> directoryStream = Files.newDire
ctoryStream(directory,"java*.exe")) {
        for (Path file : directoryStream) {
            System.out.println(file.getFileName());
}
}
catch (IOException | DirectoryIteratorException ex) {
        ex.printStackTrace();
}
```

2. Execute the application. The output should be similar to the following:

java-rmi.exe

java.exe

javac.exe

javadoc.exe

javah.exe

javap.exe

javaw.exe

javaws.exe

How it works...

First, a `Path` object representing the `bin` directory was created. It was then used as the first argument to the `newDirectoryStream` method. The second argument was the `globbing` string. In this case, it matched a directory element which started with `java` and ended with `.exe`. Any number of intermediate characters were allowed. A for each loop was then used to display the filtered files.

There's more...

Globbing strings are based on patterns, which use special characters to match string sequences. These are defined in the documentation for the `Files` class' `getPathMatcher` method. Here, we will examine those strings in more depth. There are several special characters summarized in the following table:

Special Symbols	Meaning
*	Matches zero or more characters of a name component without crossing directory boundaries
**	Matches zero or more characters crossing directory boundaries
?	Matches exactly one character of a name component
\	The escape character used to match the special symbols
[]	Matches a single character found within the brackets. A - matches a range. A ! means negation. The *, ?, and \ characters match themselves, and a - matches itself if it is the first character within the brackets or the first character after the !.
{}	Multiple subpatterns can be specified at the same time. These patterns are grouped together using the curly braces, but are separated within the curly braces by commas.

Matching is typically performed in an implementation-dependent manner. This includes whether matching is case sensitive or not. The ** symbol is not applicable here, since the `newDirectoryStream` method returns individual elements. There is no opportunity here to match sequences that cross directory boundaries. Other methods will use this capability.

The following table presents several examples of potentially useful globbing patterns:

Globbing String	Will Match
`*.java`	Any filename that ends with `.java`
`*.{java,class,jar}`	Any file that ends with `.java`, `.class`, or `.jar`
`java*[ph].exe`	Only those files that start with java and are terminated with either a `p.exe` or `h.exe`
`j*r.exe`	Those files that start with a `j` and end with an `r.exe`

Now, let's discuss the use of the `PathMatcher` interface.

Using the PathMatcher interface to filter a directory

The `java.nio.file.PathMatcher` interface provides a method of matching a filename using a **glob**. It has a single method `matches`, which accepts a `Path` argument. If the file matches the glob pattern, then it returns `true`. Otherwise, it returns `false`.

In the following code sequence, we modify the previous example by creating a `PathMatcher` object using the glob pattern: `glob:java?.exe`. Within the for loop, we use the `matches` method to further filter a subset of the file that starts with `java` and is followed by a single character and then ends with `.exe`:

```
        Path directory = Paths.get("C:/Program Files/Java/jdk1.7.0/
    bin");
        PathMatcher pathMatcher = FileSystems.getDefault().
    getPathMatcher("glob:java?.exe");
        try (DirectoryStream<Path> directoryStream =
                Files.newDirectoryStream(directory,"java*.exe")) {
            for (Path file : directoryStream) {
                if(pathMatcher.matches(file.getFileName())) {
                    System.out.println(file.getFileName());
}
}
}
    catch (IOException | DirectoryIteratorException ex) {
            ex.printStackTrace();
}
```

When you execute this sequence, you should get the following output:

javac.exe

javah.exe

javap.exe

javaw.exe

Notice the use of the **glob:** prefix used with the `matches` method. Its use is required with this method, but not with the `newDirectoryStream` method. Also, the `matches` method takes a `Path` argument. However, notice that we used the `String` returned from the `Path` class' `getFileName` method. Using the `Path` object only or using a `String` literal does not work.

Instead of using the glob: prefix, we can use regular expressions instead. To do this, use a **reg:** prefix followed by a regular expression.

Normally, for a simple filtering of a directory, we would use the more restrictive glob pattern as part of the `newDirectoryStream` method. We used it here for illustrative purposes. However, if we wanted to perform more than one filtering operation as part of a loop, then using a pattern as part of the `newDirectoryStream` method, and later with the use of one or more `matches` method invocations is a viable strategy.

See also

The *Writing your own directory filter* recipe explores how to create more powerful filters to match filenames based on attributes other than the filename.

Writing your own directory filter

A directory filter is used to control which directory elements are returned, when using the `java.nio.file.Files` class' `newDirectoryStream` method. This is useful when we need to limit the stream's output. For example, we may only be interested in those files that exceed a certain size or were last modified after a certain date. The `java.nio.file.DirectoryStream.Filter` interface, as described in this recipe will restrict the stream's output. It is more powerful than using globbing as described in the *Filtering a directory using globbing* recipe because decisions can be based on factors other than the filename.

Getting ready

To use this technique we need to:

1. Create a `DirectoryStream.Filter` object that meets our filtering requirements.
2. Create a `Path` object for the directory of interest.
3. Use these two objects as arguments to the `newDirectoryStream` method.

How to do it...

1. Create a new console application and add the following sequence to the `main` method. In this example, we will filter out only those directory elements that are hidden. We will use the Windows system directory. However, any other appropriate directory will work:

```
DirectoryStream.Filter<Path> filter = new DirectoryStream.
Filter<Path>() {
        public boolean accept(Path file) throws IOException {
            return (Files.isHidden(file));
    }
};

    Path directory = Paths.get("C:/Windows");
        try (DirectoryStream<Path> directoryStream = Files.newDire
ctoryStream(directory,filter)){
            for (Path file : directoryStream) {
                System.out.println(file.getFileName());
    }
    }
catch (IOException | DirectoryIteratorException ex) {
            ex.printStackTrace();
    }
```

2. When executed, your output should list only those files that are hidden. The following is one possible output:

SwSys1.bmp

SwSys2.bmp

WindowsShell.Manifest

How it works...

First, we created an anonymous inner class to define an object that implements the `DirectoryStream.Filter` interface. In the `accept` method, the `isHidden` method was used to determine whether the element file was hidden or not. The `DirectoryStream.Filter` interface used its `accept` method to determine whether a directory element should be returned or not. This method returned either a `true` or a `false` indicating whether the element should or should not be returned by the `newDirectoryStream` method, respectively. Thus, it filters out the **undesirables**, which in this case were non-hidden elements. A for each loop was used to display the hidden elements. When the `filter` variable was declared, it was declared using `Path` as its generic value. Interfaces that extended the `Path` interface could also be used.

This technique filters a single directory. If more than one directory needs to be filtered, then the example used in the *Using the SimpleFileVisitor class to traverse filesystems* recipe can be adapted to address multiple directories.

Monitoring file events using WatchEvents

When an application needs to be aware of changes in a directory, a watch service can listen to the changes and then inform the application of these changes. The service will register a directory to be monitored based on the type of event that is of interest. When the event occurs, a watch event is queued and can subsequently be processed as dictated by the needs of the application.

Getting ready

To monitor a directory for events, we need to do the following:

1. Create a `java.nio.file.Path` object representing the directory.
2. Create a new watch service using the `java.nio.file.FileSystem` class' `newWatchService` method.
3. Determine which events we are interested in monitoring.
4. Register the directory and events with the watch service.
5. Process the events as they occur.

How to do it...

1. Create a new console application. We will add code to the `main` method to create a watch service, determine the events we want to watch, register the `docs` directory with the service, and then process the events. Let's start by creating the watch service and a `Path` object for the directory. Add the following code to the `main` method:

```
try {
    FileSystem fileSystem = FileSystems.getDefault();
    WatchService watchService = fileSystem.
newWatchService();
    Path directory = Paths.get("/home/docs");
```

2. Next, create an array of watch events to monitor for file creation, deletion, and modification as follows:

```
WatchEvent.Kind<?>[] events = {
    StandardWatchEventKinds.ENTRY_CREATE,
    StandardWatchEventKinds.ENTRY_DELETE,
    StandardWatchEventKinds.ENTRY_MODIFY};
directory.register(watchService, events);
```

3. Add the following while loop to monitor and process any directory events:

```
while (true) {
    System.out.println("Waiting for a watch event");
    WatchKey watchKey = watchService.take();

    System.out.println("Path being watched: " +
watchKey.watchable());
    System.out.println();

    if (watchKey.isValid()) {
        for (WatchEvent<?>
          event : watchKey.pollEvents()) {
            System.out.println("Kind: " +
              event.kind());
            System.out.println("Context: " +
              event.context());
            System.out.println("Count: " +
              event.count());
            System.out.println();
}

        boolean valid = watchKey.reset();
        if (!valid) {
            // The watchKey is not longer registered
}
}
}

}
catch (IOException ex) {
        ex.printStackTrace();
}
catch (InterruptedException ex) {
        ex.printStackTrace();
}
```

4. Execute the application. You should get the following output:

    Waiting for a watch event

5. Using a text editor, create a new file called `temp.txt` and save it in the `docs` directory. The application should then display output similar to the following. Your output may differ if this is the first time you created the file in the directory. These entries indicate that the file has been created and its contents are then saved:

    Path being watched: \home\docs

    Kind: ENTRY_CREATE

    Context: temp.txt

    Count: 1

    Waiting for a watch event

    Path being watched: \home\docs

    Kind: ENTRY_MODIFY

    Context: temp.txt

    Count: 2

    Waiting for a watch event

6. Next, save the file again. You should now get the following output:

    Path being watched: \home\docs

    Kind: ENTRY_MODIFY

    Context: temp.txt

    Count: 1

    Waiting for a watch event

7. From file manager, delete the file. Your output should reflect its deletion:

    Kind: ENTRY_DELETE

    Context: temp1.txt

    Count: 1

    Waiting for a watch event

How it works...

The first thing we needed was a `WatchService` object. This was acquired by obtaining the default filesystem and then applying the `newWatchService` method to it. Next, we created a `Path` object representing the `docs` directory and an array of events that cover creation, deletion, and modification type events.

An infinite loop was then entered to monitor and handle file events that occur in the `docs` directory. The loop started by displaying a message indicating that it was waiting for events. The `WatchService` class' `take` method was executed. This method will block until an event occurs.

When an event occurred, it returned with a `WatchKey` object, which contained information about the event. Its `watchable` method returned the object being watched, which was then displayed for informational purposes.

The watch key was verified to be valid using the `isValid` method, and its `pollEvents` method was used as part of a for each loop. The `pollEvents` method returned a list of all pending events. The type, context, and count value associated with the event were displayed.

The context for the events that we monitored was the relative path between the target directory and the entry that caused the event. The count value depends on the event and is addressed in the next section.

The last activity reset the watch key. This was needed to put the key back into a ready state until it is needed again. If the method returned `false`, then the key is no longer valid.

There's more...

The `WatchService` interface possesses methods to get a watch key and to close the service. The `poll` and `take` methods retrieve the next watch key as we saw earlier. The `poll` method will return `null` if there are none present. However, the `take` method will block until a watch key is available. There is an overloaded `poll` method that takes additional arguments to specify how long to wait for an event before returning. These arguments include a time out value and a `TimeUnit` value. The use of the `TimeUnit` enumeration is discussed in the *Understanding the FileTime class section of the Setting time related attributes of a file or directory* recipe in *Chapter 4, Managing Files and Directories*.

The `Path` class' `register` method will register a file specified by the `Path` object that it is executing against. The method takes arguments that:

- Specify the watch service
- The kind of events it is to monitor
- Modifiers that determine how the `Path` object is registered

The `WatchEvent.Modifier` interface specifies how a `Path` object is to be registered with a watch service. In this release of Java, there are no defined modifiers.

The `java.nio.file.StandardWatchEventKinds` class defines the standard event types. The fields of this interface are summarized in the following table:

Kind	Meaning	Count
ENTRY_CREATE	Directory entry created	Always a 1
ENTRY_DELETE	Directory entry deleted	Always a 1
ENTRY_MODIFY	Directory entry modified	1 or greater
OVERFLOW	A special event to indicate that events may have been lost or discarded	Greater than 1

When an event occurs, the watch service will return a `WatchKey` object representing the event. This key is reused for multiple occurrences of the same event type. When an event of that type occurs, the count associated with the event is incremented. If multiple events of that type occur before the events are processed, the count value is incremented each time by some amount. The amount is dependent on the type of event.

The use of the `reset` method in the previous example will re-queue the watch key and reset the count to zero. For repeated events, the context is the same. Each directory entry will have its own watch key for that event type.

An event can be canceled using the `WatchKey` interface's `cancel` method. This will unregister the event with the watch service. Any pending events in the queue will remain in the queue until removed. Watch events are also canceled if the watch service is closed.

The watch service is thread-safe. This implies that if multiple threads are accessing events, then care should be taken when using the `reset` method. The method should not be used until all of the threads using that event have completed processing the event.

The watch service can be closed using the `close` method. If multiple threads are using this service, then subsequent attempts to retrieve a watch key will result in a `ClosedWatchServiceException`.

A filesystem may be able to report events faster than the watch service can handle them. Some implementations of a watch service may impose a limit of the number of events queued. When events are intentionally ignored, then an event of the type `OVERFLOW` is used to report this problem. Overflow events are automatically registered for a target. The context of an overflow event is implementation-dependent.

Many aspects of the watch service are implementation-dependent including:

- Whether a native event notification service is used or simulated
- How timely the events are enqueued
- The order in which events are handled
- Whether short-lived events are even reported

Understanding the ZIP filesystem provider

Handling ZIP files is much simpler than it was prior to Java 7. The ZIP filesystem provider introduced in this release handles ZIP and JAR files as though they were filesystems and, as a result, you can easily access the contents of the file. You can manipulate the file as you would do ordinary files, including copying, deleting, moving, and renaming the file. You also have the ability to modify certain attributes of the file. This recipe will show you how to create an instance of a ZIP filesystem and add directories to the system.

Getting ready

We must first create an instance of a `java.net.URI` object to represent our ZIP file, and then create the new `java.nio.file.FileSystem` before we can do any manipulations of the contents of the ZIP file. In this example, we will also use a `java.util.HashMap` to set an optional property of the `FileSystem` as follows:.

1. Create a `URI` object to represent the ZIP file.
2. Create a `HashMap` object to specify the `create` property as `true`.
3. Create a `FileSystem` object using the `newFileSystem` method.

How to do it...

1. Create a console application with a `main` method. In the `main` method, add the following code sequence. We will create a new filesystem within a ZIP file, and then add a directory to it as follows:

```
Map<String, String> attributes = new HashMap<>();
attributes.put("create", "true");
try {
    URI zipFile = URI.create("jar:file:/home.zip");
    try (FileSystem zipFileSys = FileSystems.
newFileSystem(zipFile, attributes);) {
        Path path = zipFileSys.getPath("docs");
        Files.createDirectory(path);
        try (DirectoryStream<Path> directoryStream =
                        Files.
newDirectoryStream(zipFileSys.getPath("/"));) {
```

```
                  for (Path file : directoryStream) {
                      System.out.println(file.getFileName());
        }
      }
    }
  }
catch (IOException e) {
        e.printStackTrace();
}
```

2. Execute the program. Your output should appear as follows:

   docs/

How it works...

The URI object specifies the location of your ZIP file by using a HashMap object, we specified that if the ZIP file does not exist, it should be created. The FileSystem object, zipFileSys, was created in the try-with-resources block, so the resource will automatically be closed, but if you do not wish to use the nested try-with-resources block you must use the FileSystem class' close method to close the resource manually. The try-with-resources block is detailed in *Chapter 1, Java Language Improvements*, recipe: *Using the try-with-resources block to improve exception handling code*.

To demonstrate how ZIP files can be manipulated as FileSystem objects, we invoked the createDirectory method to add a folder within our ZIP file. At this point, we also had the option to perform other FileSystem operations, such as copying files, renaming files, and deleting files. We used a java.nio.file.DirectoryStream to navigate through our ZIP file structure and print out our docs directory, but you can also navigate on your computer to the location of the ZIP file to verify its creation.

See also

See the *Using the DirectoryStream interface to process the contents of a directory* recipe for more information on the DirectoryStream class.

6
Stream IO in Java 7

In this chapter, we will cover:

- ▶ Managing simple files
- ▶ Using buffered IO for files
- ▶ Random access IO using the `SeekableByteChannel`
- ▶ Managing asynchronous communication using the `AsynchronousServerSocketChannel` class
- ▶ Writing to a file using the `AsynchronousFileChannel` class
- ▶ Reading from a file using the `AsynchronousFileChannel` class
- ▶ Using the `SecureDirectoryStream` class

Introduction

In Java 7, we found that there are numerous improvements to its IO capabilities. Most of these are found in the `java.nio` package, which has been dubbed as **NIO2**. In this chapter, we will focus on the new support for streaming and channel-based IO. A **stream** is a contiguous sequence of data. **Stream IO** acts on a single character at a time, while **channel IO** works with a buffer for each operation.

We start with the new techniques used to work with simple files. These are supported by the `Files` class and are discussed in the *Managing simple files* recipe. **Buffered IO** is usually more efficient and is explained in the *Using buffered IO for files* recipe.

The `java.nio.channels` package's `ByteChannel` interface is a channel that can read and write bytes. The `SeekableByteChannel` interface extends the `ByteChannel` interface to maintain a position within the channel. The position can be changed using seek type random IO operations. This capability is discussed in the *Random access IO using the SeekableByteChannel* recipe.

Java 7 has added support for asynchronous channel functionality. The asynchronous nature of these operations is that they do not block. An asynchronous application can continue executing without the need to wait for an IO operation to complete. When the IO completes, a method of the application is called. There are four new `java.nio.channels` package asynchronous channel classes:

- `AsynchronousSocketChannel`
- `AsynchronousServerSocketChannel`
- `AsynchronousFileChannel`
- `AsynchronousChannelGroup`

The first two are used together in a server/client environment and are detailed in the *Managing asynchronous communication using the AsynchronousServerSocketChannel class* recipe.

The `AsynchronousFileChannel` class is used for file manipulation operations that need to be performed in an asynchronous manner. The methods supporting the write and read operations are illustrated in the *Writing to a file using the AsynchronousFileChannel class* and *Reading from a file using the AsynchronousFileChannel class* recipes, respectively.

The `AsynchronousChannelGroup` class provides a means of grouping asynchronous channels together in order to share resources. The use of this class is shown in the *There's more* section of the *Reading from a file using the AsynchronousFileChannel class* recipe.

The `java.nio.file` package's `SecureDirectoryStream` class provides support for more secure access to directories. The use of this class is explained in the *Using the SecureDirectoryStream* recipe. However, the underlying operating system must provide local support for this class.

The `users.txt` file is used for several examples found in this chapter. The contents of the `users.txt` file are assumed to initially contain the following:

- Bob
- Mary
- Sally
- Tom
- Ted

Should your file's content differ, then the output of the examples will vary accordingly.

Several of the recipes in this chapter open a file. Some of these open methods that will use an enumeration argument to specify how the file should be opened. The `java.nio.file` package's `OpenOption` interface specifies how the file is opened and the `StandardOpenOption` enumeration implements this interface. The values of the enumeration are summarized in the following table:

Enumeration	Meaning
APPEND	Bytes are written to the end of the file
CREATE	Creates a new file if it does not exist
CREATE_NEW	Creates a new file only if the file does not exist
DELETE_ON_CLOSE	Deletes the file when it is closed
DSYNC	Every update to a file is written synchronously
READ	Open for read access
SPARSE	Sparse file
SYNC	Every update to the file or metadata is written synchronously
TRUNCATE_EXISTING	Truncates the length of a file to 0 when opening a file
WRITE	Opens the file for write access

While not discussed here, the `java.nio.channels` package's `NetworkChannel` interface was introduced in Java 7. This represents a channel to a network socket. Several classes including the `AsynchronousServerSocketChannel` and `AsynchronousSocketChannel` classes that are discussed in this chapter implement it. It has a `bind` method that binds a socket to a local address, allowing the retrieval and setting of various query socket options. It permits the use of operating system-specific options, which could be used for high performance servers.

The `java.nio.channels` package's `MulticastChannel` is also new to Java 7. It is used to support multicast operations for a group. It is implemented by the `DatagramChannel` class. Methods of this interface support the joining and leaving of members from a group.

The **Sockets Direct Protocol** (**SDP**) is a network protocol, which supports stream connections using **InfiniBand** (**IB**). The IB technology supports point-to-point bi-directional serial links between high-speed peripherals, such as disks. A significant part of IB is its ability to move data from the memory of one computer directly to the memory of another computer.

SDP is supported in Java 7 on Solaris and Linux operating systems. Several classes in the `java.net` and `java.nio.channels` packages support it transparently. However, SDP must be enabled before it can be used. Details on how to enable IB and then create a SDP configuration file are found at `http://download.oracle.com/javase/tutorial/sdp/sockets/index.html`.

Managing simple files

Some files are small and contain simple data. This is usually true for text files. When it is feasible to read or write the entire contents of the file at one time, there are a few `Files` class methods that will work quite well.

In this recipe, we will examine techniques for processing simple files. Initially, we will examine how to read the contents of these types of files. In the *There's more* section, we will demonstrate how to write to them.

Getting ready

To read the entire contents of a file at once:

1. Create a `java.nio.file.Path` object representing the file.
2. Use the `java.nio.file.Files` class' `readAllBytes` method.

How to do it...

1. Create a new console application. We will read and display the contents of the `users.txt` file found in the docs directory. Add the following main method to the application:

```
public static void main(String[] args) throws IOException {
  Path path = Paths.get("/home/docs/users.txt");
  byte[] contents = Files.readAllBytes(path);

  for (byte b : contents) {
    System.out.print((char)b);
  }
}
```

2. Execute the application. Your output should reflect the contents of the file. Here is one possible output:

Bob

Mary

Sally

Tom

Ted

How it works...

We started by creating a `Path` object, which represents the `users.txt` file. The `Files` class' `readAllBytes` method was executed using the `path` object as its argument. The method returned an array of bytes.

Next, a for statement was used to iterate through the array. Each `byte` was cast to a `char` and then displayed.

There's more...

The method will automatically close the file once all of the bytes have been read or should an exception occur. In addition to an `IOException` that might occur, an `OutOfMemoryError` may be thrown, if it is not possible to create an array of sufficient size to hold the contents of the file. Should this happen, then an alternative approach should be used.

We are also concerned with:

▸ Writing to a simple file

▸ Reading all of the lines of a file returned as a list

Writing to a simple file

In the following example, we are going to take the contents of the `users.txt` file and add a new name to the list. Using the previous code, comment out the for loop that prints out the values of contents. Then, after invoking the `readAllBytes` method on the `Path` object, create a new `path` object directed to a new, non-existent text file. Then declare a `String` variable called `name` and invoke the `getBytes` method on the string to return a new `byte` array.

```
Path newPath = Paths.get("/home/docs/newUsers.txt");
byte[] newContents = "Christopher".getBytes();
```

Next, we are going to use the `Files` class write method to create a new file with the same contents as our `users.txt` file, and then append our `String` name to this list. In the first invocation of the `write` method, we use `newPath` to specify where the file should be created, the contents byte array to specify what information should be used, and the `StandardOpenOption.CREATE` argument to specify that the file should be created if it does not exist. In the second invocation of the `write` method, we again use `newPath`, but then we use the byte array `newContents` and the `StandardOpenOption.APPEND` to specify that the name should be appended to the existing file.

```
Files.write(newPath, contents, StandardOpenOption.CREATE);
Files.write(newPath, newContents, StandardOpenOption.APPEND);
```

If you open the `newUsers.txt` file, you will see the list of names from your `users.txt` file, appended by the name you specified using the `newContents` byte array.

There is also an overloaded `write` method that uses the same `Path` object for its first parameter and uses the `Iterable` interface to iterate over a `CharSequence` as its second parameter. The third parameter of this method defines the `Charset` to use. The `StandardOpenOptions` are available as optional parameters as shown in the previous version. The open options were listed in the introduction to this chapter.

Reading all of the lines of a file returned as a list

In instances where you have a simple file you wish to read from, it can be efficient to use the `readAllLines` method. The method takes two arguments, namely, a `Path` object and a `Charset`. The method may throw an `IOException`. In the following example, we use the path to our `users.txt` file and the `Charset` class' `defaultCharset` method to execute the `readAllLines` method. The method returns a list of strings, which we print out within a for loop.

```
try {
  Path path = Paths.get("/home/docs/users.txt");
  List<String> contents = Files.readAllLines(path,
    Charset.defaultCharset());
  for (String b : contents) {
    System.out.println(b);
  }
} catch (IOException e) {
  e.printStackTrace();
}
```

Your output should look similar to this:

Bob
Mary
Sally
Tom
Ted

Notice that the strings returned from the `readAllLines` method does not include the end of line character.

The `readAllLines` method recognizes the following line terminators:

- \u000D followed by \u000A (CR/LF)
- \u000A, (LF)
- \u000D, (CR)

In this chapter:

- *Using buffered IO for files*: This recipe examines how buffered IO is handled in Java 7

- *Writing to a file using the AsynchronousFileChannel class*: This recipe illustrates how IO to a file can be performed in an asynchronous fashion

- *Reading from a file using the AsynchronousFileChannel class*: This recipe illustrates how IO to a file can be performed in an asynchronous fashion

Using buffered IO for files

Buffered IO provides a more efficient technique for accessing files. Two methods of the `java.nio.file` package's `Files` class return either a `java.io` package `BufferedReader` or a `BufferedWriter` object. These classes provide an easy to use and efficient technique for working with text files.

We will illustrate the read operation first. In the *There's more* section, we will demonstrate how to write to a file.

Getting ready

To read from a file using a `BufferedReader` object:

1. Create a `Path` object representing the file of interest
2. Create a new `BufferedReader` object using the `newBufferedReader` method
3. Use the appropriate `read` method to read from the file

How to do it...

1. Create a new console application using the following `main` method. In this method, we will read the contents of the `users.txt` file and then display its contents.

```
public static void main(String[] args) throws IOException {
  Path path = Paths.get("/home/docs/users.txt");
  Charset charset = Charset.forName("ISO-8859-1");
  try (BufferedReader reader = Files.newBufferedReader(path,
    charset)) {
    String line = null;
    while ((line = reader.readLine()) != null) {
      System.out.println(line);
    }
  }
}
```

2. Execute the application. Your output should reflect the contents of the `users.txt` file, which should be similar to the following:

Bob
Mary
Sally
Tom
Ted

How it works...

A `Path` object representing the `users.txt` file was created followed by the creation of a `Charset`. The ISO Latin Alphabet No. 1 was used for this example. Other character sets can be used, depending on the platform used.

A try-with-resource block was used to create the `BufferedReader` object. This type of `try` block is new to Java 7 and is detailed in the *Using the try-with-resource block to improve exception handling code* recipe in *Chapter 1, Java Language Improvements*. This will result in the `BufferedReader` object automatically being closed when the block completes.

The while loop reads each line of the file. and then displays each line to the console. Any `IOExceptions` is thrown as needed.

There's more...

When a byte is stored in a file, its meaning can differ depending upon the intended encoding scheme. The `java.nio.charset` package's `Charset` class provides a mapping between a sequence of bytes and 16-bit Unicode code units. The second argument of the `newBufferedReader` method specifies the encoding to use. There is a standard set of character sets supported by the JVM, as detailed in the Java documentation for the `Charset` class.

We also need to consider:

▸ Writing to a file using the `BufferedWriter` class
▸ Unbuffered IO support in the `Files` class

Writing to a file using the BufferedWriter class

The `newBufferedWriter` method opens or creates a file for writing and returns a `BufferedWriter` object. The method requires two arguments, a `Path` object and a specified `Charset`, and can use an optional third argument. The third argument specifies an `OpenOption` as detailed in the table found in the *Introduction*. If no option is specified, the method will behave as though the CREATE, TRUNCATE_EXISTING, and WRITE options were specified, and will either create a new file or truncate an existing file.

In the following example, we specify a new `String` object containing a name to add to our `users.txt` file. After declaring our `Path` object, we use a try-with-resource block to open a new `BufferedWriter`. In this example, we are using the default system charset and `StandardOpenOption.APPEND` to specify that we want to append the name to the end of our `users.txt` file. Within the try block, we first invoke the `newline` method against our `BufferedWriter` object to ensure that our name goes on a new line. Then we invoke the `write` method against our `BufferedWriter` object, using our `String` as the first argument, a zero to denote the beginning character of the String, and the length of our `String` to denote that the entire `String` should be written.

```
String newName = "Vivian";
Path file = Paths.get("/home/docs/users.txt");
try (BufferedWriter writer = Files.newBufferedWriter(file,
  Charset.defaultCharset(), StandardOpenOption.APPEND)) {
  writer.newLine();
  writer.write(newName, 0, newName.length());
}
```

If you examine the contents of the `users.txt` file, the new name should be appended to the end of the other names in the file.

Un-buffered IO support in the Files class

While un-buffered IO is not as efficient as buffered IO, it is still useful at times. The `Files` class provides support for the `InputStream` and `OutputStream` classes through its `newInputStream` and `newOutputStream` methods. These methods are useful in instances where you need to access very small files or where a method or constructor requires an `InputStream` or `OutputStream` as an argument.

In the following example, we are going to perform a simple copy operation where we copy the contents of the `users.txt` file to a `newUsers.txt` file. We first declare two `Path` objects, one referencing the source file, `users.txt`, and one specifying our destination file, `newUsers.txt`. Then, within a try-with-resource block, we open both an `InputStream` and an `OutputStream`, using the `newInputStream` and `newOutputStream` methods. Within the block, we read in the data from our source file and write it to the destination file.

```
Path file = Paths.get("/home/docs/users.txt");
Path newFile = Paths.get("/home/docs/newUsers.txt");
try (InputStream in = Files.newInputStream(file);
OutputStream out = Files.newOutputStream(
  newFile,StandardOpenOption.CREATE,
  StandardOpenOption.APPEND)) {
  int data = in.read();
  while (data != -1){
    out.write(data);
    data = in.read();
  }
}
```

Upon examining the `newUsers.txt` file, you should see that the content matches that of the `users.txt` file.

See also

In this chapter:

 ▸ *Managing simple files*: This recipe shows how non-buffered IO is handled in Java 7

 ▸ *Writing to a file using the AsynchronousFileChannel class*: This recipe illustrates how IO to a file can be performed in an asynchronous fashion

 ▸ *Reading from a file using the AsynchronousFileChannel class*: This recipe illustrates how IO to a file can be performed in an asynchronous fashion

Random access IO using the SeekableByteChannel

Random access to a file is useful for more complex files. It allows access to specific positions within the file in a non-sequential fashion. The `java.nio.channels` package's `SeekableByteChannel` interface provides this support, based on channel IO. Channels provide a low-level approach for bulk data transfers. In this recipe we will use a `SeekableByteChannel` to access a file.

Getting ready

To obtain a `SeekableByteChannel` object:

 1. Create a `Path` object representing a file.
 2. Get a `SeekableByteChannel` object using the `Files` class' static `newByteChannel` method.

How to do it...

 1. Create a new console application using the following `main` method. We will define a `bufferSize` variable to control the size of the buffer used by the channel. We will create a `SeekableByteChannel` object and use it to display the first two names in the `users.txt` file.

```
public static void main(String[] args) throws IOException {
    int bufferSize = 8;
    Path path = Paths.get("/home/docs/users.txt");

    try (SeekableByteChannel sbc = Files.newByteChannel(path)) {
```

```
ByteBuffer buffer = ByteBuffer.allocate(bufferSize);

sbc.position(4);
sbc.read(buffer);
for(int i=0; i<5; i++) {
   System.out.print((char)buffer.get(i));
}
System.out.println();

buffer.clear();
sbc.position(0);
sbc.read(buffer);
for(int i=0; i<4; i++) {
   System.out.print((char)buffer.get(i));
}
System.out.println();


   }
}
```

Make sure that the `users.txt` file contains the following:

```
Bob
Mary
Sally
Tom
Ted
```

2. Execute the application. The output should display the first two names in reverse order:

Mary
Bob

How it works...

We created a `bufferSize` variable to control the size of the buffer, used by the channel. Next, a `Path` object was created for the `users.txt` file. This path was used as the argument to the `newByteChannel` method, which returned a `SeekableByteChannel` object.

We moved the read position in the file to the fourth position. This placed us at the beginning of the second name in the file. The `read` method was then used, which read approximately eight bytes into buffer. The first five bytes of the buffer were then displayed.

We repeated this sequence, but moved the position to zero, that is, the beginning of the file. A `read` operation was performed again, and then we displayed the first four characters, which were the first name in the file.

This example used explicit knowledge of the size of the names in the file. Normally, this knowledge is not available unless obtained by some other technique. We used this knowledge here simply to demonstrate the nature of the `SeekableByteChannel` interface.

There's more...

The `read` method will start reading from the current position in the file. It will read until either the buffer is filled or the end of file is reached. The method returns an integer, indicating how many bytes were read. A `-1` is returned when the end of stream is reached.

The read and write operations may be accessing the same `SeekableByteChannel` object used by multiple threads. As a result, an `AsynchronousCloseException` or a `ClosedByInterruptException` exception may be thrown when another thread closes the channel or otherwise interrupts the current thread.

There is a `size` method that returns the size of the stream. A `truncate` method is available that discards all bytes past a specific position in the file. This position is passed as a long argument to the method.

The `Files` class' static `newByteChannel` method can take a second argument, which specifies the option used when opening the file. These are detailed in the *There's more* section, *Writing to a file using the BufferedWriter class*, of the *Using buffered IO for files* recipe.

In addition, we need to consider:

 ▸ Processing the contents of the entire file
 ▸ Writing to a file using the `SeekableByteChannel` interface
 ▸ Querying the position

Processing the contents of the entire file

Add the following code to the application. The purpose is to demonstrate how to process the entire file in a sequential fashion and to gain an understanding of various `SeekableByteChannel` interface methods.

```
// Read the entire file
System.out.println("Contents of File");
sbc.position(0);
buffer = ByteBuffer.allocate(bufferSize);
String encoding = System.getProperty("file.encoding");
int numberOfBytesRead = sbc.read(buffer);
System.out.println("Number of bytes read: " + numberOfBytesRead);
```

```
while (numberOfBytesRead > 0) {
  buffer.rewind();
  System.out.print("[" + Charset.forName(encoding).
    decode(buffer) + "]");
  buffer.flip();
  numberOfBytesRead = sbc.read(buffer);
  System.out.println("\nNumber of bytes read: " + numberOfBytesRead);
}
```

Execute the application. Your output should be similar to the following:

Contents of File
Number of bytes read: 8
[Bob
Mar]
Number of bytes read: 8
[y
Sally]
Number of bytes read: 8
[
Tom
T]
Number of bytes read: 2
[edTom
T]
Number of bytes read: -1

We started by repositioning the `read` to the beginning of the file, using the `position` method. The encoding string for the system was determined for the system by accessing the `system` property: `file.encoding`. We kept track of how many bytes are read with each read operation and displayed this count.

In the while loop, we displayed the contents of the buffer by enclosing it in a set of brackets. This made it easier to see what was read in. The `rewind` method sets the position within the buffer to 0. This is not to be confused with the position within the file.

To display the actual buffer, we need to apply the `forName` method to obtain a `Charset` object, and then use the `decode` method against it to convert the bytes in the buffer into Unicode characters. This was followed by the `flip` method, which sets the limit of the buffer to the current position and then sets the position in the buffer to 0. This sets up the buffer for subsequent reads.

You may want to adjust the `bufferSize` value to see how the application behaves with different values.

Writing to a file using the SeekableByteChannel interface

The `write` method takes a `java.nio` package's `ByteBuffer` object and writes it to the channel. The operation starts at the current position in the file. For example, if the file was opened with an append option, the first write will be at the end of the file. The method returns the number of bytes written.

In the following example, we will append three names to the end of the `users.txt` file. We use the `StandardOpenOption.APPEND` as the open option for the `newByteChannel` method. This will move the cursor to the end of the file and begin writing at that position. A `ByteBuffer` is created with three names separated by the system line separator property. Using this property makes the code more portable. The `write` method is then executed.

```
final String newLine = System.getProperty("line.separator");
try (SeekableByteChannel sbc = Files.newByteChannel(path,
  StandardOpenOption.APPEND)) {
  String output = newLine + "Paul" + newLine + "Carol" + newLine +
    "Fred";
  ByteBuffer buffer = ByteBuffer.wrap(output.getBytes());
  sbc.write(buffer);
}
```

The initial contents of the `users.txt` file should be:

Bob
Mary
Sally
Tom
Ted

Add the code sequence to the application and execute the program. Examine the contents of the `users.txt` file. It should now appear as follows:

Bob
Mary
Sally
Tom
Ted
Paul
Carol
Fred

Query the position

The overloaded `position` method returns a long value indicating the position within the file. This is complemented by a `position` method that takes a long argument and sets the position to that value. If the value exceeds the size of the stream, then the position is set to the end of the stream. The `size` method will return the size of the file used by the channel.

To demonstrate the use of these methods, we will duplicate the example in the previous section. This means we will position the file cursor to the end of the `users.txt` file and then write three different names on separate lines.

In the following code sequence, we use the `size` method to determine how big the file is, and then use this value as the argument to the `position` method. This moves the cursor to the end of the file.

Next, a `ByteBuffer` is created thrice, and written to the file each time using a different name. The position is displayed for informational purposes.

```
Path path = Paths.get("/home/docs/users.txt");

final String newLine = System.getProperty("line.separator");
try (SeekableByteChannel sbc = Files.newByteChannel(path,
  StandardOpenOption.WRITE)) {
  ByteBuffer buffer;
  long position = sbc.size();
  sbc.position(position);
  System.out.println("Position: " + sbc.position());

  buffer = ByteBuffer.wrap((newLine + "Paul").getBytes());
  sbc.write(buffer);
  System.out.println("Position: " + sbc.position());
  buffer = ByteBuffer.wrap((newLine + "Carol").getBytes());
  sbc.write(buffer);
  System.out.println("Position: " + sbc.position());
  buffer = ByteBuffer.wrap((newLine + "Fred").getBytes());
  sbc.write(buffer);
  System.out.println("Position: " + sbc.position());
}
```

The contents of the `users.txt` file should initially contain:

```
Bob
Mary
Sally
Tom
Ted
```

Add this sequence to the application and execute the program. Examine the contents of the `users.txt` file. It should now appear as follows:

Bob
Mary
Sally

Tom
Ted
Paul
Carol
Fred

See also

In this chapter

> ▸ *There's more* section of the *Random access IO using the SeekableByteChannel* recipe: This recipe briefs you on the options used to open a file

> ▸ *Writing to a file using the BufferedWriter class* of the *Using buffered IO for files* recipe.

Managing asynchronous communication using the AsynchronousServerSocketChannel class

Java 7 supports asynchronous communications between a server and a client. The `java.nio.channels` package's `AsynchronousServerSocketChannel` class supports server operations for streaming IO in a thread-safe manner. Communication is conducted using an `AsynchronousSocketChannel` object that acts as a client. Together we can use these classes to build a server/client application that communicates in an asynchronous fashion.

Getting ready

Both a server and a client need to be created. To create a server:

1. Use the static `AsynchronousServerSocketChannel` class' open method to get an instance of a `AsynchronousServerSocketChannel` object
2. Bind the channel to a local address and port number
3. Use the `accept` method to accept a connection request from a client
4. Process messages as they are received

To create a client:

1. Create an `AsynchronousSocketChannel` object using the static `open` method
2. Create an instance of an `InetSocketAddress` object for the server
3. Connect to the server
4. Send messages as needed

How to do it...

We will create two applications: one on the server and one on the client. Together, they will support a simple server/client application, which will explain how asynchronous communication is performed using an AsynchronousSocketChannel.

1. Create a new console application that will be on the server and add the following main method. The server will simply display any messages sent to it. It opens a server socket and binds it to an address. It will then use the accept method with a CompletionHandler to process any requests from a client.

```java
public static void main(String[] args) {throws Exception
   final AsynchronousServerSocketChannel listener =
      AsynchronousServerSocketChannel.open();
   InetSocketAddress address = new InetSocketAddress("localhost",
      5000);
   listener.bind(address);

   listener.accept(null, new
      CompletionHandler<AsynchronousSocketChannel, Void>() {

      public void completed(AsynchronousSocketChannel channel, Void
         attribute) {
         try {
            System.out.println("Server: completed method executing");
            while(true) {
               ByteBuffer buffer = ByteBuffer.allocate(32);
               Future<Integer> readFuture = channel.read(buffer);
               Integer number = readFuture.get();
               System.out.println("Server: Message received: " + new
                  String(buffer.array()));
            }

         } catch (InterruptedException | ExecutionException ex) {
            ex.printStackTrace();
         }
      }

      public void failed(Throwable ex, Void atttribute) {
         System.out.println("Server: CompletionHandler exception");
         ex.printStackTrace();
      }
   });
   while(true) {
      // wait - Prevents the program from
```

```
        // terminating before the client can connect
      }
    } catch (IOException ex) {
      ex.printStackTrace();
    }
}
```

2. Next, create a second console application that will act as a client. It will use the `open` method to create an `AsynchronousSocketChannel` object and then connect to the server. A `java.util.concurrent` package's `Future` object's `get` method is used to block until the connection is complete, and then a message is sent to the server.

```
public static void main(String[] args) {throws Exception
  try {
  AsynchronousSocketChannel client =
    AsynchronousSocketChannel.open();
  InetSocketAddress address = new InetSocketAddress("localhost",
    5000);

  Future<Void> future = client.connect(address);
  System.out.println("Client: Waiting for the connection to
    complete");
  future.get();

  String message;
  do {
    System.out.print("Enter a message: ");
    Scanner scanner = new Scanner(System.in);
    message = scanner.nextLine();
    System.out.println("Client: Sending ...");
    ByteBuffer buffer = ByteBuffer.wrap(message.getBytes());
    System.out.println("Client: Message sent: " + new
      String(buffer.array()));
    client.write(buffer);
  } while(!"quit".equals(message)) {

  }
}
```

You will need to execute both the applications. Depending on your environment, you may need to execute one of the applications in a command window and the second in your IDE. This will be the case if you can have only one instance of your IDE running at a time.

3. Execute the server application first. Next, execute the client application. It should prompt you for a message and then send the message to the server where it will be displayed. Your output should have the following general output. The client and the server output are shown in separate columns in the following table:

Client	Server
Client: Waiting for the connection to complete	
Enter a message: First message	
Client: Sending ...	
Client: Message sent: First message	
	Server: completed method executing
	Server: Message received: First message
Enter a message: `Most excellent message`	
Client: Sending ...	
Client: Message sent: Most excellent message	
	Server: Message received: Most excellent message
Enter a message: `quit`	
Client: Sending ...	
Client: Message sent: quit	
	Server: Message received: quit
	java.util.concurrent.ExecutionException: java.io.IOException: The specified network name is no longer available.
	...

Notice that when the client application was terminated, an `ExecutionException` occurred in the server. Normally, we would handle this exception more gracefully in a production application.

How it works...

Let's examine the server application first. An `AsynchronousServerSocketChannel` object was created using the `open` method. The `bind` method was then used to associate the socket with a socket address, determined by the system and a port number of `5000`.

Next, the `accept` method was invoked to accept a connection. The first argument specified a `null` value, which was used for attachments. Later, we will see how to use an attachment. The second argument was a `CompletionHandler` object. This object was created as an anonymous inner class, and its methods will be called when a communication request made by a client makes a communication request.

In the `completed` method, we displayed a message indicating that the method is executing. We then entered an infinite while loop where we allocated 32 bytes to a buffer, and then attempted to read from a client. The `read` method returned a `Future` object that we subsequently used the `get` method against. This effectively blocked the execution until the client sent a message. The message was then displayed.

Notice that the `get` method returned a generic `Future` object of type `Integer`. We could have used this to determine how many bytes were actually read. It was used here simply to block until the IO was complete. The `failed` method would have been called if an exception had occurred with the channel communication.

The infinite while loop at the end of the try block prevents the server from terminating. This is acceptable here for simplicity's sake, but normally, we would handle this in a more graceful fashion.

In the client application, we used the `open` method to create an `AsynchronousSocketChannel` object. A network address corresponding to the server was created and then used with the connect method to connect to the server. This method returned a `Future` object. We used this object with the `get` method to block until a connection with the server was established.

Notice that the `connect` method returned a `Future` object of the type `Void`. The `Void` class is found in the `java.lang` package and is a wrapper class for `void`. It was used here as nothing was effectively returned by the `connect` method.

A while loop was entered, which terminated when the user entered `quit`. The user was prompted for a message, and then a `ByteBuffer` object was created using the message. The buffer was then written to the server.

Notice the use of multiple exceptions in the catch blocks of both applications. This is a new Java 7 language improvement and is discussed in the *Catching multiple exception types to improve type checking* recipe in *Chapter 1, Java Language Improvements*.

There's more...

The `bind` method is overloaded. Both versions' first argument is a `SocketAddress` object, corresponding to a local address. A `null` value can be used, which will automatically assign a socket address. The second `bind` method accepts an integer value for the second argument. This configures the maximum number of pending connections allowed in an implementation-dependent manner. A value less than or equal to zero will use an implementation-specific default value.

There are two aspects of this communication technique that we should address:

▸   Using the `Future` object in a server

▸   Understanding the `AsynchronousServerSocketChannel` class options

Using the Future object in a server

The `AsynchronousServerSocketChannel` class' `accept` method is overloaded. There is a no argument method that accepts a connection and returns a `Future` object for the channel. The `Future` object's `get` method will return an `AsynchronousSocketChannel` object for the connection. The advantage of this approach is that it returns an `AsynchronousSocketChannel` object, which can be used in other contexts.

Instead of using the `accept` method, which uses a `CompletionHandler`, we can use the following sequence to do the same thing. Comment out the previous `accept` method and add the following code:

```
try {
    Future<AsynchronousSocketChannel> future = listener.accept();
    AsynchronousSocketChannel worker = future.get();

    while (true) {
        // Wait
        stem.out.println("Server: Receiving ...");
        ByteBuffer buffer = ByteBuffer.allocate(32);
        Future<Integer> readFuture = worker.read(buffer);
        Integer number = readFuture.get();
        ystem.out.println("Server: Message received: " + new
            String(buffer.array()));
    }
} catch (IOException | InterruptedException | ExecutionException ex) {
    ex.printStackTrace();
}
```

Execute the applications again. You should get the same output as before.

Understanding the AsynchronousServerSocketChannel class options

The `supportedOptions` method returns a set of options used by the `AsynchronousServerSocketChannel` class. The `getOption` method will return the value of the option. Add the following code after the use of the `bind` method in the previous example:

```
Set<SocketOption<?>> options = listener.supportedOptions();
for (SocketOption<?> socketOption : options) {
  System.out.println(socketOption.toString() + ": " +
    listener.getOption(socketOption));
}
```

Execute the code. The default values will be displayed and should be similar to the following:

```
SO_RCVBUF: 8192
SO_REUSEADDR: false
```

The options can be set using the `setOption` method. This method takes the name of the option and a value. The following illustrates how to set the receive buffer size to 16,384 bytes:

```
listener.setOption(StandardSocketOptions.SO_RCVBUF, 16384);
```

The `StandardSocketOptions` class defines socket options. Only the `SO_REUSEADDR` and `SO_RCVBUF` options are supported for the `AsynchronousServerSocketChannel` channel.

See also

> ▸   In this chapter: There's more section, of the *Reading from a file using the AsynchronousFileChannel class* recipe: This recipe explains the use of attachments with a completion handler and the use of the `AsynchronousChannelGroup` class

Writing to a file using the AsynchronousFileChannel class

The `java.nio.channels` package's `AsynchronousFileChannel` class permits file IO operations to be performed in an asynchronous manner. When an IO method is invoked, it will return immediately. The actual operation may occur at some other time (and potentially using a different thread). In this recipe, we will explore how the `AsynchronousFileChannel` class performs asynchronous **write** operations. **Read** operations will be demonstrated in the *Reading from a file using the AsynchronousFileChannel class* recipe.

Getting ready

To perform a write operation:

1. Create a `Path` object representing the file to be read from.

2. Use this path with the `open` method to open a file channel.

3. Use the `write` method to write data to the file, optionally using a completion handler.

How to do it...

In this example, we will perform a series of write operations against a file. There are two overloaded `write` methods. Both take as their initial arguments a `java.nio` package's `ByteBuffer`, containing the data to be written and a second argument specifying the position to write to in the file.

The two arguments' `write` method returns a `java.util.concurrent` package's `Future<Integer>` object, which can also be used to write to a file, as demonstrated in the *There's more* section. The second `write` method has a third argument, an attachment, and a fourth argument, a `CompletionHandler` object. The completion handler is executed when the write operation completes.

1. Create a new console application. Use the following `main` method. We open a file called `asynchronous.txt` for writing. A completion handler is created and used with the `write` method. Two write operations are performed. Thread information is displayed to explain the asynchronous nature of the operation and how completion handlers work.

```java
public static void main(String[] args) {throws Exception
  try (AsynchronousFileChannel fileChannel =
    AsynchronousFileChannel.open(Paths.get(
    "/home/docs/asynchronous.txt"),
    READ, WRITE,
    StandardOpenOption.CREATE)) {
    CompletionHandler<Integer, Object> handler =
      new CompletionHandler<Integer, Object>() {

      @Override
      public void completed(Integer result, Object attachment) {
        System.out.println("Attachment: " + attachment +
          " " + result + " bytes written");
        System.out.println("CompletionHandler Thread ID: " +
          Thread.currentThread().getId());
      }

      @Override
```

```
      public void failed(Throwable e, Object attachment) {
        System.err.println("Attachment: " +
          attachment + " failed with:");
        e.printStackTrace();
      }
    };

    System.out.println("Main Thread ID: " +
      Thread.currentThread().getId());
    fileChannel.write(ByteBuffer.wrap("Sample".getBytes()), 0,
      "First Write", handler);
    fileChannel.write(ByteBuffer.wrap("Box".getBytes()), 0,
      "Second Write", handler);

  }
}
```

2. Execute the application. Your application may not behave as you expect. Due to the asynchronous nature of the operations, the order of execution of the various elements may vary from execution to execution. The following is one possible output:

    Main Thread ID: 1
    Attachment: Second Write 3 bytes written
    Attachment: First Write 6 bytes written
    CompletionHandler Thread ID: 13
    CompletionHandler Thread ID: 12

    Re-executing the application may give a different order of execution. This behavior is explained in the following section.

How it works...

We started by creating an `AsynchronousFileChannel` object using a `Path` object for the `asynchronous.txt` file in the `docs` directory. The file was opened for read and write operations, and was supposed to be created if it did not already exist. A `CompletionHandler` object was created. This was used in this example to confirm the execution of the write operations.

The `write` method was executed twice. The first time the string, `Sample`, was written to the file, starting at position `0` in the file. The second write operation wrote the string, `Box`, to the file, also starting at position `0`. This resulted in an overwrite, with the contents of the file containing the string, `Boxple`. This was intentional, and illustrates the use of the `position` argument of the `write` method.

The ID of the current thread was displayed at various points in the code. It shows one thread used for the `main` method, and two other threads used for the content handlers. When the `write` method was executed, it was performed in an asynchronous fashion. The `write` method executes and immediately returns. The actual write may occur at a later time. Upon completion of the write operation, a successful completion results in the content handler's `completed` method executing. This displays the ID for its thread, and a message showing the attachment and the number of bytes written. If an exception occurs, the `failed` method will be executed.

As you can see from the output, a separate thread was used to execute the completion handler. The completion handler was defined to return an `Integer` value. This value represents the number of bytes written. The attachment can be any object needed. In this case, we used it to show which `write` method has completed. The asynchronous nature of the write operations resulted in an unpredictable execution order of the content handlers. However, the `write` methods did execute in the anticipated order.

Notice the use of the try-with-resource block. This Java 7 feature is explored in the *Using the try-with-resource block to improve exception handling code* recipe in *Chapter 1, Java Language Improvements*.

There's more...

The two arguments' `write` method returns a `Future<Integer>` object. Later, in the program, we can use its `get` method, which blocks until the write operation has completed. Comment out the previous example's write operations, and replace them with the following code sequence:

```
Future<Integer> writeFuture1 =
    fileChannel.write(ByteBuffer.wrap("Sample".getBytes()), 0);
Future<Integer> writeFuture2 =
    fileChannel.write(ByteBuffer.wrap("Box".getBytes()), 0);

int result = writeFuture1.get();
System.out.println("Sample write completed with " + result + " bytes
    written");
result = writeFuture2.get();
System.out.println("Box write completed with " + result + " bytes
    written");
```

Execute the application. The output should be similar to the following:

Main Thread ID: 1
Sample write completed with 6 bytes written
Box write completed with 3 bytes written

The `write` methods returned a `Future` object. The `get` method was blocked until the write operation was completed. We used the result to display a message indicating which write operation executed and how many bytes were written.

There are considerably more aspects of asynchronous file channel IO that could be addressed. Other aspects that may be of interest include:

 ▸ Forcing the updates to a channel to be written

 ▸ Locking parts or all of a file for exclusive access

 ▸ Using `AsynchronousChannelGroup` to manage related asynchronous operations

See also

 ▸ In this chapter *Reading from a file using the AsynchronousFileChannel class*: This recipe demonstrates how to perform asynchronous reads, and the use of the `AsynchronousChannelGroup` class.

Reading from a file using the AsynchronousFileChannel class

Asynchronous read operations are also possible using either of two overloaded `read` methods. We will demonstrate how this is accomplished using a `java.nio.channels` package's `AsynchronousChannelGroup` object. This will provide us with a way of observing these methods in action and provide an example of an `AsynchronousChannelGroup`.

Getting ready

To perform a write operation:

1. Create a `Path` object representing the file to be read from.
2. Use this path with the `open` method to open a file channel.
3. Use the `read` method to read data from the file.

How to do it...

1. Create a new console application. In the `main` method, create an instance of a `java.util.concurrent` package's `ScheduledThreadPoolExecutor` object of size three. We will use the `ScheduledThreadPoolExecutor` class primarily because it is easy to create. A size of three will help illustrate how threads are managed.

   ```
   ExecutorService pool = new ScheduledThreadPoolExecutor(3);
   ```

2. Next, add a try-with-resource block and create an `AsynchronousFileChannel` object for the file `items.txt`. Use an `open` option of `StandardOpenOption.READ`, and the previously created pool object.

```
try (AsynchronousFileChannel fileChannel =
  AsynchronousFileChannel.open(
    Paths.get("/home/docs/items.txt"),
    EnumSet.of(StandardOpenOption.READ), pool)) {
```

3. Next, display the main thread ID and then create a `CompletionHandler` object, which we will use to display the results of the asynchronous read operation.

```
System.out.println("Main Thread ID: " +
  Thread.currentThread().getId());
CompletionHandler<Integer, ByteBuffer> handler =
  new CompletionHandler<Integer, ByteBuffer>() {

  @Override
  public synchronized void completed(Integer result, ByteBuffer
    attachment) {
    for (int i = 0; i < attachment.limit(); i++) {
      System.out.print((char) attachment.get(i));
    }
    System.out.println("");
    System.out.println("CompletionHandler Thread ID: "
      + Thread.currentThread().getId());
    System.out.println("");
  }

  @Override
  public void failed(Throwable e, ByteBuffer attachment) {
    System.out.println("Failed");
  }
};
```

4. Next, add code to create an array of `ByteBuffer` objects. Allocate 10 bytes for each buffer, and then use a buffer as the first argument of the `read` method and as the attachment. Using it as the attachment, allows us to access the result of the read operation in the completion handler. The starting read position is specified in the second argument, and is set up to read every 10-byte segment of the file.

```
final int bufferCount = 5;
ByteBuffer buffers[] = new ByteBuffer[bufferCount];
for (int i = 0; i < bufferCount; i++) {
  buffers[i] = ByteBuffer.allocate(10);
  fileChannel.read(buffers[i], i * 10, buffers[i], handler);
}
```

5. Add a call to the `awaitTermination` method to allow the read operations to complete. Then display the buffers a second time.

```
pool.awaitTermination(1, TimeUnit.SECONDS);

System.out.println("Byte Buffers");
for (ByteBuffer byteBuffer : buffers) {
  for (int i = 0; i < byteBuffer.limit(); i++) {
    System.out.print((char) byteBuffer.get(i));
  }
  System.out.println();
}
```

6. Use the following as the content of the `items.txt` file, where each entry is a 10-byte sequence consisting of an item and a quantity:

```
Nail     34Bolt      12Drill    22Hammer   24Auger    24
```

7. Execute the application. Your output should be similar to the following:

Main Thread ID: 1
Nail   34
CompletionHandler Thread ID: 10

Drill 22
CompletionHandler Thread ID: 12

Bolt   12
CompletionHandler Thread ID: 11

Auger 24
CompletionHandler Thread ID: 12

Hammer 24
CompletionHandler Thread ID: 10

Byte Buffers
Nail   34
Bolt   12
Drill 22
Hammer 24
Auger 24

Notice the use of three IDs for the completion handler threads. These correspond to the three threads created as part of the thread pool.

How it works...

A `java.util.concurrent` package's `ExecutorService` was created with a thread pool of size three to demonstrate the use of a thread group and to force the reuse of threads. The `items.txt` file contained data of equal lengths. This simplified the example.

In the content handler, upon successful completion, the `completed` method was executed. The attachment contained the buffer `read`, which was then displayed along with the content handler's thread ID. Notice the use of the `synchronized` keyword for the `completed` method. While not always required for the method, it was used here, so that the output would be more readable. The removal of the keyword would result in an interleaving of the buffer's output, making it unreadable.

Notice the non-deterministic behavior of the completion handler threads. They did not execute in the order that the corresponding `read` methods were executed. Repeated execution of the application should produce differing output.

Knowing that the input file contained only five items, we created five `ByteBuffer` objects each of size `10`. The `read` method was executed five times using a different buffer.

The `awaitTermination` method was executed, which effectively paused the application for a second. This allowed the completion handler's threads to complete. The buffers were then displayed a second time to verify the operation.

There's more...

Whenever an asynchronous channel is created, it is assigned to a channel group. By defining your own group, you can exercise better control over the threads used in the group. When a channel is created using an `open` method, it belongs to a global channel group.

An asynchronous channel group provides techniques needed for the completion of asynchronous IO operations that are bound to a group. Each group has a thread pool. These threads are used for the IO operations and `CompletionHandler` objects.

In the previous example, we used the `open` method to associate a thread pool with the asynchronous operations. An asynchronous channel group can also be created using one of the following static `AsynchronousChannelGroup` methods:

- `withFixedThreadPool`: A fixed size pool that uses a `ThreadFactory` to create new threads. The size of the pool is specified by its first argument.
- `withCachedThreadPool`: This pool uses an `ExecutorService` to create new threads. The second argument specifies a suggested number of initial threads for the pool.
- `withThreadPool`: This also uses an `ExecutorService`, but without an initial size specified.

An asynchronous channel group provides the ability to perform an orderly shutdown of a group. Once the shutdown is initiated:

▸ Its attempts to create a new channel result in a `ShutdownChannelGroupException`

▸ Threads running completion handlers are not interrupted

A group terminates when:

▸ All of its channels are closed

▸ All completion handlers have run to completion

▸ All group resources have been released

Other methods of interest include:

▸ The `isShutdown` method, which will determine if a group is shutdown or not.

▸ The `isTerminated` method, which will determine if a group has been terminated.

▸ The `shutdownNow` method, which will force the shutdown of a group. All channels are closed but content handlers are not interrupted.

See also

In this chapter:

▸ *Writing to a file using the AsynchronousFileChannel class*: This recipe demonstrates how to perform asynchronous writes

Using the SecureDirectoryStream class

The `java.nio.file` package's `SecureDirectoryStream` class is designed to be used with applications that depend on tighter security than that provided by other IO classes. It supports race-free (sequentially consistent) operations on a directory, where the operations are performed concurrently with other applications.

This class requires support from the operating system. An instance of the class is obtained by casting the return value of the `Files` class' `newDirectoryStream` method to a `SecureDirectoryStream` object. If the cast fails, then the underlying operating system does not support this type of stream.

Getting ready

To get and use a `SecureDirectoryStream` object:

1. Create a `Path` object representing the directory of interest.

2. Use the `Files` class' `newDirectoryStream` method, and cast the result to a `SecureDirectoryStream`.

3. Use this object to affect `SecureDirectoryStream` operations.

How to do it...

1. Create a new console application. In the `main` method, add the following code. We will create a `Path` object for the `docs` directory and then obtain a `SecureDirectoryStream` object for it. This will be used to view the POSIX permissions for the directory.

```
public static void main(String args[]) throws IOException {
    Path path = Paths.get("home/docs");
    SecureDirectoryStream<Path> sds = (SecureDirectoryStream)
        Files.newDirectoryStream(path);
    PosixFileAttributeView view =
        sds.getFileAttributeView(PosixFileAttributeView.class);
    PosixFileAttributes attributes = view.readAttributes();
    Set<PosixFilePermission> permissions = attributes.permissions();

    for (PosixFilePermission permission : permissions) {
        System.out.print(permission.toString() + ' ');
    }
    System.out.println();
}
```

2. Execute the application on a system that supports the `SecureDirectoryStream` class. The following output was obtained by running the application on an Ubuntu system:

GROUP_EXECUTE OWNER_WRITE OWNER_READ OTHERS_EXECUTE GROUP_READ OWNER_EXECUTE OTHERS_READ

How it works...

A `Path` object for the `docs` directory was obtained and then used as the argument of the `Files` class' `newDirectoryStream` method. The result of the method was cast to a `SecureDirectoryStream` class. The `getFileAttributeView` method was then executed to obtain a view, which was used to display the POSIX file permissions for the directory. The use of the `PosixFileAttributeView` class is discussed in the *Using the PosixFileAttributeView to maintain POSIX file attributes* recipe, in *Chapter 3, Obtaining File and Directory Information*.

There's more...

Other methods supported by the SecureDirectoryStream class include the ability to delete a file or directory, a move method to move a file to a different directory, and the creation of a `SeekableByteChannel` to access a file.

7
Graphical User Interface Improvements

In this chapter, we will cover the following:

- ▶ Mixing heavyweight and lightweight components
- ▶ Managing window types
- ▶ Managing the opacity of a window
- ▶ Creating a varying gradient translucent window
- ▶ Managing the shape of a window
- ▶ Using the new border types in Java 7
- ▶ Handling multiple file selection in the FileDialog class
- ▶ Controlling the print dialog box type
- ▶ Using the new JLayer decorator for a password field

Introduction

The ability to develop applications that have a **Graphical User Interface** (**GUI**) interface has been enhanced in Java 7. Some of these are minor improvements and are discussed in this introduction. Others, such as using the `javax.swing.JLayer` decorator class are more involved and are discussed in separate recipes.

It is now possible to mix heavyweight and lightweight components in an application without adding special code to make it work as desired. This improvement is largely transparent to users of Java 7. However, the essence of this approach, and special situations that might arise from their use, are detailed in the *Mixing heavyweight and lightweight components* recipe.

To ease the development of applications, three basic window types have been introduced. These should simplify the creation of certain types of applications and are discussed in the *Managing window types* recipe.

The overall appearance of an application may include such characteristics as its opacity and shape. The *Managing the opacity of a window* recipe illustrates how to control a window's opacity and the *Creating a varying gradient translucent window* recipe looks into creating gradients for such windows. Controlling the shape of a window, such as making it round or some irregular shape, is detailed in the *Managing the shape of a window* recipe.

The translucency-related capabilities were added originally as part of the **Java 6 Update 10** release. However, they were implemented as part of the private `com.sun.awt.AWTUtilities` class. This capability has been moved to the `java.awt` package.

`Javax.swing.JComponents` have borders whose appearance can be controlled. In Java 7, several new borders have been added. These are illustrated in the *Using the new border types in Java 7* recipe.

Improvements have also been made in the use of the file dialog and print dialog boxes. These enhancements are discussed in the *Handling multiple file selection in the FileDialog class* and *Controlling the print dialog box type* recipes, respectively.

The ability to draw over a `JComponent` has been added. This allows the use of special effects, which were not easily achieved in earlier versions of Java. The *Using the new JLayer decorator for a password field* recipe illustrates this process and also demonstrates how to create a watermark for windows.

All the recipes of this chapter use a `JFrame`-based application. The following is the code used to develop a minimal window-based application, upon which the recipe's examples are based. An `ApplicationDriver` class is used to start and display the `JFrame`-derived `ApplicationWindow` class. The `ApplicationDriver` class is shown as follows:

```
public class ApplicationDriver {

    public static void main(String[] args) {

        SwingUtilities.invokeLater(new Runnable() {

            @Override
            public void run() {
                ApplicationWindow window = new ApplicationWindow();
                window.setVisible(true);
```

```
    }
  });


    }
}
```

The `invokeLater` method uses an inner class to create and then display the `ApplicationWindow`. This window is set up in its constructor. It is a simple window that has an **Exit** button, which we will use to close the application and enhance in later recipes:

```
public class ApplicationWindow extends JFrame {

    public ApplicationWindow() {
        this.setTitle("Example");
        this.setSize(200, 100);
        this.setLocationRelativeTo(null);
        this.setDefaultCloseOperation(JFrame.EXIT_ON_CLOSE);

        JButton exitButton = new JButton("Exit");
        exitButton.addActionListener(new ActionListener() {
            public void actionPerformed(ActionEvent event) {
                System.exit(0);
    }
  });
        this.add(exitButton);
    }
}
```

When this code is executed, the output should appear as shown in the following screenshot:

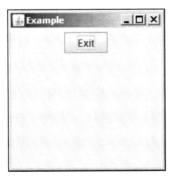

There are a number of minor improvements introduced in Java 7. For example, the protected static `java.awt.Cursor` array has been deprecated. Instead, use the `getPredefinedCursor` method. This method takes an integer argument and returns a `Cursor` object.

A new **HSV** tab was introduced to the `java.swing.JColorChooser` dialog box. It appears as shown in the following screenshot:

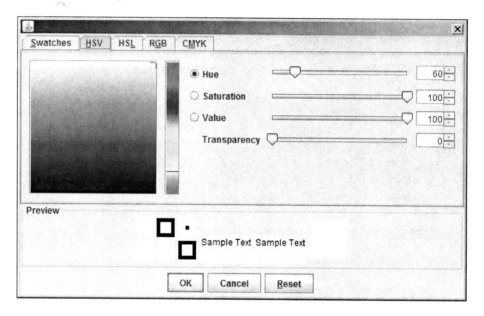

Also in Java 7, it is possible to customize a dragged JApplet's title and to specify whether it should be decorated or not. This is accomplished from a `script` tag as follows:

```
<script src="http://javascript source file"></script>
<script>
    var attributes = { code:'AppletName', width:100, height:100 };
    var parameters = {jnlp_href: 'appletname.jnlp',
                        java_decorated_frame: 'true',
                        java_applet_title: 'A Custom Title'
                     };
    deployJava.runApplet(attributes, parameters, '7'7);
</script>
```

The `java_decorated_frame` parameter is set to `true` to specify that the window should be decorated. The title of the window is specified using the `java_applet_title` parameter.

This example is adapted from `http://download.oracle.com/javase/tutorial/deployment/applet/draggableApplet.html`. More details on how to create draggable applets can be found at that site.

A couple of miscellaneous changes need to be noted. The **Nimbus Look and Feel** has been moved from the `com.sun.java.swing` package to the `javax.swing` package. The `isValidateRoot` method has been added to the `Applet` class to indicate that the container is a valid root. Lastly, a new **Java2D** graphics pipeline based upon the **X11 XRender** extension has been added to provide better access to **Graphical Processing Units** (**GPU**).

Mixing heavyweight and lightweight components

Java provides two basic sets of components for developing GUI applications: **Abstract Window Toolkit** (**AWT**) and **Swing**. AWT is dependent upon the native systems' underlying code, and these components are therefore referred to as heavyweight components. Swing components, on the other hand, operate fully independent of the native system, are completely implemented in Java code, and are thus referred to as lightweight components. In previous versions of Java, it was inefficient and troublesome to mix heavyweight and lightweight components. In `Java 6 Update 12`, and continuing into Java 7, the JVM handles the mixing of heavyweight and lightweight components.

Getting ready

If you are working with code that implements both heavyweight and lightweight components, there is no need to make any changes to the code, as Java 7 automatically handles the components. We are going to modify code from the beginning of this chapter to demonstrate this:

1. Create a new application using the code examples from the introduction section.
2. Modify the code to use both heavyweight and lightweight examples.
3. Run the application using an older version of Java and then again using Java 7.

How to do it...

1. Create a new window application as specified in the introduction to this chapter. Add the following section of code to the `ApplicationWindow` constructor:

```
JMenuBar menuBar = new JMenuBar();
JMenu menu = new JMenu("Overlapping Menu");
JMenuItem menuItem = new JMenuItem("Overlapping Item");
menu.add(menuItem);
menuBar.add(menu);
this.setJMenuBar(menuBar);
this.validate();
```

2. Next, modify the declaration of the **Exit** button so that you are now using a heavyweight `Button` rather than a lightweight `JButton` as follows:

```
Button exitButton = new Button("Exit");
```

3. Execute the application. You need to run the application using a version of Java prior to **Java 6 Build 10** or the overlapping issue will not display. When the window opens, click on the menu and notice that, although the menu item overlaps the **Exit** button, the button shows through and covers the menu text. The following is an example of the overlap:

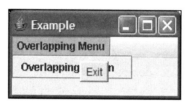

4. Now, run the application again using Java 7. When you click on the menu this time, you should notice the overlapping issue has been resolved, as shown in the following screenshot:

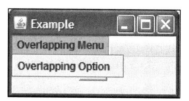

How it works...

The JVM handles the mixing of components automatically. In this example, we created a scenario to illustrate the overlapping problem, and then showed how it was resolved in the latest Java releases. However, it is a good practice to call the `validate` method on the top-level frame to ensure that all shapes are redrawn properly. There is also the potential that previous work-arounds for mixing components may need to be removed.

There's more...

The following are some specific areas to consider, when using mixed components with Java 7:

▶ Advanced swing events may not work correctly, particularly those events maintained by a `javax.swing.InputMap`.

▸ Partially transparent lightweight components that are intended to allow heavyweight components to be seen through them are not supported. The heavyweight items will not be displayed beneath translucent pixels.

▸ Heavyweight components must be created as part of the frame's or applet's process.

▸ If the mixing of heavyweight and lightweight components has already been handled in your application and the Java 7 additions have caused problems, you can use the private `sun.awt.disableMixing` system property to turn off mixing support.

Managing window types

The `JFrame` class supports a `setType` method, which configures the general appearance of a window to one of the three types. This can simplify the setting of a window's appearance. In this recipe we will examine these types and their appearance on Windows and Linux platforms.

Getting ready

To set the window type, use the `setType` method with one of the three window types, as found in the `java.awt.Window` class:

▸ `Type.NORMAL`: This represents a normal window and is the default value for windows

▸ `Type.POPUP`: This is a temporary window intended to be used for small areas, such as tool tips

▸ `Type.UTILITY`: This is also a small window for objects, such as a palette

How to do it...

1. Create a new window application as specified in the introduction to this chapter. Add the following statement before the **Exit** button is created:

   ```
   this.setType(Type.POPUP);
   ```

2. Execute the application. On a Windows system, the window should appear as follows:

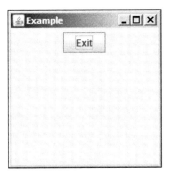

How it works...

The use of the method is simple enough. The `Type` enumeration is found in the `java.awt` package. On Windows, the windows appear as shown in the following screenshots. The normal and popup styles have the same appearance. The utility type is missing the minimize and maximize buttons:

The following screenshot shows an example of the window type `Type.NORMAL`:

The following screenshot shows an example of the window type `Type.POPUP`:

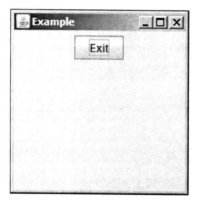

The following screenshot shows an example of the window type `Type.UTILITY`:

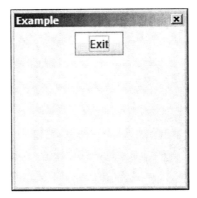

On Ubuntu, the windows appear as shown in the following screenshots. The normal and utility have the same appearance, while the popup type is missing its buttons:

The following screenshot shows an example of the window type `Type.NORMAL`:

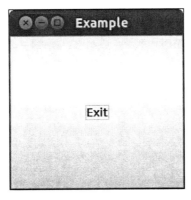

The following screenshot shows an example of the window type `Type.POPUP`:

The following screenshot shows an example of the window type `Type.UTILITY`:

Managing the opacity of a window

The opacity of a window refers to how transparent the window is. When a window is completely opaque, then nothing behind the window on the screen can be seen. A partially opaque window allows the background to bleed through. In this recipe we will learn how to control the opacity of a window.

Getting ready

To control the opacity of a window, use the `JFrame` class' `setOpacity` method with a float value representing how opaque the window should be.

How to do it...

1. Create a new standard GUI application as described in the chapter's introduction. Replace the `invokeLater` method invocation with the following code:

```
JFrame.setDefaultLookAndFeelDecorated(true);

SwingUtilities.invokeLater(new Runnable() {

    @Override
    public void run() {
        ApplicationWindow window = new
ApplicationWindow();
        window.setOpacity(0.75f);
        window.setVisible(true);
    }
});
```

2. Execute the application. The window should appear as follows:

Notice how the window behind this application can be seen. In this case, the background is the code for the application.

How it works...

The `setOpacity` used `0.75f` to set the opacity of the window. This results in it being 75 percent transparent, as can be seen by the code bleed through.

The range of values for opacity is 0.0f through 1.0f. A value of 1.0f represents a completely opaque window, and a value of 0.0f represents a completely transparent window. If the opacity is set to 0.0f, the mouse may or may not be enabled. This is determined by the underlying system. To set a value less than 1.0f:

▶ Translucency must be supported

▶ The window must be undecorated

▶ The window cannot be in full screen mode

To determine whether translucency is supported or not is covered in the next section. The `getOpacity` method can be used to determine what the current level of opacity is.

There's more...

To determine if the platform supports opacity, we need to use an instance of the `java.awt.GraphicsDevice` class. The `java.awt.GraphicsEnvironment` class contains a list of `GraphicsDevice` objects for the current platform. A `GraphicsDevice` normally refers to the screens available, but can include printers or image buffers. Each `GraphicsDevice` may also contain a set of `GraphicsConfiguration` objects that specify the configurations possible for a device, such as its resolution and what color model it supports.

In the following code sequence, we get an instance of the `GraphicsEnvironment` object and then use its `getDefaultScreenDevice` method to get a `GraphicsDevice` object. The `isWindowTranslucencySupported` method is used against the `GraphicsDevice` object to determine if transparency is supported:

```
GraphicsEnvironment graphicsEnvironment =
    GraphicsEnvironment.getLocalGraphicsEnvironment();
GraphicsDevice graphicsDevice = graphicsEnvironment.
getDefaultScreenDevice();

if (!graphicsDevice.isWindowTranslucencySupported(
        GraphicsDevice.WindowTranslucency.TRANSLUCENT)) {
    System.err.println(
        "Translucency is not supported on this platform");
        System.exit(0);
}
```

The `GraphicsDevice.WindowTranslucency` enumeration represents the types of transparency that may be supported by the platform. Its values are summarized in the following table. The alpha value refers to the level of transparency:

Value	Meaning
PERPIXEL_TRANSLUCENT	Represents the system support for some of the pixels to be set with potentially different alpha values
PERPIXEL_TRANSPARENT	Represents the system support for all of the pixels to be set to either 0.0f or 1.0f
TRANSLUCENT	Represents the system support for all of the pixels to be set with an alpha value

See also

The *Using the new JLayer Decorator for a password field* recipe addresses how to draw over the top of a `JComponent`.

Creating a varying gradient translucent window

There are instances when an application window can be aesthetically enhanced by the addition of special graphics features. Java 7 supports the use of gradient translucent windows, and the translucency can be both visually interesting as well as functional.

This recipe will demonstrate using both the transparency feature as well as a color gradient on a window.

Getting ready

In order to create a translucent, gradient color window, you need to:

1. Perform a check to ensure that the system environment supports per-pixel translucency.
2. Set the background color, such that the window initially is completely transparent.
3. Create a `java.awt.GradientPaint` object to specify the color and position of the gradient.

How to do it...

1. Create a new standard GUI application as described in the chapter's introduction. Add the following code to the `ApplicationDriver` class, before the start of the thread:

```
GraphicsEnvironment envmt =
        GraphicsEnvironment.getLocalGraphicsEnvironment();
GraphicsDevice device = envmt.getDefaultScreenDevice();

  if (!device.isWindowTranslucencySupported
    (WindowTranslucency.PERPIXEL_TRANSLUCENT)) {
    System.out.println("Translucent windows are not supported
on your system.");
        System.exit(0);
}

    JFrame.setDefaultLookAndFeelDecorated(true);
```

2. Next, replace the body of the `ApplicationWindow` constructor with the following code sequence:

```
this.setTitle("Gradient Translucent Window");
setBackground(new Color(0, 0, 0, 0));
this.setSize(500, 700);
this.setLocationRelativeTo(null);
this.setDefaultCloseOperation(JFrame.EXIT_ON_CLOSE);

JPanel panel = new JPanel() {
 @Override
 protected void paintComponent(Graphics gradient) {
   if (gradient instanceof Graphics2D) {
      final int Red = 120;
      final int Green = 50;
      final int Blue = 150;
      Paint paint = new GradientPaint(0.0f, 0.0f,
        new Color(Red, Green, Blue, 0),
```

```
                     getWidth(), getHeight(),
                        new Color(Red, Green, Blue, 255));
                Graphics2D gradient2d = (Graphics2D) gradient;
                gradient2d.setPaint(paint);
                gradient2d.fillRect(0, 0, getWidth(), getHeight());
        }
    }
};
    this.setContentPane(panel);
    this.setLayout(new FlowLayout());

    JButton exitButton = new JButton("Exit");
    this.add(exitButton);
    exitButton.addActionListener(new ActionListener() {
        public void actionPerformed(ActionEvent event) {
            System.exit(0);
        }
    });
```

3. Execute the application. Your window should resemble the following:

First, we added code to the `ApplicationDriver` class to test whether per-pixel translucency was supported by the system. In our example, if it were not supported, the application would exit. This is discussed in more detail in the *There's more...* section of the *Managing the opacity of a window* recipe.

Gradients should not be used on decorated windows. We called the `setDefaultLookAndFeelDecorated` method to ensure that the default look and feel is used. When executed on Windows 7, this results in an undecorated window.

In the `ApplicationDriver` class, we first set the background color of the window. We used `(0, 0, 0, 0)` to specify the saturation levels of each color, red, green, and blue, and the alpha value, as zero. Color values can be any integer between 0 and 255, but we want to start our window without any color. The alpha value of zero means our window will be completely transparent.

Next, we created a new `JPanel`. Within the `JPanel`, we overrode the `paintComponent` method and created a new `GradientPaint` object. There are four constructors for the `GradientPaint` class. We chose to use the one requiring floating numbers for the X and Y coordinates of the points referenced in the gradient, and the `Color` objects to specify the color of the gradient. You also have the option of passing `Point2D` objects rather than floating point numbers.

The first points specified, either by floating point number or `Point2D` objects, represent the start of the gradient. The second two, in our example, determined by the `getWidth` and `getHeight` methods, determine the ending points of the gradient. The result in our example was a gradient that started out light in the upper-left-hand corner, and became progressively darker as it moved down and to the right.

Finally, we cast the gradient as a `Graphics2D` object and called the `setPaint` and `fillRect` method to paint our gradient across the window.

See also

The use of the `GraphicsDevice` object to determine the level of transparency support is discussed in more detail in the *There's more...* section of the *Managing the opacity of a window* recipe.

Managing the shape of a window

There are times in application development when it can be fun and useful to create specially-shaped windows. This feature is now available in Java as of version 7. In this recipe we will develop a stop sign shape window to ensure that the user wants to continue some operation.

Getting ready

To create a specially-shaped window, you must:

1. Verify that per-pixel translucency is supported on the given system.
2. Create a component listener to catch `componentResized` events.
3. Create an instance of a shape and pass it to the `setShape` method.

How to do it...

1. Create a new standard GUI application as described in the chapter's introduction. In the `main` method, prior to starting the thread, test to ensure that shaped windows are supported on the system by adding the following code:

```
GraphicsEnvironment envmt =
        GraphicsEnvironment.getLocalGraphicsEnvironment();
GraphicsDevice device = envmt.getDefaultScreenDevice();

if (!device.isWindowTranslucencySupported(
        WindowTranslucency.PERPIXEL_TRANSLUCENT)) {
    System.out.println("Shaped windows not supported");
    System.exit(0);
}
```

2. Create a new class called `StopPanel` that is derived from `JPanel` and add the following constructor to it:

```
public StopPanel() {
    this.setBackground(Color.red);
    this.setForeground(Color.red);
    this.setLayout(null);

    JButton okButton = new JButton("YES");
    JButton cancelButton = new JButton("NO");
    okButton.setBounds(90, 225, 65, 50);
    cancelButton.setBounds(150, 225, 65, 50);

    okButton.addActionListener(new ActionListener() {
        public void actionPerformed(ActionEvent event) {
            System.exit(0);
        }
    });

    cancelButton.addActionListener(new ActionListener() {
        public void actionPerformed(ActionEvent event) {
            System.exit(0);
        }
    });

    this.add(okButton);
    this.add(cancelButton);

}
```

3. You also need to implement a paintComponent method for the StopPanel class. It is responsible for displaying text to our window. The following is one way to implement this method:

```
@Override
public void paintComponent(Graphics g) {
    super.paintComponent(g);
    Graphics2D g2d = (Graphics2D) g;
    int pageHeight = this.getHeight();
    int pageWidth = this.getWidth();
    int bigHeight = (pageHeight+80)/2;
    int bigWidth = (pageWidth-305)/2;
    int smallHeight = (pageHeight+125)/2;
    int smallWidth  = (pageWidth-225)/2;

    Font bigFont = new Font("Castellar", Font.BOLD, 112);
    Font smallFont = new Font("Castellar", Font.PLAIN, 14);

    g2d.setFont(bigFont);
    g2d.setColor(Color.white);
    g2d.drawString("STOP", bigWidth, bigHeight);
    g2d.setFont(smallFont);
    g2d.drawString("Are you sure you want to continue?",
smallWidth, smallHeight);
}
```

4. Within the ApplicationWindow class, create a new instance of a StopPanel before the **Exit** button is created. Next, create a new instance of a Shape. In our example, we created a Polygon object by using the getPolygon method as follows:

```
this.add(new StopPanel());
    final Polygon myShape = getPolygon();
```

5. Then add a componentListener in front of the code to create the **Exit** button to catch the componentResized event. Within the listener, invoke the setShape method against the Shape object. We will also set the foreground and background colors at this point:

```
        this.addComponentListener(new ComponentAdapter() {
            @Override
            public void componentResized(ComponentEvent e) {
                setShape(myShape);
                ((JFrame) e.getSource()).setForeground(Color.red);
                ((JFrame) e.getSource()).setBackground(Color.red);
}
});
```

6. Add a call to the `setUndecorated` method and set the property to `true`:

```
setUndecorated(true);
```

7. Next, add the `getPolygon` method to the class. This method creates an octagon using the two arrays of integers in conjunction with the `addPoint` method of the `Polygon` class:

```
private Polygon getPolygon() {
    int x1Points[] = {0, 0, 100, 200, 300, 300, 200, 100};
    int y1Points[] = {100, 200, 300, 300, 200, 100, 0, 0};
    Polygon polygon = new Polygon();
    for (int i = 0; i < y1Points.length; i++) {
        polygon.addPoint(x1Points[i], y1Points[i]);
}
    return polygon;
}
```

8. When the application is executed, you should see an octagonal window formatted like the following one:

How it works...

Our initial test to verify per-pixel translucency allowed us to tailor the application to the needs of the system it is running on. In our example, if the property was not supported we simply exited the application, though in a real-world environment you would probably want to open a less sophisticated window. Detecting the operating system support is discussed in more detail in the *There's more...* section of the *Managing the opacity of a window* recipe.

The `StopPanel` class implemented the `JPanel` interface and allowed us to add the custom text and buttons we used in our window. Because we were using a special shape for our window, we chose to call the `setLayout` method with a `null` argument, which in turn allowed us to use the `setBounds` methods to explicitly place our buttons where we wanted them on the window. It is important to note that although the window is displayed as an octagon, or whatever other shape you choose, in actuality the window is still a rectangle, as specified by the `setSize` method. Therefore, buttons and other objects may be placed on the window, but not visible if they are outside the bounds set by your shape.

The `paintComponent` method was used to customize the text on the window. Within this method, we set the size, style, and location of the text, and called the `drawString` method to actually paint it to the screen.

To actually create an octagonal window, we created our `getPolygon` method and manually drew the polygon. However, if you wanted to use a window with a shape already defined by a class implementing the `Shape` interface, you would not need to create a separate method. You simply pass the `Shape` object to the `setShape` method. If the `setShape` method's argument is `null`, the window will resize to the default for the given system, typically a rectangle.

It is important to execute the `setShape` method within a `componentResized` event. This ensures that anytime the window is redrawn, the `setShape` method will be called and the shape will be maintained. It is also important to call the `setUndecorated` method because, at the present time, decorations will be lost with specially-shaped windows. Also, the window may not be in full-screen mode.

See also

The use of the `GraphicsDevice` object to determine the level of transparency support is discussed in more detail in the *There's more...* section of the *Managing the opacity of a window* recipe.

Using the new border types in Java 7

Borders are used for the outline of swing components. In Java 7, several new border options are available. In this recipe we will develop a simple application to demonstrate how to create borders and how these borders appear.

Getting ready

To create and use a border:

1. Create a new border using a `javax.swing.BorderFactory` method.
2. Use the border object as an argument of the `setBorder` method applied against a `JComponent` object.

How to do it...

1. Create a new standard GUI application as described in the chapter's introduction. Modify the `ApplicationWindow` class to replace the following lines:

    ```
    JButton exitButton = new JButton("Exit");
    this.add(exitButton);
    ```

2. With the following code:

    ```
    JPanel panel = new JPanel();
    panel.setBorder(BorderFactory.
    createRaisedSoftBevelBorder());
        this.setLayout(new FlowLayout());

        JButton exitButton = new JButton("Exit");
        panel.add(exitButton);
        this.add(panel);
    ```

3. Execute the application. The window should appear as follows:

How it works...

The `setBorder` method changed the border of the `JPanel` to a raised soft-beveled border. The `BorderFactory` method possesses a number of static methods to create borders. The following table summarizes the new borders available in Java 7:

Method	Visual effect
The default border	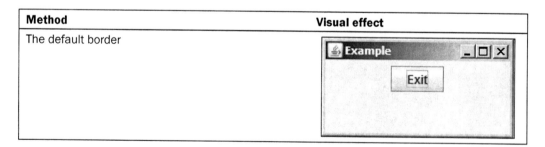

Method	Visual effect
createRaisedSoftBevelBorder()	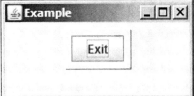
createLineBorder(Color.BLACK, 1, true) The first argument is the color of the border. The second is its thickness, while the third argument specifies whether the corners should be rounded or not.	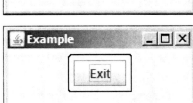
createLoweredSoftBevelBorder()	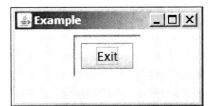
createSoftBevelBorder(BevelBorder.LOWERED) This has the same effect as createLoweredSoftBevelBorder()	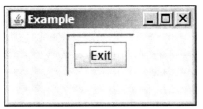
createSoftBevelBorder(BevelBorder.RAISED) This has the same effect as createRaisedSoftBevelBorder()	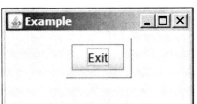

Method	Visual effect
`createSoftBevelBorder(BevelBorder.LOWERED, Color.lightGray, Color.yellow)` The first argument is the type of border: `RAISED` or `LOWERED`. The second argument is the color of the outer highlighted area The third argument is the color of the inner edge	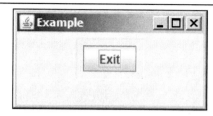
`createSoftBevelBorder(BevelBorder.RAISED,Color.lightGray, Color.yellow)` The same arguments as `createSoftBevelBorder`	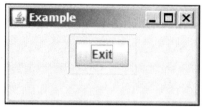
`createSoftBevelBorder(BevelBorder.LOWERED, Color.lightGray, Color.lightGray, Color.white, Color.orange)` The arguments are used for the inner and outer edges of the highlighted and shadowed areas of the border	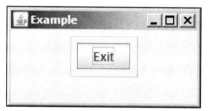
`createStrokeBorder(new BasicStroke(1.0f))` A second overloaded method takes a `Paint` object as a second argument, and is used to generate a color	
`createDashedBorder(Color.red)`	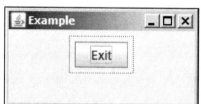
`createDashedBorder(Color.red, 4.0f, 1.0f)` The second argument is the relative length of a dash line and the third parameter is the relative length of a space.	

Method	Visual effect
`createDashedBorder(Color.red, 2.0f, 10.0f, 1.0f, true)` The second parameter specifies the thickness of the line. The third and fourth parameters specify the length and spacing respectively, while the last Boolean parameter determines whether the ends are rounded or not.	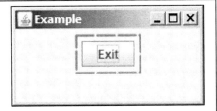

The border can be changed for any `JComponent` class. However, the appearance is not always acceptable. As we did in this example, it is sometimes better to change the border on an enclosing `JPanel` object.

Handling multiple file selection in the FileDialog class

The ability to select two or more files or directories in a file dialog box is achieved using the *Ctrl* and/or *Shift* keys in conjunction with the mouse. In Java 7, the file dialog box enables or disables this capability using the `java.awt.FileDialog` class' `setMultipleMode` method. This simple enhancement is illustrated in this recipe.

Getting ready

To enable or disable the selection of multiple files in a print dialog box:

1. Create a new `FileDialog` object.
2. Use its `setMultipleMode` method to determine its behavior.
3. Display the dialog box.
4. Use the return value to determine which files were selected.

How to do it...

1. Create a new standard GUI application as described in the chapter's introduction. Modify the `ApplicationWindow` class to add a button to display a file dialog box as shown in the following code. In an anonymous inner class, we will display the dialog box:

```
public ApplicationWindow() {
    this.setTitle("Example");
    this.setSize(200, 100);
    this.setLocationRelativeTo(null);
    this.setDefaultCloseOperation(JFrame.EXIT_ON_CLOSE);

    this.setLayout(new FlowLayout());

    final FileDialog fileDialog = new FileDialog(this,
"FileDialog");
    fileDialog.setMultipleMode(true);

    JButton fileDialogButton = new JButton("File Dialog");
    fileDialogButton.addActionListener(new ActionListener() {
        public void actionPerformed(ActionEvent event) {
            fileDialog.setVisible(true);
}
});

    this.add(fileDialogButton);

    JButton exitButton = new JButton("Exit");
    exitButton.addActionListener(new ActionListener() {
        public void actionPerformed(ActionEvent event) {
            System.exit(0);
}
});

    this.add(exitButton);
}
```

2. Execute the application. The application window should appear as follows:

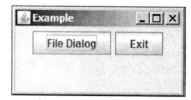

3. Select the **File Dialog** button and the following dialog box should appear. Navigate to a directory and select a few files. In the window that follows, two files of the /home/ music directory have been selected:

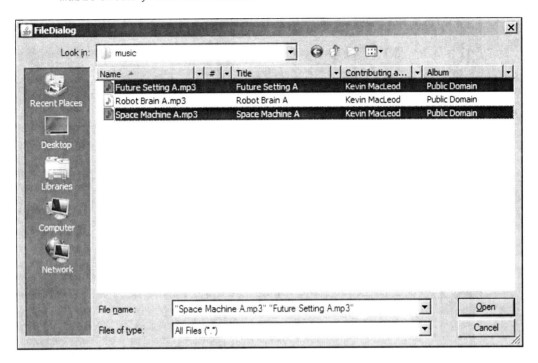

How it works...

The fileDialog class' setMultipleMode method was executed with an argument of true. This enabled multiple selections of files. An anonymous inner class was created to handle the selection of the file button event. In the actionPerformed method, the dialog box was made visible.

There's more...

To determine which files were selected, we can use the fileDialog class' getFiles method. Add the following code after the fileDialog class' setVisible method:

```
File files[] = fileDialog.getFiles();
for (File file : files) {
    System.out.println("File: " + file.getName());
}
```

The method returns an array of `File` objects. Using a for each loop, we can display the name of each file selected. Execute the application and select a few files. The output for the selected music files should appear as follows:

File: Future Setting A.mp3

File: Space Machine A.mp3

Controlling the print dialog box type

The standard print dialog that comes as part of the `java.awt.PrintJob` class allows the use of both a common and a native dialog box. This provides the ability to better tailor the application to a platform. The specification of the dialog box type is simple.

Getting ready

To specify the print dialog type and to use the print dialog, the following steps need to be followed:

1. Create a `javax.print.attribute.PrintRequestAttributeSet` object.
2. Assign the dialog type desired to this object.
3. Create a `PrinterJob` object.
4. Use the `PrintRequestAttributeSet` object as an argument to the `PrinterJob` class' `printDialog` method.

How to do it...

1. Create a new standard GUI application as described in the chapter's introduction. Modify the `ApplicationWindow` class to add a button to display a print dialog shown as follows. In an anonymous inner class, we will display a printer dialog box:

```
public ApplicationWindow() {
    this.setTitle("Example");
    this.setSize(200, 100);
    this.setLocationRelativeTo(null);
    this.setDefaultCloseOperation(JFrame.EXIT_ON_CLOSE);

    this.setLayout(new FlowLayout());

    JButton printDialogButton = new JButton("Print Dialog");
    printDialogButton.addActionListener(new ActionListener() {
        public void actionPerformed(ActionEvent event) {
            final PrintRequestAttributeSet attributes = new
HashPrintRequestAttributeSet();
```

```
                     attributes.add(DialogTypeSelection.COMMON);
                     PrinterJob printJob = PrinterJob.getPrinterJob();
                     printJob.printDialog(attributes);
      }
   });
          this.add(printDialogButton);

          JButton exitButton = new JButton("Exit");
          exitButton.addActionListener(new ActionListener() {
              public void actionPerformed(ActionEvent event) {
                  System.exit(0);
      }
   });
          this.add(exitButton);
   }
```

2. Execute the application and select the **Print** button. The dialog box that appears should use the common appearance type, as shown in the following screenshot:

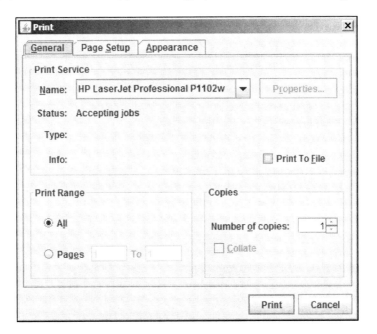

How it works...

A new **Print** button was created allowing the user to display a print dialog box. In the anonymous inner class used to handle the button's action event, we created a `PrintRequestAttributeSet` object based on the `javax.print.attribute. HashPrintRequestAttributeSet` class. This permitted us to add the `DialogTypeSelection.NATIVE` attribute to the set. The `DialogTypeSelection` class is new to Java 7 and provides two fields: `COMMON` and `NATIVE`.

Next, we created a `PrinterJob` object and executed the `printDialog` method against this object. The print dialog box was then displayed. If we had used the `NATIVE` type instead, shown as follows:

```
attributes.add(DialogTypeSelection.NATIVE);
```

Then the print dialog would appear as follows on a Windows platform:

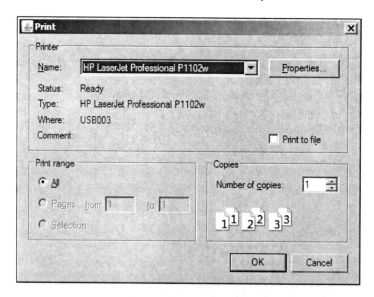

Using the new JLayer decorator for a password field

Java 7 supports the decoration of GUI components, such as textboxes and panels. Decoration is the process of drawing on top of the component to give it a special appearance. For example, we may want to watermark an interface to show that it is a beta version, or possibly to provide an indication of an error with a graphical X in a text field that is not otherwise possible.

The `javax.swing.JLayer` class provided a way of tying components of a display, the drawing of extra graphics over the components, and the interception of the events together. The handling of the events and the display is delegated to a `javax.swing.plaf.LayerUI` derived object. When an event occurs, a method to handle the event will be executed. When the component is drawn, the `LayerUI` derived object's `paint` method will be executed displaying graphics as needed.

In this recipe we will learn how Java supports this capability. In the first section, we will demonstrate how to display an error message for a password field. In the *There's more...* section, we will show how to create a watermark for a window.

Getting ready

To decorate a component:

1. Create the components to be decorated.
2. Create a `LayerUI` derived class that implements the decoration graphics operations.
3. Create a `JLayer` object based on the component and the `LayerUI` derived class.
4. Add the `JLayer` object to the application.

How to do it...

1. Create a new standard GUI application as described in the chapter's introduction. Use the following `ApplicationWindow`. In its constructor, we will perform the essential steps using a `getPanel` method to return our password `JPanel` object. When the user enters a password, the window will be decorated with a message indicating that the password is too short, until at least six characters are entered:

```
public ApplicationWindow() {
    this.setTitle("Example");
    this.setSize(300, 100);
    this.setLocationRelativeTo(null);
    this.setDefaultCloseOperation(JFrame.EXIT_ON_CLOSE);

    LayerUI<JPanel> layerUI = new PasswordLayerUI();
    JLayer<JPanel> jlayer = new JLayer<JPanel>(getPanel(),
layerUI);

    this.add(jlayer);
}

    private JPanel getPanel() {
        JPanel panel = new JPanel(new BorderLayout());
```

```
            JPanel gridPanel = new JPanel(new GridLayout(1, 2));
            JLabel quantityLabel = new JLabel("Password");
            gridPanel.add(quantityLabel);
            JPasswordField passwordField = new JPasswordField();
            gridPanel.add(passwordField);
            panel.add(gridPanel, BorderLayout.CENTER);

            JPanel buttonPanel =
              new JPanel(new FlowLayout(FlowLayout.LEFT));
            JButton okButton = new JButton("OK");
            buttonPanel.add(okButton);
            JButton cancelButton = new JButton("Cancel");
            buttonPanel.add(cancelButton);
            panel.add(buttonPanel, BorderLayout.SOUTH);

            return panel;
    }
```

2. Next, create the `PasswordLayerUI` class as shown in the following code.
    The `paint` method will perform the actual decoration. The remaining methods
    are used to enable keyboard events and handle them as they occur:

```
class PasswordLayerUI extends LayerUI<JPanel> {

    private String errorMessage = "Password too short";

    @Override
    public void paint(Graphics g, JComponent c) {
        FontMetrics fontMetrics;
        Font font;
        int height;
        int width;

        super.paint(g, c);
        Graphics2D g2d = (Graphics2D) g.create();
        int componentWidth = c.getWidth();
        int componentHeight = c.getHeight();

        // Display error message
        g2d.setFont(c.getFont());
        fontMetrics = g2d.getFontMetrics(c.getFont());
        height = fontMetrics.getHeight();
        g2d.drawString(errorMessage,
```

```
                          componentWidth / 2 + 10, componentHeight / 2 +
height);

            g2d.dispose();
    }

    @Override
    public void installUI(JComponent component) {
        super.installUI(component);
        ((JLayer) component).setLayerEventMask(AWTEvent.KEY_EVENT_
MASK);
    }

    @Override
    public void uninstallUI(JComponent component) {
        super.uninstallUI(component);
        ((JLayer) component).setLayerEventMask(0);
    }

    protected void processKeyEvent(KeyEvent event, JLayer layer) {
        JTextField f = (JTextField) event.getSource();
        if (f.getText().length() < 6) {
            errorMessage = "Password too short";
    }
    else {
            errorMessage = "";
    }
            layer.repaint();
    }

}
```

3. Execute the application. Enter a few characters in the textbox. Your window should appear similar to the following:

4. Enter at least six characters. At that point the decoration should disappear as follows:

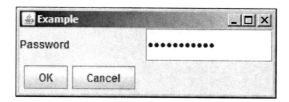

How it works...

In the `ApplicationWindow`, we created an instance of the `PasswordLayerUI` class. We used this object along with the `JPanel` returned by the `getPanel` method to create `JLayer` object. The `JLayer` object was then added to the window.

Notice the use of generics for the `LayerUI` and `JLayer` objects. This was used to ensure that the elements are all compatible. We used `JPanel` because that was the composite component we were decorating.

The `JLayer` class provided a way of tying the password box, the display of the error message, and the interception of the key events together. The handling of the key events and the display of the error message was delegated to the `PasswordLayerUI` object. When a key was pressed, the `processKeyEvent` method was executed. When the component was drawn, the `paint` method was executed displaying the error message by the password box.

In the `PasswordLayerUI` class, we declared a private `String` variable to hold our error message. It was declared at this level, because it was used in more than one method.

The `paint` method does the actual decorating. It was passed a `Graphics` object representing the area that we can draw to, and a `JComponent` component, which in this case was a `JPanel`. In the `paint` method, we used both the component's font and we also created a new `font` for the error message. The `height` and `width` of the component and the error string were calculated and used to position the error string that was displayed.

The `installUI` and `uninstallUI` methods were concerned with performing any initialization required to perform decoration. In this case, they were used to enable keyboard events to be intercepted and processed by the class. The `setLayerEventMask` method was used with the `AWTEvent.KEY_EVENT_MASK` argument to enable the processing of keyboard events. The `processKeyEvent` method performed the actual processing of keyboard events. In this method, the length of the password text field contents was used to determine which error message was to be displayed.

There's more...

This example could conceivably be performed using a label instead. However, this example was intended to provide a simple demonstration of how to use decorations. The creation of other decorations, such as a watermark is not as easily performed without the use of `JLayer` and `LayerUI` classes.

Add the following code before the `dispose` method. This sequence will add a watermark to the window indicating that this is a beta version of the interface. The `Castellar` font is used to provide a more stenciled look to the text. A `Composite` object is used to change the alpha value for the string. This effectively controls the transparency of the string displayed. The `getComposite` method is used to get the current composite for the window, and is then used to determine the rule being used. The rule along with an alpha value of `0.25f` is used to allow the watermark to fade into the background as follows:

```
// Display watermark
String displayText = "Beta Version";
font = new Font("Castellar",Font.PLAIN, 16);
fontMetrics = g2d.getFontMetrics(font);
g2d.setFont(font);
width = fontMetrics.stringWidth(displayText);
height = fontMetrics.getHeight();

Composite com = g2d.getComposite();
AlphaComposite ac = AlphaComposite.getInstance(
        ((AlphaComposite)com).getRule(),0.25f);
g2d.setComposite(ac);
g2d.drawString(displayText,
        (componentWidth - width) / 2,
        (componentHeight - height) / 2);
```

When executed, your application should appear similar to the following screenshot. Notice that the watermark is in all caps. This is the result of using the `Castellar` font, which is an all-capital letter font patterned after the letters used on a Roman column dedicated to Augustus.

8
Handling Events

In this chapter, we will cover the following:

- ▶ Managing extra mouse buttons and high resolution mouse wheels
- ▶ Controlling focus when displaying a window
- ▶ Using secondary loops to mimic modal dialog boxes
- ▶ Handling spurious thread wakeups
- ▶ Handling applet initialization status with event handlers

Introduction

There have been several additions to Java 7 that address events or are related to events. This includes the handling of mouse events where enhanced support is provided for the detection of mouse buttons and for using high resolution mouse wheels, as we will see in the *Managing extra mouse buttons and high resolution mouse wheels* recipe.

When a window is made visible with either the `setVisible` or `toFront` methods, we now have the ability to control whether they should gain focus or not. Some windows may be displayed for informational or status purposes and do not necessarily need or warrant focus. How to control this behavior is explained in the *Controlling AutoRequestFocus* recipe.

The reader should be familiar with the behavior of modal dialog boxes. Essentially, the modal dialog box will not return focus to the main window until it is closed. There are times when it is desirable to mimic this behavior without using a dialog box. For example, the selection of a button that performs a relatively long running calculation may benefit from this behavior. The *Using secondary loops to mimic modal dialog boxes* recipe examines how this can be done.

While not common, spurious interrupts can occur when using the `wait` method. The `java.awt.event.InvocationEvent` class' `isDispatched` method can be used to handle spurious interrupts as detailed in the *Handling spurious thread wakeups* recipe.

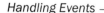

Applets have also been enhanced with regards to their ability to communicate with JavaScript code. The *Handling Applet initialization status with event handlers* recipe describes how JavaScript code can be made aware of and take advantage of knowing when an applet loads.

Other minor event-related improvements in Java 7 that don't warrant recipes include the availability of accessing extended key codes and the implementation of the `java.awt.iamg.ImageObserver` interface for the `JSlider` class.

The `KeyEvent` class has been augmented with two new methods: `getExtendedKeyCode` and `getExtendedKeyCodeForChar`. The first method returns a unique integer for a key, but unlike the `getKeyCode` method, its value depends on how the keyboard is currently configured. The second method returns the extended key code for a given Unicode character.

The `imageUpdate` method has been added to the `JSlider` class. This permits the class to monitor the status of an image being loaded, though this capability is probably best used with classes that are derived from `JSlider`.

Managing extra mouse buttons and high resolution mouse wheels

Java 7 has provided more options for handling mouse events. The `java.awt.Toolkit` class' `areExtraMouseButtonsEnabled` method allows you to determine whether more than the standard set of buttons is supported by the system. The `java.awt.event.MouseWheelEvent` class' `getPreciseWheelRotation` method can be used to control action on high resolution mouse wheels. In this recipe we will write a simple application to determine the number of mouse buttons enabled and test the mouse wheel rotation.

Getting ready

First, create a new application using the starter classes `ApplicationWindow` and `ApplicationDriver` found in the introduction of *Chapter 7, Graphical User Interface Improvements*:

1. Implement the `MouseListener` and `MouseWheelListener` interfaces to capture mouse events.

2. Use the `areExtraMouseButtonsEnabled` and `getPreciseWheelRotation` methods to determine specific information about the mouse.

How to do it...

1. First, we will set up basic information about the JFrame we are creating, using the following code example:

```
public class ApplicationWindow extends JFrame {

    public ApplicationWindow() {
        this.setTitle("Example");
        this.setSize(200, 100);
        this.setLocationRelativeTo(null);
        this.setDefaultCloseOperation(JFrame.EXIT_ON_CLOSE);
        this.setLayout(new FlowLayout());
        JButton exitButton = new JButton("Exit");
        this.add(exitButton);

    }
}
```

2. Next, we want to gather some information about the mouse. We execute the getNumberOfButtons method to determine how many buttons are present on our mouse. Then we use the areExtraMouseButtonsEnabled method to determine how many buttons on our mouse are available to us. We print this information to the console as follows:

```
int totalButtons = MouseInfo.getNumberOfButtons();
System.out.println(Toolkit.getDefaultToolkit().
areExtraMouseButtonsEnabled());
System.out.println("You have " + totalButtons + " total
buttons");
```

3. Next, we enable our listeners:

```
this.addMouseListener(this);
this.addMouseWheelListener(this);

exitButton.addActionListener(new ActionListener() {
    public void actionPerformed(ActionEvent event) {
        System.exit(0);
}
});
```

4. In the mousePressed event method, simply print out the button number pressed using the getButton method as follows:

```
public void mousePressed(MouseEvent e) {
    System.out.println("" + e.getButton());
}
```

5. Implement the remainder of the `MouseListener` interface methods. In the `mouseWheelMoved` event method, use both the `getPreciseWheelRotation` and the `getWheelRotation` methods to print out specific information about the movement of the mouse wheel:

```
public void mouseWheelMoved(MouseWheelEvent e) {
    System.out.println("" + e.getPreciseWheelRotation() +
        " - " + e.getWheelRotation());
}
```

6. Execute the application. You should see a `JFrame` window similar to the following:

7. When you click in the window, you will see varying output in your console depending upon your mouse, which button you click, and in which direction you move your mouse wheel. Here is one possible output:

true

You have 5 total buttons

1

2

3

4

5

0.75 - 0

1.0 - 1

1.0 - 1

1.1166666666666667 - 1

-1.0 - 0

-1.0 - -1

-1.2916666666666667 - -1

-1.225 - -1

How it works...

The getNumberOfButtons method returned the total number of buttons on our mouse. In the previous example, there were five buttons, but if the application was executed on a system with no mouse, it would have returned a -1. In our mousePressed method, we printed the name of the button clicked, as returned by the getButton method.

We executed the areExtraMouseButtonsEnabled method to determine that extra buttons are, in fact, supported and allowed to be added to an EventQueue. If you want to change the value of this, you must do so before the Toolkit class is initialized as explained in the *There's more...* section.

Because multiple mouse buttons were enabled, our output displayed the number for all five mouse buttons. In most instances, the mouse wheel is also considered a button and is included in the count.

The last several lines of the previous console output are indications of movement of the mouse wheel. The first one, **0.75 - 0**, is an indication that the mouse wheel was moved backwards, or toward the user. This is evident by the return value of 0.75 from the getPreciseWheelRotation method and the 0 from the getWheelRotation method. The last line of output, **-1.225 - -1**, is conversely an indication of forward mouse wheel movement, or away from the user. This is indicated by a negative return value by both methods.

This application was executed using a high resolution mouse wheel. A lower resolution mouse wheel will only return integer values.

There's more...

There are two ways of controlling whether extra mouse buttons are enabled or not. The first technique is to start the application with the following command line and set the sun.awt. enableExtraMouseButtons property to either true or false:

```
java -Dsun.awt.enableExtraMouseButtons=false ApplicationDriver
```

The -D option used a false value specifying that the extra mouse buttons were not to be enabled. The second approach is to set the same property before the Toolkit class is initialized. This can be accomplished with the following code:

```
System.setProperty("sun.awt.enableExtraMouseButtons", "true");
```

Controlling a focus when displaying a window

The `setAutoRequestFocus` method has been added to the `java.awt.Window` class and is used to specify whether a window should receive focus when it is displayed using either the `setVisible` or `toFront` methods. There may be times when a window is made visible, but we don't want the window to have focus. For example, if the window being displayed contains status information, making it visible will be sufficient. Giving it focus may not make sense and may frustrate the user by forcing them to change focus back to the original window.

Getting ready

To control the focus when a window is made visible, we will invoke the `setAutoRequestFocus` method with `true` if it should receive focus and a `false` value otherwise.

How to do it...

1. To demonstrate this technique we will create two windows. One will be used to hide and then display a second window. By using the `setAutoRequestFocus` method in the second window, we can control whether it receives focus or not.

2. Start by creating a new project with the following driver. In the driver, we will create the first window as follows:

```
public class ApplicationDriver {

    public static void main(String[] args) {

        SwingUtilities.invokeLater(new Runnable() {

            @Override
            public void run() {
                ApplicationWindow window = new
ApplicationWindow();
                window.setVisible(true);
}
});

}
}
```

3. Next, add the `ApplicationWindow` class. In this class, we add two buttons to hide and reveal the second window and a third one to exit the application as follows:

```java
public class ApplicationWindow extends JFrame {

    private SecondWindow second;

    public ApplicationWindow() {
        this.setTitle("Example");
        this.setBounds(100, 100, 200, 200);
        this.setDefaultCloseOperation(JFrame.EXIT_ON_CLOSE);
        this.setLayout(new FlowLayout());

        second = new SecondWindow();
        second.setVisible(true);

        JButton secondButton = new JButton("Hide");
        this.add(secondButton);
        secondButton.addActionListener(new ActionListener() {
            public void actionPerformed(ActionEvent event) {
                second.setVisible(false);
            }
        });

        JButton thirdButton = new JButton("Reveal");
        this.add(thirdButton);
        thirdButton.addActionListener(new ActionListener() {
            public void actionPerformed(ActionEvent event) {
                second.setVisible(true);
            }
        });

        JButton exitButton = new JButton("Exit");
        this.add(exitButton);
        exitButton.addActionListener(new ActionListener() {
            public void actionPerformed(ActionEvent event) {
                System.exit(0);
            }
        });
    }
}
```

4. Add the `SecondWindow` class next. This simple window does nothing but use the `setAutoRequestFocus` method to control how it behaves:

```
public class SecondWindow extends JFrame {

    public SecondWindow() {
        this.setTitle("Second Window");
        this.setBounds(400, 100, 200, 200);
        this.setDefaultCloseOperation(JFrame.EXIT_ON_CLOSE);

        this.setAutoRequestFocus(false);
    }
}
```

5. Execute the application. Both windows should appear with the focus on the first window, as shown in the following screenshot:

6. The second window appears as follows:

7. Select the **Hide** button. The second window should disappear. Next, select the **Reveal** button. The second window should reappear and should not have focus. This is the effect of the setAutoRequestFocus method, when used with a value of false.

8. Stop the application and change the argument of the setAutoRequestFocus method to true. Re-execute the application and hide and then reveal the second window. When it is revealed, the second window should receive focus.

How it works...

The application driver displayed the application window. In the ApplicationWindow class, the second window was created and displayed. Also, the three buttons were created and inner classes were created to affect each of their operations. The setAutoRequestFocus method was passed a value of false to specify that focus was not to be retained when the window was displayed.

There's more...

This approach may be useful for applications that run from the system tray.

 Please note that the isAutoRequestFocus method is available to determine the value of the autoRequestFocus value.

Using secondary loops to mimic modal dialog boxes

The java.awt.EventQueue class' SecondaryLoop interface provides a convenient technique for mimicking the behavior of a modal dialog box. A modal dialog box has two behaviors. The first one is from the user's perspective. The user is not permitted to interact with the main window, until the dialog box is complete. The second perspective is from the program execution standpoint. The thread in which the dialog box is called is blocked until the dialog box is closed.

A SecondaryLoop permits the execution of some task while blocking the current thread, until the secondary loop is complete. It may not have a user interface associated with it. This can be useful when the user selects a button that, while it does not display a dialog box, does involve a long running calculation. In this recipe we will demonstrate how to use a secondary loop and examine its behavior.

Getting ready

To create and use a secondary loop, the following steps need to be followed:

1. Get an instance of the default `java.awt.Toolkit` for the application.
2. Use this to obtain a reference to the system event queue.
3. Create a `SecondaryLoop` object using the event queue.
4. Use the `SecondaryLoop` interface's `enter` method to start the loop.
5. Implement the desired behavior in the secondary loop.
6. Use the `SecondaryLoop` interface's `exit` method to terminate the loop.

How to do it...

1. Create a new application with the following `ApplicationDriver` class. It simply displays the application's window as follows:

```
public class ApplicationDriver {

    public static void main(String[] args) {

        SwingUtilities.invokeLater(new Runnable() {

            @Override
            public void run() {
                ApplicationWindow window = new
    ApplicationWindow();
                window.setVisible(true);
        }
        });


    }
}
```

2. Add the following `ApplicationWindow` class. It creates two buttons, which will be used to demonstrate the behavior of secondary loops:

```
public class ApplicationWindow extends JFrame implements
ActionListener {

    private JButton firstButton;
    private JButton secondButton;

    public ApplicationWindow() {
        this.setTitle("Example");
```

```
        this.setBounds(100, 100, 200, 200);
        this.setDefaultCloseOperation(JFrame.EXIT_ON_CLOSE);
        this.setLayout(new FlowLayout());

        firstButton = new JButton("First");
        this.add(firstButton);
        firstButton.addActionListener(this);

        secondButton = new JButton("Second");
        this.add(secondButton);
        secondButton.addActionListener(this);
    }


}
```

3. Next, add the following `actionPerformed` method. A `SecondaryLoop` object is created and, depending on the button selected, `WorkerThread` objects are created as follows:

```
    @Override
    public void actionPerformed(ActionEvent e) {
        Thread worker;
        JButton button = (JButton) e.getSource();
        Toolkit toolkit = Toolkit.getDefaultToolkit();
        EventQueue eventQueue = toolkit.getSystemEventQueue();
        SecondaryLoop secondaryLoop = eventQueue.
createSecondaryLoop();

        Calendar calendar = Calendar.getInstance();
        String name;

        if (button == firstButton) {
            name = "First-"+calendar.get(Calendar.MILLISECOND);
    }
    else {
            name = "Second-"+calendar.get(Calendar.MILLISECOND);
    }
        worker = new WorkerThread(secondaryLoop, name);
        worker.start();

        if (!secondaryLoop.enter()) {
            System.out.println("Error with the secondary loop");
    }
    else {
            System.out.println(name + " Secondary loop returned");
    }
    }
```

4. Add the following `WorkerThread` class as an inner class. Its constructor saves the `SecondaryLoop` object and a message is passed to it. The message will be used to help us interpret the results. The `run` method displays the messages before and after it sleeps for two seconds:

```
class WorkerThread extends Thread {

    private String message;
    private SecondaryLoop secondaryLoop;

    public WorkerThread(SecondaryLoop secondaryLoop,
        String message) {
            this.secondaryLoop = secondaryLoop;
            this.message = message;
    }

    @Override
    public void run() {
        System.out.println(message + " Loop Sleeping ... ");
        try {
            Thread.sleep(2000);
    }
catch (InterruptedException ex) {
                ex.printStackTrace();
    }
            System.out.println(message + " Secondary loop
completed with a result of " +
                secondaryLoop.exit());
    }
}
```

5. Execute the application. The following window should appear. It has been resized here:

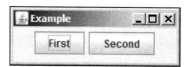

6. Next, select the **First** button. The following console output should illustrate the execution of the secondary loop. The number following **First-** will probably differ from your output:

First-433 Loop Sleeping ...

First-433 Secondary loop completed with a result of true

First-433 Secondary loop returned

7. While a secondary loop blocks the current thread, it does not prevent the window from continuing to execute. The window's UI thread is still active. To demonstrate this, restart the application and select the **First** button. Before two seconds have elapsed, select the **Second** button. The console output should be similar to the following:

First-360 Loop Sleeping ...

Second-416 Loop Sleeping ...

First-360 Secondary loop completed with a result of true

Second-416 Secondary loop completed with a result of true

Second-416 Secondary loop returned

First-360 Secondary loop returned

This illustrates two aspects of secondary loops. The first is that the application can still interact with the user, and the second is the behavior of two secondary loops executing at the same time. Specifically, if a second secondary loop is started before the first one is complete, the first one will not resume until the nested (second) one is terminated.

Notice that the application still responds to user input. Also, notice that the **Second-416** loop started execution after the **First-360**. However, while the **First-360** completed before the **Second-416**, as you would expect, the **First-360** loop did not return and resume the execution of the blocked thread, until after the **Second-416** loop returned. We will witness the same behavior if the **First** button is selected twice within two seconds.

How it works...

In the `ApplicationWindow`, we created two buttons. The buttons were added to the application and then associated with the application's implementation of the `ActionListener` interface. We used the **First** button to illustrate the execution of a secondary loop.

In the `actionPerformed` method, we used the `Toolkit` class' `getSystemEventQueue` method to get an instance of the `EventQueue`. This queue was then used with the `createSecondaryLoop` method to create a secondary loop.

In order to keep track of potential multiple secondary loops, we created an instance of the `Calendar` class and created a unique name derived from either **First-** or **Second-** suffixed with the current time in milliseconds. While this technique would not guarantee unique names, it is unlikely that two loops will have the same name and this is sufficient for our example.

Depending on which button was pressed, an instance of `WorkerThread` was created using `secondaryLoop` object and a unique name. The worker thread was then started and the `enter` method was executed against `secondaryLoop`.

At this point, the secondary loop will execute and the current thread will be blocked. In the `WorkerThread` class, a message was displayed indicating which secondary loop was executed. It was then suspended for two seconds followed by a second message indicating that the secondary loop completed along with the `exit` method return value.

The `actionPerformed` method's thread was then unblocked and a last message was displayed indicating that the secondary loop completed Notice that this thread blocked until the secondary loop completed.

This mimicked the behavior of a modal dialog box from the application's perspective. The thread where the secondary loop was created is blocked until the loop is completed. While other threading approaches could have been used to achieve a similar result, this approach is convenient and easy to use.

There's more...

It is not possible to use the same `SecondaryLoop` object to start a new loop if one is already active. Any attempt to do so will result in the `enter` method returning a value of `false`. However, once the loop has completed, the loop can be reused for other loops. This means the `enter` method can subsequently be executed against the same `SecondaryLoop` object.

See also

See the *Using the new JLayer Decorator for a password field* recipe in *Chapter 7, Graphical User Interface Improvements*. This recipe can be useful if you need to create a timer-hour hourglass type animation that could be displayed over the button indicating a long running process.

Handling spurious thread wakeups

When multiple threads are used, one thread may need to wait until the completion of one or more other threads. When this is necessary, one approach is to use the `Object` class' `wait` method to wait for the other threads to complete. These other threads need to use either the `Object` class' `notify` or `notifyAll` methods to permit the thread that is waiting to continue.

However, spurious wakeup calls can occur in some situations. In Java 7, the `java.awt.event.InvocationEvent` class' `isDispatched` method has been introduced to address this problem.

Getting ready

To avoid spurious wakeup calls:

1. Add a synchronized block.

2. Create a `while` loop based on the results of an application-specific condition and the `isDispatched` method.

3. Use the `wait` method in the body of the loop.

How to do it...

1. Due to the nature of spurious interrupts, it is not feasible to create a demonstration application that will consistently demonstrate this behavior. The recommended way of handling a `wait` is illustrated as follows:

```
synchronized (someObject) {
        Toolkit toolkit = Toolkit.getDefaultToolkit();
        EventQueue eventQueue = toolkit.getSystemEventQueue();
        while(someCondition && !eventQueue.isDispatchThread()) {
                try {
                wait();
        }
catch (InterruptedException e) {
        }
        }
        // Continue processing
        }
```

2. This approach will eliminate spurious interrupts.

How it works...

First, we used a synchronized block for the object we are working with. Next, we obtain an instance of the `EventQueue`. The `while` loop will test an application-specific condition to determine if it should be in a `wait` state. This could be simply a Boolean variable indicating that a queue is ready to be processed. The loop will continue executing while the condition is `true` and the `isDispatched` method returns `false`. This means if the method returns `true`, then the event was actually dispatched from the event queue. This will also occur with the `EventQueue.invokeAndWait` method.

A thread may wake up from a `wait` method for no reason at all. The `notify` or `notifyAll` methods may not have been called. This can occur due to conditions external to the JVM that are usually low-level and subtle.

In earlier versions of the **Java Language Specification**, this issue was not mentioned. However, in Java 5 the `wait` method documentation included a discussion of this issue. Clarification of this issue is found in the third edition of the Java Language Specification, **section 17.8.1 Wait**, found at `http://java.sun.com/docs/books/jls/third_edition/html/memory.html#17.8.1`.

Handling applet initialization status with event handlers

JavaScript code is able to call applet methods. However, this is not possible until the applet has been initialized. Any attempt to communicate with the applet will be blocked until the applet is loaded. In order to determine when the applet has been loaded, Java 7 has introduced a load status variable, which is accessible from JavaScript code. We will explore how to set up an HTML file to detect and respond to these events.

Getting ready

To use the loading status of an applet:

1. Create JavaScript functions to handle applet load events.
2. Deploy the applet, setting the parameter `java_status_events` to `true`.

How to do it...

1. Create a new application for the Java applet. In the `java.applet.Applet` class' `init` method, we will create a `Graphics` object to display a simple blue rectangle and then sleep for two seconds. This delay will simulate the loading of the applet:

```java
public class SampleApplet extends Applet {
    BufferedImage image;
    Graphics2D g2d;

    public void init() {
        int width = getWidth();
        int height = getHeight();
        image = new BufferedImage(width, height, BufferedImage.
TYPE_INT_RGB);
        g2d = image.createGraphics();
        g2d.setPaint(Color.BLUE);
        g2d.fillRect(0, 0, width, height);
        try {
            Thread.sleep(2000);
    }
```

```
catch (InterruptedException ie) {
            ie.printStackTrace();
    }
}


    public void paint(Graphics g) {
        g.drawImage(image, 0, 0, this);
    }
}
```

2. Package the applet in a `SampleApplet.jar` file. Next, create an HTML file as follows. The first part consists of declaring a title and creating the `determineAppletState` function to check on the load status of the applet as follows:

```
<HTML>
<HEAD>
<TITLE>Checking Applet Status</TITLE>
<SCRIPT>
    function determineAppletState() {
        if (sampleApplet.status == 1) {
            document.getElementById("statediv").innerHTML =
"Applet loading ...";
            sampleApplet.onLoad = onLoadHandler;
    }
    else if (sampleApplet.status == 2) {
            document.getElementById("statediv").innerHTML =
                "Applet already loaded";
    }
    else {
            document.getElementById("statediv").innerHTML =
                "Applet entered error while loading";
    }
    }


    function onLoadHandler() {
        document.getElementById("loadeddiv").innerHTML =
            "Applet has loaded";
    }

</SCRIPT>
</HEAD>
```

3. Follow this with the body of the HTML file. It uses an `onload` event to call the `determineAppletState` function. This is followed by a header field and two division tags. The divisions will be used for display purposes as follows:

```
<BODY onload="determineAppletState()">
<H3>Sample Applet</H3>
<DIV ID="statediv">state</DIV>
<DIV ID="loadeddiv"></DIV>
```

4. Complete the HTML file with a JavaScript sequence that configures and executes the applet as follows:

```
<DIV>
    <SCRIPT src="http://www.java.com/js/deployJava.js"></SCRIPT>
    <SCRIPT>
        var attributes = {id:'sampleApplet', code:'SampleApplet.
class', archive:'SampleApplet.jar', width:200,

height:100};
        var parameters = {java_status_events: 'true'};
        deployJava.runApplet(attributes, parameters, '7'7);
    </SCRIPT>
</DIV>
</BODY>
</HTML>
```

5. Load the applet into a browser. Here, it is loaded into Chrome as follows:

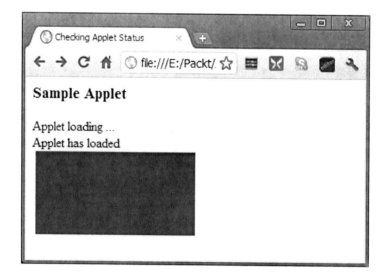

How it works...

The `SampleApplet` possessed two methods: `init` and `paint`. The `init` method created a `BufferedImage` object, which it used to display a blue square whose size is determined by the area allocated to the applet. Initially, the load was delayed for two seconds using the `sleep` method to simulate a slow loading applet. The `paint` method simply displayed the image. When the status is loading, the `onLoadHandler` was specified as the function to invoke when the applet completes loading. When this function is executed, a message to that effect was displayed in the `loadeddiv` division element.

In the body tag of the HTML file, the `determineAppletState` function was specified as the function to execute when the HTML was loaded into the browser. This ensured that the load status was checked when the HTML file was loaded.

The variable and attributes associated the `sampleApplet` ID with the `SampleApplet` class. The archive file containing the class and the size of the applet were also specified. In order to take advantage of this capability, the applet needed to be deployed with the `java_status_events` parameter set to `true`.

The function `determineAppletState` used the load status variable, status to display the status of the load process. Messages displayed in HTML division elements showed the sequence of operations.

The `deployJava.js` is part of the **Java Deployment Toolkit** and is used to detect the presence of a JRE, install one if necessary, and then run an applet. It can also be used for other **Web Start** programs. In this case, it was used to execute the applet using the attributes and parameters along with the version of JRE to use, that is Java 7.

 More information about executing Java applications deployment using `deployJava.js` is found at `http://download.oracle.com/javase/7/docs/technotes/guides/jweb/index.html`.

There are three applet status values as detailed in the following table:

Status	Value	Meaning
LOADING	1	The applet is loading
READY	2	The applet has loaded

9
Database, Security, and System Enhancements

In this chapter, we will cover the following:

- ▶ Using the RowSetFactory class
- ▶ Java 7 database enhancements
- ▶ Using the ExtendedSSLSession interface
- ▶ Using the platform MXBeans for JVM or system process load monitoring
- ▶ Redirecting input and output from operating systems processes
- ▶ Embedding a JNLP file in an HTML page

Introduction

This chapter covers database, security, and system type enhancements that have been made to Java 7. Some of these enhancements are minor and will be addressed in this introduction. Others are more significant and are detailed in this chapter's recipes. Due to the rather specialized nature of some topics, such as those typified by some of the security enhancements, they will be mentioned but not explained here.

Multiple enhancements have been made to JDBC in Java 7, which now supports **JDBC 4.1**. Some of the improvements depend on third party driver support not available in early driver versions. When this happens, you may receive an `AbstractMethodException`. When testing the database recipes for this chapter, ensure that you are working with a driver that supports the JDBC 4.1 functionality. Drivers can be found at `http://developers.sun.com/product/jdbc/drivers`.

The *Using the RowSetFactory* recipe deals with the use of the `javax.sql.rowset.RowSetFactory` interface and the `javax.sql.rowset.RowSetProvider` class, which permits the creation of any row sets as supported by a given JDBC driver. There are a number of other improvements in database's support included in Java 7. These are addressed in the *Java 7 database enhancements* recipe, and include such issues as determining the name of the current schema and providing access to hidden columns. The **Derby** database engine will be used for the database examples. If you prefer to use other databases and tables, you can do so by adjusting the code for the different databases.

In addition to these database recipes, the try-with-resource statement can be used with any object that implements the `java.sql` package's `Connection`, `ResultSet`, or `Statement` interfaces. This language improvement simplifies the process of opening and closing resources. The general use of the try-with-resource statement is detailed in the *Using the try-with-resource block to improve exception handling code* recipe, in *Chapter 1, Java Language Improvements*. An example of using this with a `ResultSet`-derived class is shown in the *Using the RowSetFactory class* recipe.

The `Statement` interface has been enhanced with two new methods. The first method, `closeOnCompletion`, is executed to specify that the `Statement` object will be closed when result sets that use the connection are closed. The second method, `isCloseOnCompletion`, returns a Boolean value indicating whether the statement will be closed when this criteria is met.

Network enhancements to Java 7 include the addition of two methods to the `java.net.URLClassLoader` class:

- `close`: This method will close the current `URLClassLoader`, so that it is no longer able to load classes or resources. This addresses a problem found on Windows, as detailed at `http://download.oracle.com/javase/7/docs/technotes/guides/net/ClassLoader.html`

- `getResourceAsStream`: This method returns an `InputStream` for the resource specified by its `String` argument

Assistance is also provided to support stream connections using the **InfiniBand** (**IB**). This technology uses **Remote Direct Memory Access** (**RDMA**) to move data directly between the memories of different computers. This support is provided through the **Sockets Direct Protocol** (**SDP**) network protocol. The specialized nature of this technology precludes further discussion.

The *Using the platform MXBeans for JVM or system process load monitoring* recipe, examines the improvements made in the support of `MXBeans`. This includes different methods for accessing these management type beans.

The `java.lang.ProcessBuilder` class has improved redirect capabilities as introduced by the `ProcessBuilder.Redirect` class. This topic is explored in the *Redirecting input and output from operating systems processes* recipe.

Java 7 has also improved the way applets can be embedded in an HTML page. The *Embedding a JNLP file in an HTML page* recipe provides a demonstration of this technique.

The **Java Secure Socket Extension** (**JSSE**) is used to secure Internet communications using **Secure Sockets Layer** (**SSL**) and **Transport Layer Security** (**TLS**). JSSE assists in data encryption, authentication, and maintaining message integrity. In Java 7, several enhancements have occurred. The *Using the ExtendedSSLSession interface* recipe uses SSL, and is used to illustrate the use of the `ExtendedSSLSession` interface and new security features.

Security enhancements include the incorporation of **Elliptic Curve Cryptography** (**ECC**) algorithms. This class of encryption algorithms is more resistant to brute force attacks. A portable implementation of the algorithm has been provided.

New exception classes have been added or enhanced to enhance security. The new `java.security.cert.CertificateRevokedException`, when thrown, means that an **X.509** certificate has been revoked. The `java.security.cert.CertPathValidatorException` class has been enhanced with the addition of a new constructor that takes a `CertPathValidatorException.Reason` object. This object implements the `CertPathValidatorException.BasicReason` enumeration that enumerates the reason for the exception. The `CertPathValidatorException` class's `getReason` method returns a `CertPathValidatorException.Reason` object.

Java 7 also supports TLS 1.1 and 1.2 specifications and improves upon this support. The **Sun JSSE** provider supports TLS 1.1 and TLS 1.2 as defined in RFC 4346 (`http://tools.ietf.org/html/rfc4346`) and RFC 5246 (`http://tools.ietf.org/html/rfc5246`) respectively. These include support to protect against cipher block chaining attacks and new cryptographic algorithms.

In addition, there are a few other TKS-related enhancements:

▶ The **SSLv2Hello** protocol has been removed from the list of protocols that are enabled by default.

▶ A flaw relating to TLS renegotiation has been fixed in Java 7. Details regarding this flaw can be found at `http://www.oracle.com/technetwork/java/javase/documentation/tlsreadme2-176330.html`.

▶ During TLS 1.1/1.2 handshaking, Java 7 has improved the process of version number checking.

Weak cryptographic algorithms can be disabled using the `jdk.certpath.disabledAlgorithms` property for the **Sun** provider. By default, the MD2 algorithm is disabled. This property is specified in the `jre/lib/security/java.security` file. The default setting is shown as follows:

```
jdk.certpath.disabledAlgorithms=MD2
```

It is also possible to specify not only the algorithm, but restrictions on the key size.

Algorithm restrictions can also be placed at the TLS level. This is accomplished using the `jdk.tls.disabledAlgorithms` security property in the `jre/lib/security/java.security` file. An example is as follows:

```
jdk.tls.disabledAlgorithms=MD5, SHA1, RSA keySize < 2048
```

Currently, this property is specific to the **Oracle JSSE** implementation and may not be recognized by other implementations.

The **Server Name Indication** (**SNI**) JSSE extension (RFC 4366) enables TLS clients to connect to virtual servers, that is, multiple servers with different network names that use the same supporting network address. This is enabled to `true` by default, but can be set to `false` for systems where the extension is not supported.

The `jsse.enableSNIExtension` system property is used to control this setting. It can be set using the `-D` java command option shown as follows:

```
java -D jsse.enableSNIExtension=true ApplicationName
```

It is also possible to set this property using the `setProperty` method shown as follows:

```
System.setProperty("jsse.enableSNIExtension", "true");
```
Note that the property name may change in the future.

Using the RowSetFactory class

Row sets can now be created using the new `javax.sql.rowset` package's `RowSetFactoryInterface` interface and the `RowSetProvider` class. This permits the creation of any type of row set supported by JDBC. We will use the Derby database to illustrate the process of creating row sets. The COLLEAGUES table will be used. A description of how to create this table is found at `http://netbeans.org/kb/docs/ide/java-db.html`. The SQL code to create the table is as follows:

```
CREATE TABLE COLLEAGUES (
    "ID" INTEGER not null primary key,
    "FIRSTNAME" VARCHAR(30),
    "LASTNAME" VARCHAR(30),
    "TITLE" VARCHAR(10),
```

```
    "DEPARTMENT" VARCHAR(20),
    "EMAIL" VARCHAR(60)
);

INSERT INTO COLLEAGUES VALUES (1,'Mike','Johnson','Manager','Engineeri
ng','mike.johnson@foo.com');
INSERT INTO COLLEAGUES VALUES
(2, 'James', 'Still', 'Engineer', 'Engineering', 'james.still@foo.
com');
INSERT INTO COLLEAGUES VALUES
(3, 'Jerilyn', 'Stall', 'Manager', 'Marketing', 'jerilyn.stall@foo.
com');
INSERT INTO COLLEAGUES VALUES
(4, 'Jonathan', 'Smith', 'Manager', 'Marketing', 'jonathan.smith@foo.
com');
```

Getting ready

To create a new row set:

1. Create an instance of the `RowSetFactory`.

2. Use one of the several `create` methods to create a `RowSet` object.

How to do it...

1. Create a new console application. In the `main` method, add the following code
   sequence. We will create a new `javax.sql.rowset.JdbcRowSet` object and use
   it to display some of the fields in the `COLLEAGUES` table. Start by setting up `String`
   variables to establish connectivity to the database and create a `RowSetFactory`
   object as follows:

```
        String databaseUrl = "jdbc:derby://localhost:1527/
contact";
        String username = "userName";
        String password = "password";

        RowSetFactory rowSetFactory = null;
        try {
            rowSetFactory = RowSetProvider.newFactory("com.sun.
rowset.RowSetFactoryImpl", null);
}
catch (SQLException ex) {
            ex.printStackTrace();
            return;
}
```

2. Next, add a try block to catch any `SQLExceptions`, and then use the `createJdbcRowSet` method to create the row set. Next, display the selected elements of the table.

```
        try (JdbcRowSet rowSet = rowSetFactory.
createJdbcRowSet();) {

                rowSet.setUrl(databaseUrl);
                rowSet.setUsername(username);
                rowSet.setPassword(password);
                rowSet.setCommand("SELECT * FROM COLLEAGUES");
                rowSet.execute();

                while (rowSet.next()) {
                    System.out.println(rowSet.getInt("ID") + " - "
                            + rowSet.getString("FIRSTNAME"));
        }
        }
        catch (SQLException ex) {
                ex.printStackTrace();
        }
```

3. Execute the application. The output should appear as follows:

1 - Mike

2 - James

3 - Jerilyn

4 - Jonathan

How it works...

String variables were created for the database URL, username, and password. The `RowSetFactory` object was created using the static `newFactory` method. Any exceptions generated will result in the termination of the application.

In the try-with-resources block, the `createJdbcRowSet` method was used to create an instance of the `JdbcRowSet` class. The URL, username, and password were then assigned to the row set. The select command retrieved all of the fields from the `COLLEAGUES` table. The query was then executed.

Next, a `while` loop was used to display the ID and the first name for each row of the row set.

There's more...

There may be more than one `RowSetFactory` implementation available. The `newFactory` method will look for a `RowSetFactory` class in the following order:

1. The one specified in the system property, `javax.sql.rowset.RowSetFactory`, if defined.

2. Using the `ServiceLoader` API.

3. The platform default instance.

In addition to the creation of a `JdbcRowSet` row set, other methods are available to create different types of row sets as listed in the following table:

Method	Row set created
`createCachedRowSet`	`CachedRowSet`
`createFilteredRowSet`	`FilteredRowSet`
`createJdbcRowSet`	`JdbcRowSet`
`createJoinRowSet`	`JoinRowSet`
`createWebRowSet`	`WebRowSet`

A `RowSetFactory` can also be created using the overloaded `newFactory` method that takes two arguments, shown as follows:

```
rowSetFactory = RowSetProvider.newFactory("com.sun.rowset.RowSetFactoryImpl", null);
```

This approach provides more control to the application, enabling it to specify the provider to use. When there are multiple providers found in the class path, this can be useful. The first argument specifies the class name of the provider and the second argument specifies the class loader to use. Using `null` as the second argument specifies that the context class loader is to be used.

Java 7 database enhancements

There are numerous small enhancements to the database support provided by Java 7. This recipe addresses these enhancements and provides examples where practical. Due to the immaturity of many JDBC 4.1 drives, not all of the code examples will be completely functional.

Most of the examples start by:

1. Creating a connection to a Derby database.
2. Using the connection methods to access needed functionality.

How to do it...

1. Create a new console application. In the `main` method, add the following code sequence. It will establish a connection to the database and determine if auto-generated keys will always be returned and what the current schema is:

```
try {
        Connection con = DriverManager.getConnection(
                "jdbc:derby://localhost:1527/contact",
"userName", "password");

        System.out.println("Schema: " + con.getSchema());

        System.out.println("Auto Generated Keys: " + metaData.
generatedKeyAlwaysReturned());

}
catch (SQLException ex) {
        ex.printStackTrace();
}
```

2. When executed, your output should appear similar to the following:

Auto Generated Keys: true

Schema: SchemaName

How it works...

The `Statement` interface's `getGeneratedKeys` method was introduced in Java 1.4 and returns any auto-generated keys for that statement. The `java.sql.DatabaseMetaData` interface's `generatedKeyAlwaysReturned` method returned a Boolean value, indicating that auto-generated keys will always be returned.

It is possible to set and get the schema for a connection using the `Connection` interface's `setSchema` and `getSchema` methods. The `getSchema` method was executed, which returned the schema name.

There's more...

Three other topics bear further discussion:

- ▸ Retrieving pseudo-columns
- ▸ Controlling the type value of the `OUT` parameter
- ▸ Other database enhancements

Retrieving pseudo-columns

Databases will often use hidden columns to represent a unique key for every row of a table. These hidden columns are sometimes called **pseudo-columns**. In Java 7, two new methods have been added to address pseudo-columns. The `DatabaseMetaData` interface's `getPseudoColumns` method will retrieve a `ResultSet`. The method asks for the following:

- ▸ Catalog: This needs to match the catalog name used in the database. If no catalog is used, then use an empty string. A null value means that the catalog name will not be used when searching for the columns.

- ▸ Schema pattern: This needs to match the schema name used in the database. If no schema is used then use an empty string. A null value means that the schema name will not be used when searching for the columns.

- ▸ Table name pattern: This needs to match the table name used in the database

- ▸ Column name pattern: This needs to match the column name used in the database

The `ResultSet` returned will have the following organization as shown in the following table:

Column	Type	Meaning
TABLE_CAT	String	The name of the catalog which may be null
TABLE_SCHEM	String	The name of the schema which may be null
TABLE_NAME	String	The name of the table
COLUMN_NAME	String	The name of the column
DATA_TYPE	int	SQL type (`java.sql.Types`)
COLUMN_SIZE	int	The size of the column
DECIMAL_DIGITS	int	The number of fractional digits. A null value means there are no fractional digits.
NUM_PREC_RADIX	int	The radix
COLUMN_USAGE	String	Specifies how the column is used as defined by the new PsuedoColumnUsage enumeration
REMARKS	String	Comment regarding the column
CHAR_OCTET_LENGTH	int	The maximum number of characters for a char column

Column	Type	Meaning
IS_NULLABLE	String	YES: Column can contain null
		NO: Column cannot contain nulls
		"": Unknown

The hidden columns represent a unique key, which provides a fast way of accessing a row. Derby does not support hidden columns. However, the following code sequence illustrates how this can be accomplished:

```
        try {
            Connection con = DriverManager.getConnection(
                "jdbc:derby://localhost:1527/contact", "userName",
    "password");
            DatabaseMetaData metaData = con.getMetaData();
            ResultSet resultSet = metaData.getPseudoColumns("",
    "schemaName", "tableName", "");

            while (rs.next()) {
                System.out.println(
                    resultSet.getString("TABLE_SCHEM ")+" - "+
                    resultSet.getString("COLUMN_NAME "));
    }

    }
catch (SQLException ex) {
            ex.printStackTrace();
    }
```

Derby will return an empty `ResultSet` consisting of the columns listed previously.

Controlling the type value of the OUT parameter

The `java.sql.CallableStatement` has two overloaded `getObject` methods that return an object, which is given a column name or index. Support is currently limited. However, the basic approach is illustrated as follows:

```
        try {
            Connection conn = DriverManager.getConnection(
                "...", "username", "password");
            String query = "{CALL GETDATE(?,?)}";
```

```
            CallableStatement callableStatement = (CallableStatement)
    conn.prepareCall(query);

            callableStatement.setInt(1,recordIdentifier);
            callableStatement.registerOutParameter(1, Types.DATE);
            callableStatement.executeQuery();

            date = callableStatement.getObject(2,Date.class));

    }
    catch (SQLException ex) {
            ex.printStackTrace();
    }
```

The query string contains a call to a stored procedure. This procedure is assumed to use an integer value as the first parameter to identify a record in a table. The second argument is to be returned and is of the type `Date`.

Once the query is executed, the `getObject` method will return the specified column using the data type specified. The method will convert the SQL type to the Java data type.

Other database enhancements

The `java.sql` package's `Driver` interface has a new method, which returns the parent logger for the driver. This is illustrated with the following code sequence:

```
    try {
            Driver driver = DriverManager.getDriver("jdbc:derby://
    localhost:1527");
            System.out.println("Parent Logger" + driver.
    getParentLogger());
    }
    catch (SQLException ex) {
            ex.printStackTrace();
    }
```

However, when executed, the current version of the driver will generate the following exception:

Java.sql.SQLFeatureNotSupportedException: Feature not implemented: getParentLogger.

Derby does not use the `java.util.logging` package, so it throws this exception. The `javax.sql.CommonDataSource` interface has also added the `getParentLogger` method.

In addition, when a series of database operations are performed in conjunction with an `Executor`, three methods are available to support those operations, which are as follows:

- ▶ `abort`: This method will abort an open connection using the `Executor` passed to the method
- ▶ `setNetworkTimeout`: This method specifies the timeout period in milliseconds to wait for the response to a request. It also uses an `Executor` object.
- ▶ `getNetworkTimeout`: This method returns the number of milliseconds that the connection will wait for database requests

The last two methods are optional and are not supported by Derby.

Using the ExtendedSSLSession interface

The `javax.net.ssl` package provides a series of classes used to effect secure socket communication. Improvements introduced in Java 7 include the addition of the `ExtendedSSLSession` interface, which can be used to determine the specific local and peer supported signature algorithms that are used. In addition, when an `SSLSession` is created, an endpoint identification algorithm can be used to ensure that the host computer's address matches that of the certificate. This algorithm is accessible through the `SSLParameters` class.

Getting ready

To demonstrate the use of the `ExtendedSSLSession` interface, we will:

1. Create an `SSLServerSocket`-based `EchoServer` application to accept messages from a client.
2. Create a client application, which uses a `SSLSocket` instance to communicate with the server.
3. Use the `EchoServer` application to obtain an instance of the `ExtendedSSLSession` interface.
4. Use a `SimpleConstraints` class to demonstrate the use of algorithm constraints.

How to do it...

1. Let's start by creating a class called `SimpleConstraints`, which is adapted from the **Java PKI Programmer's Guide** (http://download.oracle.com/javase/7/docs/technotes/guides/security/certpath/CertPathProgGuide.html). We will use this to associate algorithm constraints to the application. Add the following class to your project:

```
public class SimpleConstraints implements AlgorithmConstraints {
    public boolean permits(Set<CryptoPrimitive> primitives,
```

```
        String algorithm, AlgorithmParameters parameters) {
      return permits(primitives, algorithm, null, parameters);
  }

    public boolean permits(Set<CryptoPrimitive> primitives, Key key) {
      return permits(primitives, null, key, null);
  }

    public boolean permits(Set<CryptoPrimitive> primitives,
          String algorithm, Key key, AlgorithmParameters parameters) {
      if (algorithm == null) algorithm = key.getAlgorithm();

      if (algorithm.indexOf("RSA") == -1) return false;

      if (key != null) {
        RSAKey rsaKey = (RSAKey)key;
        int size = rsaKey.getModulus().bitLength();
        if (size < 2048) return false;
  }

      return true;
  }
  }
```

2. To create the `EchoServer` application, create a new console application. Add the following code to the `main` method. In this initial sequence, we create and start up the server:

```
        try {
            SSLServerSocketFactory sslServerSocketFactory =
                    (SSLServerSocketFactory)
SSLServerSocketFactory.getDefault();
            SSLServerSocket sslServerSocket =
                    (SSLServerSocket) sslServerSocketFactory.
createServerSocket(9999);
            System.out.println("Waiting for a client ...");
            SSLSocket sslSocket = (SSLSocket) sslServerSocket.
accept();

        }
        catch (Exception exception) {
            exception.printStackTrace();
        }
```

3. Next, add the following code sequence to set up algorithm constraints for the application. It also returns the name of the end point algorithm:

```
SSLParameters parameters = sslSocket.
getSSLParameters();
    parameters.setAlgorithmConstraints
        (new SimpleConstraints());


    String endPoint = parameters.
getEndpointIdentificationAlgorithm();
    System.out.println("End Point: " + endPoint);
```

4. Add the following code to display local supported algorithms:

```
    System.out.println("Local Supported Signature
Algorithms");
        if (sslSocket.getSession() instanceof
ExtendedSSLSession) {
            ExtendedSSLSession extendedSSLSession =
                (ExtendedSSLSession) sslSocket.
getSession();
            String algorithms[] =
                extendedSSLSession.
getLocalSupportedSignatureAlgorithms();
            for (String algorithm : algorithms) {
                System.out.println("Algorithm: " + algorithm);
        }
    }
```

5. The following sequence displays peer-supported algorithms:

```
    System.out.println("Peer Supported Signature
Algorithms");
        if (sslSocket.getSession() instanceof
ExtendedSSLSession) {
            String algorithms[] = ((ExtendedSSLSession)
sslSocket.getSession()).getPeerSupportedSignatureAlgorithms();
            for (String algorithm : algorithms) {
                System.out.println("Algorithm: " + algorithm);
        }
    }
```

6. Add the following code to buffer the input stream coming from a client application:

```
    InputStream inputstream = sslSocket.getInputStream();
    InputStreamReader inputstreamreader = new
InputStreamReader(inputstream);
    BufferedReader bufferedreader = new BufferedReader
(inputstreamreader);
```

7. Finish the method by adding code to display the input from the client:

```
        String stringline = null;
        while ((stringline = bufferedreader.readLine()) !=
null) {
            System.out.println(string);
            System.out.flush();
}
```

8. To execute the server, we need to create key store. This is accomplished from the command prompt by executing the following command:

   keytool -genkey -keystore mySrvKeystore -keyalg RSA

9. Provide a password and other information requested by the program. Next, navigate to the echo server's location and enter the following command:

   java -Djavax.net.ssl.keyStore=mySrvKeystore

   Djavax.net.ssl.keyStorePassword=password package.EchoServer

10. The **password** above, is the password that you used to create the key store, and package, is your EchoServer's package, if any. When the program executes, you get the following output:

    Waiting for a client ...

11. We now need to create a client console application called `EchoClient`. In the `main` method, add the following code where we create a connection to the server and then send the input from the keyboard to the server:

```
        try {
            SSLSocketFactory sslSocketFactory =
                    (SSLSocketFactory) SSLSocketFactory.
getDefault();
            SSLSocket sslSocket = (SSLSocket)
                    sslSocketFactory.createSocket("localhost",
9999);

            InputStreamReader inputStreamReader =
                    new InputStreamReader(System.in);
            BufferedReader bufferedReader =
                    new BufferedReader(inputStreamReader);

            OutputStream outputStream = sslSocket.
getOutputStream();
            OutputStreamWriter outputStreamWriter =
                    new OutputStreamWriter(outputStream);
            BufferedWriter bufferedwriter =
```

```
                    new BufferedWriter(outputStreamWriter);

        String line = null;
        while ((line = bufferedReader.readLine()) != null) {
            bufferedwriter.write(line + '\n');
            bufferedwriter.flush();
    }
    }
    catch (Exception exception) {
            exception.printStackTrace();
    }
```

12. Copy the key store file to the client application's directory. In a separate command window, execute the following command:

    ```
    java -Djavax.net.ssl.trustStore=mySrvKeystore
    -Djavax.net.ssl.trustStorePassword=password package.EchoClient
    ```

13. The **password** above, is the password that you used to create the key store, and package, is your EchoServer's package, if any. When the program executes, enter the word **cat**, and then press the *Enter* key. In the server command window, you should see an end point name, which may be null, a list of local supported signature algorithms, and **cat** similar to the following:

End Point: null

Local Supported Signature Algorithms

Algortihm: SHA512withECDSA

Algortihm: SHA512withRSA

Algortihm: SHA384withECDSA

Algortihm: SHA384withRSA

Algortihm: SHA256withECDSA

Algortihm: SHA256withRSA

Algortihm: SHA224withECDSA

Algortihm: SHA224withRSA

Algortihm: SHA1withECDSA

Algortihm: SHA1withRSA

Algortihm: SHA1withDSA

Algortihm: MD5withRSA

Peer Supported Signature Algorithms

cat

14. As you enter more input lines, they should be reflected in the server command window. To terminate the program, enter a *Ctrl + C* in the client command window.

How it works...

The `SimpleConstraints` class allows only RSA algorithms and then with keys that use 2048 bits or more. This was used as an argument to the `setAlgorithmConstraints` method. The class implemented the `java.security.AlgorithmConstraints` interface, which represents the restrictions of the algorithm.

A `SSLServerSocketFactory` instance was created followed by the creation of a `SSLServerSocket`. The `accept` method was executed against the socket, which blocks until a client connects to it.

Next, the `SimpleConstraints` was set followed by the use of the `getEndpointIdentificationAlgorithm` method, which returned an empty string. For this example, no endpoint identification algorithm was used.

The local and peer supported signature algorithms were listed. The remaining code was concerned with reading and then displaying the string sent by a client.

The `EchoClient` application is simpler. It created an instance of the `SSLSocket` class and then used its `getOutputStream` method to write the user's input to the echo server.

Using the platform MXBeans for JVM or system process load monitoring

Java Management Extensions (**JMX**) is a standard way of adding a management interface to an application. A **managed bean** (**MBean**) provides the management services for the application and is registered with a `javax.management.MBeanServer`, which holds and administers the MBean. A `javax.management.MXBean` is a type of MBean, which permits clients to access the bean without the need to access specific classes.

The `java.lang.management` package's `ManagementFactory` class has added several new methods to gain access to an MBean. These can then be used to access process and load monitoring.

Getting ready

To access an `MXBean`:

1. Use the `getPlatformMXBean` method with the `MXBean` type needed for the application.
2. Use the `MXBean` methods as required.

How to do it...

1. Create a new console application. Use the `main` method that follows. In this application, we will obtain an `MXBean` for the runtime environment and display basic information about it:

```
public static void main(String[] args) {
    RuntimeMXBean mxBean = ManagementFactory.
getPlatformMXBean(RuntimeMXBean.class);

    System.out.println("JVM Name: " + mxBean.getName());
    System.out.println("JVM Specification Name: " + mxBean.
getSpecName());
    System.out.println("JVM Specification Version: " + mxBean.
getSpecVersion());
    System.out.println("JVM Implementation Name: " + mxBean.
getVmName());
    System.out.println("JVM Implementation Vendor: " + mxBean.
getVmVendor());
    System.out.println("JVM Implementation Version: " +
mxBean.getVmVersion());

}
```

2. Execute the application. Your output should be similar to the following:

JVM Name: 5584@name-PC

JVM Specification Name: Java Virtual Machine Specification

JVM Specification Version: 1.7

JVM Implemenation Name: Java HotSpot(TM) 64-Bit Server VM

JVM Implemenation Vendor: Oracle Corporation

JVM Implemenation Version: 21.0-b17

How it works...

We used the `ManagementFactory` class' static `getPlatformMXBean` method with an argument of `RuntimeMXBean.class`. This returned an instance of a `RuntimeMXBean`. Specific methods of this instance were then applied and their values were displayed.

There's more...

The `ManagementFactory` introduced several new methods in Java 7:

- `getPlatformMXBean`: This is an overloaded method that returns a `PlatformManagedObject`-derived object supporting a particular management interface using a `Class` argument
- `getPlatformMXBeans`: This is an overloaded method that returns a `PlatformManagedObject`-derived object supporting a particular management interface using an `MBeanServerConnection` object and a `Class` argument
- `getPlatformManagementInterfaces`: This method returns a set of `Class` objects for `PlatformManagedObject`-derived objects on the current Java platform

In addition, a new interface was added to the `java.lang.management` package. The `PlatformManagedObject` interface serves as the base interface for all `MXBeans`.

Using the getPlatformMXBeans method

The `getPlatformMXBeans` method is passed the `MXBean` type and returns a list of the platform `MXBeans` that implements the `MXBean` type. In the following example, we obtain a list for the `OperatingSystemMXBean`. Several attributes of the `MXBean` are then displayed:

```
        List<OperatingSystemMXBean> list =
ManagementFactory.getPlatformMXBeans(OperatingSystemMXBean.class);
        for (OperatingSystemMXBean bean : list) {
            System.out.println("Operating System Name: " + bean.
getName());
            System.out.println("Operating System Architecture: " +
bean.getArch());
            System.out.println("Operating System Version: " + bean.
getVersion());
        }
```

When executed, you should get an output similar to the following. The exact output is dependent on the operating system and hardware used to execute the application:

Operating System Name: Windows 7

Operating System Architecture: amd64

Operating System Version: 6.1

Obtaining the platform's management interfaces

The ManagementFactory class' static getPlatformManagementInterfaces method returns a set of Class objects representing the platform-supported MXBeans. However, this method generated a ClassCastException on both the Windows 7 and the Ubuntu platforms when running the JDK 7.01 release. Future versions should correct this problem.

The **jconsole** application that is available as part of the JDK, provides an alternative technique for determining which MXBeans are available. The following is the console displaying the attributes for the operating system, specifically the ProcessCpuLoad attribute:

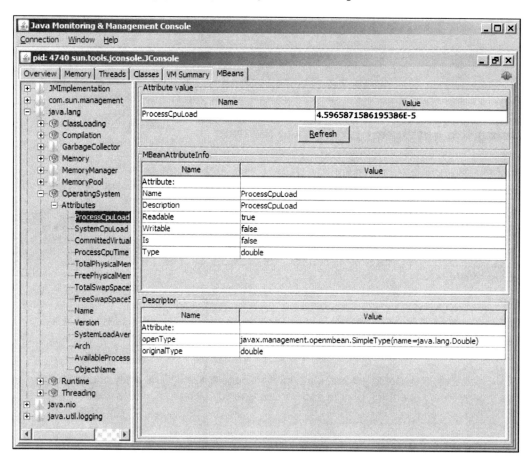

Redirecting input and output from operating system's processes

The `java.lang.ProcessBuilder` class has several new methods that are useful for redirecting the input and output of external processes executed from a Java application. The nested `ProcessBuilder.Redirect` class has been introduced to provide these additional redirect capabilities. To demonstrate this process, we are going to send command-line arguments from a text file to a DOS prompt and record the output in another text file.

Getting ready

In order to control input and output from external processes, you must:

1. Create a new `ProcessBuilder` object.
2. Direct the input and output of the process to the appropriate locations.
3. Execute the process via the `start` method.

How to do it...

1. First, create a new console application. Create three new file instances to represent the three files involved in our process execution: input, output, and errors as follows:

   ```
   File commands = new File("C:/Projects/ProcessCommands.txt");
   File output = new File("C:/Projects/ProcessLog.txt");
   File errors = new File("C:/Projects/ErrorLog.txt");
   ```

2. Create the file `ProcessCommands.txt` using the path specified for the file and enter the following text:

   cd C:

   dir

   mkdir "Test Directory"

   dir

3. Make sure that there is a carriage return after the last line.

4. Next, create a new instance of a `ProcessBuilder`, passing the string `"cmd"` to the constructor to specify the external process that we want to launch, which is the operating system command window. Call the `redirectInput`, `redirectOutput`, and `redirectError` methods with no arguments and print out the default locations:

   ```
   ProcessBuilder pb = new ProcessBuilder("cmd");
   System.out.println(pb.redirectInput());
   System.out.println(pb.redirectOutput());
   System.out.println(pb.redirectError());
   ```

5. Then we want to call the overloaded form of the previous methods, passing the respective file to each one. Once again, call the no argument form of each method executed using the `toString` method to verify that the IO sources have been changed:

```
pb.redirectInput(commands);
pb.redirectError(errors);
pb.redirectOutput(output);
System.out.println(pb.redirectInput());
System.out.println(pb.redirectOutput());
System.out.println(pb.redirectError());
```

6. Finally, call the `start` method to execute the process as follows:

```
pb.start();
```

7. Run the application. You should see output similar to the following:

PIPE

PIPE

PIPE

redirect to read from file "C:\Projects\ProcessCommands.txt"

redirect to write to file "C:\Projects\ProcessLog.txt"

redirect to write to file "C:\Projects\ErrorLog.txt"

8. Examine each of the text files. Your output file should have text similar to this:

Microsoft Windows [Version 6.7601]

Copyright (c) 2009 Microsoft Corporation. All rights reserved.

C:\Users\Jenn\Documents\NetBeansProjects\ProcessBuilderExample>cd C:

C:\>dir

Volume in drive C has no label.

Volume Serial Number is 927A-1F77

Directory of C:

03/05/2011 10:56   <DIR>   Dell

11/08/2011 16:04   <DIR>   Miscellaneous

11/08/2011 11:08   <DIR>   MOVE

10/31/2011 10:57   <DIR>   MUSIC

```
11/08/2011  19:44   <DIR>        Projects
10/27/2011  21:09   <DIR>        temp
10/28/2011  10:46   <DIR>        Users
11/08/2011  17:11   <DIR>        Windows
           0 File(s)          0 bytes
          34 Dir(s)  620,819,542,016 bytes free


C:\>mkdir "Test Directory"


C:\>dir
 Volume in drive C has no label.
 Volume Serial Number is 927A-1F77


 Directory of C:\


03/05/2011  10:56   <DIR>        Dell
11/08/2011  16:04   <DIR>        Miscellaneous
11/08/2011  11:08   <DIR>        MOVE
10/31/2011  10:57   <DIR>        MUSIC
11/08/2011  19:44   <DIR>        Projects
10/27/2011  21:09   <DIR>        temp
10/28/2011  10:46   <DIR>        Test Directory
10/28/2011  10:46   <DIR>        Users
11/08/2011  17:11   <DIR>        Windows
```

9. Execute the program again and examine the contents of your error log. Because your test directory had already been created with the first process execution, you should now see the following error message:

A subdirectory or file Test Directory already exists.

How it works...

We created three files to handle the input and output of our process. When we created the instance of the `ProcessBuilder` object, we specified the application to launch to be the command window. The information required to perform actions within the application was stored in our input file.

When we first called the `redirectInput`, `redirectOutput`, and `redirectError` methods, we did not pass any arguments. These methods all return a `ProcessBuilder.Redirect` object, which we printed. This object represents the default IO source, which in all three cases was `Redirect.PIPE`, one of the `ProcessBuilder.Redirect.Type` enumerations. A pipe takes the output of one source and sends it to another.

The second form of the methods that we used involved passing a `java.io.File` instance to the `redirectInput`, `redirectOutput`, and `redirectError` methods. These methods return a `ProcessBuilder` object as well, but they also have the function of setting the IO source. In our example, we then called the no argument form of each method once more to verify that the IO had been redirected.

The first time the program was executed, your error log should have been empty, assuming you used valid file paths for each `File` object, and you have write permissions on your computer. The second execution was intended to display how the capture of errors can be directed to a separate file. If the `redirectError` method is not invoked, the errors will inherit the standard location and will be displayed in your IDE's output window. See the *There's More...* section for information about inheriting standard IO locations.

It is important to note that the `start` method must be called after the redirect methods. Starting the process before redirecting input or output will cause the process to disregard your redirects and the application will execute using the standard IO locations.

There's more...

In this section, we will examine the use of the `ProcessBuilder.Redirect` class and the `inheritIO` method.

Using the ProcessBuilder.Redirect class

The `ProcessBuilder.Redirect` class provides another way to specify how the IO data is redirected. Using the previous example, add a new line prior to calling the `start` method:

```
pb.redirectError(Redirect.appendTo(errors));
```

This form of the `redirectError` method allows you to specify that the errors should be appended to the error log text file rather than overwritten. If you execute the application with this change, you will see two instances of the error when the process tries to create the `Test Directory` directory again:

A subdirectory or file Test Directory already exists.

A subdirectory or file Test Directory already exists.

This is an example of using the overloaded form of the `redirectError` method, passing a `ProcessBuilder.Redirect` object instead of a file. All three methods, `redirectError`, `redirectInput`, and `redirectOutput`, have this overloaded form.

The `ProcessBuilder.Redirect` class has two special values, namely, `Redirect.PIPE` and `Redirect.INHERIT`. `Redirect.PIPE` is the default way external process IO is handled, and simply means that the Java process will be connected to the external process via a pipe. The `Redirect.INHERIT` value means that the external process will have the same input or output location as the current Java process. You can also redirect the input or output of data using the `Redirect.to` and `Redirect.from` methods.

Using the inheritIO method to inherit the default IO locations

If you execute an external process from a Java application, you can set the location of the source and destination data to be the same as that of the current Java process. The `ProcessBuilder` class' `inheritIO` method is a convenient way to accomplish this. If you have a `ProcessBuilder` object pb, executing the following code:

```
pb.inheritIO()
```

Then it has the same effect as executing the following three statements together:

```
pb.redirectInput(Redirect.INHERIT)
pb.redirectOutput(Redirect.INHERIT)
pb.redirectError(Redirect.INHERIT)
```

In both cases, the input, output, and error data will be located in the same places as the current Java process' input, output, and error data.

Embedding a JNLP file in an HTML page

Java 7 provides a new option to speed up the deployment of an applet in a web page. Prior to 7, when applets were launched using the **Java Network Launch Protocol** (**JNLP**), the JNLP file must first be downloaded from the network before the applet can be launched. With the new release, the JNLP file can be embedded directly into the HTML code, reducing the amount of time the applet needs to launch. In this example, we are going to build a basic applet and launch it using a JNLP-embedded HTML page.

Getting ready

To speed up applet launch in Java 7, you must:

1. Create a new Applet.
2. Create and encode a JNLP file.
3. Add the reference to the JNLP file to an HTML page.

How to do it...

1. First create an applet to use in an HTML window. The following is a simple applet that can be used for the purposes of this recipe. This applet has two input fields, `subtotal` and `taxRate`, and a `calculate` button is used to calculate the grand total:

```java
public class JNLPAppletExample extends Applet {

    TextField subtotal = new TextField(10);
    TextField taxRate = new TextField(10);
    Button calculate = new Button("Calculate");
    TextArea grandTot = new TextArea("Total = $", 2, 15, TextArea.
SCROLLBARS_NONE);

    @Override
    public void init() {
        this.setLayout(new GridLayout(3,2));
        this.add(new Label("Subtotal = "));
        this.add(subtotal);
        this.add(new Label("Tax Rate = "));
        this.add(taxRate);
        this.add(calculate);
        grandTot.setEditable(false);
        this.add(grandTot);
        calculate.addActionListener(new CalcListener());
    }

    class CalcListener implements ActionListener {

        public void actionPerformed(ActionEvent event) {
            double subTot;
            double tax;
            double grandTot;

            subTot = validateSubTot(subtotal.getText());
```

```
                tax = validateSubTot(taxRate.getText());
                grandTot = calculateTotal(subTot, tax);
                JNLPAppletExample.this.grandTot.setText("Total = $" +
grandTot);
        }
    }


    double validateSubTot(String s) {
        double answer;
        Double d;
        try {
            d = new Double(s);
            answer = d.doubleValue();
    }
    catch (NumberFormatException e) {
            answer = Double.NaN;
    }
        return answer;
    }


    double calculateTotal(double subTot, double taxRate) {
        double grandTotal;
        taxRate = taxRate / 100;
        grandTotal = (subTot * taxRate) + subTot;
        return grandTotal;
    }
    }
}
```

2. Next, create a JNLP file called `JNLPExample.jnlp`. The following is a sample JNLP file to accompany our previous applet. Notice that within the resources tag a JAR file is referenced. This JAR file, containing your applet, must be in the same location as your JNLP file and the HTML file, which we will create in a moment:

```xml
<?xml version="1.0" encoding="UTF-8"?>
<jnlp href="JNLPExample.jnlp">
    <information>
        <title>Embedded JNLP File</title>
        <vendor>Sample Vendor</vendor>
    </information>
    <resources>
        <j2se version="7" />
        <jar href="JNLPAppletExample.jar"
            main="true" />
    </resources>
    <applet-desc
```

```
            name="Embedded JNLP Example"
            main-class="packt.JNLPAppletExample"
            width="500"
            height="500">
      </applet-desc>
        <update check="background"/>
  </jnlp>
```

3. After you have created the JNLP file, it must be encoded. There are several resources available online to convert the JNLP file to BASE64, but the one used for this example was `http://base64encode.org/`. Use the UTF-8 charset. Once you have your encoded data, you will use this in the creation of an HTML file. Create an HTML file shown as follows. Notice that the BASE64-encoded string highlighted has been shortened for purposes of brevity, but your string will be much longer:

```
<HTML>
<HEAD>
<TITLE>Embedded JNLP File Example</TITLE>
</HEAD>
<BODY>
<H3>Embedded JNLP Applet</H3>
<script src="http://www.java.com/js/deployJava.js"></script>
<script>
    var jnlpFile = "JNLPExample.jnlp";
    deployJava.createWebStartLaunchButtonEx(jnlpFile);
</script>
<script>
    var attributes = {} ;
    var parameters = {jnlp_href: 'JNLPExample.jnlp',
    jnlp_embedded: 'PD94bWw...'};
    deployJava.runApplet(attributes, parameters, '7');
</script>
</BODY>
</HTML>
```

4. Also, notice the first script tag. To avoid using a `codebase` attribute, we are utilizing another new feature of Java 7 by using a Development Toolkit script.

5. Load your application in a browser window. You may need to enable JavaScript depending upon your current browser settings. Your applet should load quickly and appear similar to the following screenshot:

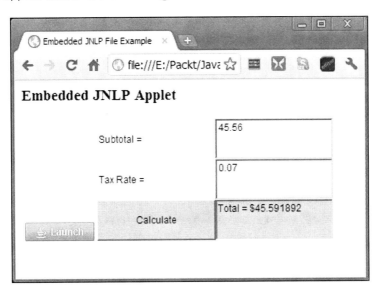

How it works...

Embedding the JNLP file in the HTML page allowed the applet to be loaded immediately, rather than having to be downloaded from the server first. The JNLP file had to have a relative path in the `href` attribute and the `codebase` should not be specified. By leaving the `codebase` attribute blank, it was determined by the URL of the applet's web page.

The `resources` tag specified the location of your JAR file and the version of Java to use. The path for your JAR file was assumed to be the default working directory as was the location of your JNLP file. Also included in your JNLP file was a description of your applet, surrounded by the `applet-desc` tag. The name of your applet and the name of your main class file was specified in this tag.

The HTML file contained information necessary to load the applet without having to download the applet information from a server. We first specified that we are going to load the application using a JavaScript call. Then, in our first script tag, we added a section to allow us to call the applet without a `codebase`. This is advantageous because the application can be loaded and tested in different environments without changing the `codebase` attribute. It is, instead, inherited from the web page that the application is running from.

There are two functions of the Deployment Toolkit that can be used to deploy Java applets in a web page without a `codebase` attribute: the `launchWebStartApplication` and `createWebStartLaunchButtonEx`. We chose to use the `createWebStartLaunchButtonEx` for this recipe, but the `launchWebStartApplication` option is also discussed as follows. In both instances, the client must have the Java SE 7 release to launch the applet, and if they do not, they will be directed to the Java website to download the most recent version.

The `createWebStartLaunchButtonEx` function created a launch button for the application. Within the `script` tag, the `jnlpFile` variable specified the name of the JNLP file and was relative to the applet's web page. This filename is then passed to the `deployJava.createWebStartLaunchButtonEx` function.

Alternatively, the `launchWebStartApplication` function could be embedded in an HTML link. The function is invoked within an `href` tag, shown as follows:

```
<script src="http://www.java.com/js/deployJava.js"></script>
<a href="javascript:deployJava.launchWebStartApplication('JNLPExample.
jnlp');">Launch</a>
</script>
```

The second `script` tag within your HTML file contained information about your JNLP file. The `jnlp_href` variable stored the name of the JNLP file. The JNLP file's encoded form was specified by the `jnlp_embedded` parameter. The BASE64 encoder encoded binary data for instances where the data needs to be stored and transferred across textual mediums, such as e-mail and XML files.

10
Concurrent Processing

In this chapter, we will cover the following:

- ▶ Using join/fork framework in Java 7
- ▶ Using the reusable synchronization barrier Phaser
- ▶ Using the ConcurrentLinkedDeque class safely with multiple threads
- ▶ Using the LinkedTransferQueue class
- ▶ Supporting multiple threads using the ThreadLocalRandom class

Introduction

Support for concurrent applications has been improved in Java 7. Several new classes have been introduced that support the parallel execution of tasks. The `ForkJoinPool` class is used for applications, which use the divide-and-conquer technique to solve a problem. Each subproblem is forked (split) as a separate thread and later joined, if necessary to provide a solution. The threads used by this class are normally subclasses of the `java.util. concurrent.ForkJoinTask` class and are lightweight threads. The use of this approach is illustrated in the *Using join/fork framework in Java* recipe.

In addition, the `java.util.concurrent.Phaser` class has been introduced to support the execution of a collection of threads in a series of phases. A group of threads are synchronized, so that they all execute and then wait for the completion of the others. Once they have all completed, they can be re-executed for a second phase or subsequent phase. The *Using the reusable synchronization barrier Phaser* recipe illustrates the use of this class in a game engine setting.

The *Using the java.util.concurrent.ConcurrentLinkedDeque class safely with multiple threads* and *Using the java.util.concurrent.LinkedTransferQueue class* recipes introduced two new classes designed to work safely with multiple threads. Examples of their use in support of the producer/consumer framework are illustrated.

The `java.util.concurrent.ThreadLocalRandom` class is new and provides better support for random number generation used between multiple threads. It is discussed in the *Supporting multiple threads using the ThreadLocalRandom class* recipe.

Two new constructors have been added to the `java.util.ConcurrentModificationException` class. They both accept a `Throwable` object used to specify the cause of the exception. One of the constructors also accepts a string that provides a detail message regarding the exception.

Java 7 has improved the use of class loaders by modifying the locking mechanism to avoid deadlocks. In multi-threaded custom class loaders prior to Java 7, certain custom class loaders were prone to deadlocks, when they used a cyclic delegation model.

Consider the following scenario. Thread1 tries to use a ClassLoader1 (locking ClassLoader1) to load class1. It then delegates the loading of class2 to ClassLoader2. At the same time, Thread2 uses ClassLoader2 (locking ClassLoader2) to load class3, and then delegates the loading of class4 to ClassLoader1. Since both class loaders are locked and both the threads need both loaders, a deadlock situation occurs.

The desired behavior of a concurrent class loader is to load different classes from the same instance of the class loader concurrently. This requires locking at a finer level of granularity, such as locking a class loader by the name of the class being loaded.

Synchronization should not be done at the class loader level. Instead, a lock should be made on a class level, where the class loader allows only a single instance of the class to be loaded at a time by that class loader.

Some class loaders are capable of loading classes concurrently. This type of class loader is called **parallel capable class loaders**. They are required to register themselves during their initialization process using the `registerAsParallelCapable` method.

If the custom class loader uses an acyclic hierarchal delegation model, no changes are needed in Java. In a hierarchal delegation model, delegation is first made to its parent class loader. Class loaders that do not use the hierarchical delegation model should be constructed as parallel capable class loaders in Java.

To avoid deadlock for custom class loaders:

> ▸ Use the `registerAsParallelCapable` method in the class initialization sequence. This indicates that all instances of the class loader are multi-thread safe.

- Make sure that the class loader code is multi-thread safe. This involves:

  - Using an internal locking scheme, such as the class name locking scheme used by `java.lang.ClassLoader`

  - Removing any synchronization on the class loader lock

  - Ensuring that critical sections are multi-thread safe

- It is recommended that the class loader overrides the `findClass(String)` method

- If the `defineClass` methods are overridden, then ensure that they are only called once per class name

More detail about this problem can be found at `http://openjdk.java.net/groups/core-libs/ClassLoaderProposal.html`.

Using join/fork framework in Java

The **join/fork** framework is an approach that supports breaking a problem into smaller and smaller pieces, solving them in parallel, and then combining the results. The new `java.util.concurrent.ForkJoinPool` class supports this approach. It is designed to work with multi-core systems, ideally with dozens or hundreds of processors. Currently, few desktop platforms support this type of concurrency, but future machines will. With fewer than four processors, there will be little performance improvement.

The `ForkJoinPool` class is derived from the `java.util.concurrent.AbstractExecutorService` making it an `ExecutorService`. It is designed to work with `ForkJoinTasks`, though it can be used with normal threads. The `ForkJoinPool` class differs from other executors, in that its threads attempt to find and execute subtasks created by other currently running tasks. This is called **work-stealing**.

The `ForkJoinPool` class can be used for problems where the computation on the subproblems is either modified or returns a value. When a value is returned, a `java.util.concurrent.RecursiveTask` derived class is used. Otherwise, the `java.util.concurrent.RecursiveAction` class is used. In this recipe we will illustrate the use of the `RecursiveTask` derived class.

Getting ready

To use the fork/join framework for a task that returns a result for each subtask:

1. Create a subclass of `RecursiveTask` that implements the computation needed.

2. Create an instance of the `ForkJoinPool` class.

3. Use the `ForkJoinPool` class' `invoke` method with the instance of the subclass of the `RecursiveTask` class.

How to do it...

This application is not intended to be implemented in the most efficient manner, but is used to illustrate the fork/join task. As a result, on systems with a small number of processors, there may be little or no performance improvement.

1. Create a new console application. We will use a static inner class that is derived from RecursiveTask to compute the sum of squares of the integers in the numbers array. First, declare the numbers array as follows:

```
private static int numbers[] = new int[100000];
```

2. Add the SumOfSquaresTask class as follows. It creates a subrange of array elements and either uses an iterative loop to compute their sum of squares or breaks the array into smaller pieces based on a threshold size:

```
private static class SumOfSquaresTask extends
RecursiveTask<Long> {

    private final int thresholdTHRESHOLD = 1000;
    private int from;
    private int to;

    public SumOfSquaresTask(int from, int to) {
        this.from = from;
        this.to = to;
    }

    @Override
    protected Long compute() {
        long sum = 0L;
        int mid = (to + from) >>> 1;

        if ((to - from) < thresholdTHRESHOLD) {
            for (int i = from; i < to; i++) {
                sum += numbers[i] * numbers[i];
            }

            return sum;
        }
        else {
            List<RecursiveTask<Long>> forks =
                new ArrayList<>();
            SumOfSquaresTask task1 =
                    new SumOfSquaresTask(from, mid);
            SumOfSquaresTask task2 =
                    new SumOfSquaresTask(mid, to);
```

```
                    forks.add(task1);
                    task1.fork();
                    forks.add(task2);
                    task2.fork();

                    for (RecursiveTask<Long> task : forks) {
                        sum += task.join();
        }

                    return sum;
        }
        }
        }
```

3. Add the following `main` method. For comparison purposes, the sum of squares is computed using a for loop and then using the `ForkJoinPool` class. The execution time is calculated and displayed as follows:

```
        public static void main(String[] args) {
            for (int i = 0; i < numbers.length; i++) {
                numbers[i] = i;
        }

            long startTime;
            long stopTime;

            long sum = 0L;
            startTime = System.currentTimeMillis();
            for (int i = 0; i < numbers.length; i++) {
                sum += numbers[i] * numbers[i];
        }
            System.out.println("Sum of squares: " + sum);
            stopTime = System.currentTimeMillis();
            System.out.println("Iterative solution time: " + (stopTime
    - startTime));

            ForkJoinPool forkJoinPool = new ForkJoinPool();
            startTime = System.currentTimeMillis();
            long result = forkJoinPool.invoke(new SumOfSquaresTask(0,
    numbers.length));
            System.out.println("forkJoinPool: " + forkJoinPool.
    toString());
            stopTime = System.currentTimeMillis();
            System.out.println("Sum of squares: " + result);
            System.out.println("Fork/join solution time: " + (stopTime
    - startTime));
        }
```

4. Execute the application. Your output should be similar to the following. However, you should observe different execution times depending on your hardware configuration:

    Sum of squares: 18103503627376

    Iterative solution time: 5

    Sum of squares: 18103503627376

    Fork/join solution time: 23

Notice that the iterative solution is faster than the one using the fork/join strategy. As mentioned earlier, this approach is not always more efficient, unless there are a large number of processors.

Running the application repeatedly will result in different results. A more aggressive testing approach would be to execute the solution repeatedly under possibly different processor loading conditions and then take the average of the result. The size of the threshold will also affect its performance.

How it works...

The `numbers` array was declared as a 100,000 element integer array. The `SumOfSquaresTask` class was derived from the `RecursiveTask` class using the generic type `Long`. A threshold of 1000 was set. Any subarray smaller than this threshold was solved using iteration. Otherwise the segment was divided in half and two new tasks were created, one for each half.

The `ArrayList` was used to hold the two subtasks. This was strictly not needed and actually slows down the computation. However, it would be useful if we decided to partition the array into more than two segments. It provides a convenient way of recombining the elements when the subtasks are joined.

The `fork` method was used to split up the subtasks. They entered the thread pool and will eventually be executed. The `join` method returned the results when the subtask completed. The sum of the subtasks was added together and then returned.

In the `main` method, the first code segment computed the sum of squares using a `for` loop. The start and stop time were based on the current time measured in milliseconds. The second segment created an instance of the `ForkJoinPool` class, and then used its `invoke` method with a new instance of the `SumOfSquaresTask` object. The arguments passed to the `SumOfSquaresTask` constructor, instructed it to start with the first element of the array and end with the last. Upon completion, the execution time was displayed.

There's more...

The `ForkJoinPool` class has several methods that report on the state of the pool, including:

- `getPoolSize`: This method returns the number of threads that are started but are not completed
- `getRunningThreadCount`: This method returns an estimate of the number of threads that are not blocked but are waiting to join other tasks
- `getActiveThreadCount`: This method returns an estimate of the number of threads executing tasks

The `ForkJoinPool` class' `toString` method returns several aspects of the pool. Add the following statement immediately after the `invoke` method is executed:

```
out.println("forkJoinPool: " + forkJoinPool);
```

When the program executes, you will get an output similar to the following:

forkJoinPool: java.util.concurrent.ForkJoinPool@18fb53f6[Running, parallelism = 4, size = 55, active = 0, running = 0, steals = 171, tasks = 0, submissions = 0]

See also

The *Using the reusable synchronization barrier Phaser* recipe offers a different approach for executing multiple threads.

Using the reusable synchronization barrier Phaser

The `java.util.concurrent.Phaser` class is concerned with the synchronization of threads that work together in cyclic type phases. The threads will execute and then wait for the completion of the other threads in the group. When all of the threads are completed, one phase is done. The `Phaser` can then be used to coordinate the execution of the same set of threads again.

The `java.util.concurrent.CountdownLatch` class provided a way of doing this, but required a fixed number of threads, and is executed once by default. The `java.util. concurrent.CyclicBarrier`, which was introduced in Java 5, also used a fixed number of threads, but is reusable. However, it is not possible to advance to the next phase. This is useful when a problem is characterized by a series of steps/phases that advance from one phase to the next based on some criteria.

With the introduction of the `Phaser` class in Java 7, we now have a concurrency abstraction that combines the features of `CountDownLatch` and `CyclicBarrier` and adds support of a dynamic number of threads. The term, phase, refers to the idea that the threads can be coordinated to execute in distinct phases, or steps. All of the threads will execute and then wait for the others to complete. Once they have completed, they will then begin anew and complete a second or subsequent phase of operation.

A barrier is a type of block that prevents a task from proceeding further until some condition is met. A common condition is when all of the related threads have completed.

The `Phaser` class provides several features, which makes it useful:

- Parties can be added and removed from the thread pool dynamically
- There is a unique phase number associated with each phase
- The `Phaser` can be terminated causing any waiting threads to return immediately
- Exceptions that occur do not affect the state of the barrier

The `register` method increments the number of parties that are participating. The termination of a phaser occurs when the internal count reaches zero or as determined by some other criteria set.

Getting ready

We will develop an application that mimics the operation of a game engine. The first version will create a series of tasks representing participants in a game. We will use the `Phaser` class to coordinate their interaction.

To use the `Phaser` class to synchronize the start of a set of tasks:

1. Create a collection of `Runnable` objects that will participate in the phaser.
2. Create an instance of the `Phaser` class.
3. For each participant:
   - Register the participant
   - Create a new thread using the participants' `Runnable` object
   - Use the `arriveAndAwaitAdvance` method to wait for the other tasks to be created
   - Execute the thread
4. Use the `Phaser` object's `arriveAndDeregister` to start the execution of the participants.

How to do it...

1. Create a new console application with a class called `GamePhaserExample`. We will create a simple hierarchy of inner classes that represent the participants in a game. Add the `Entity` class as the base abstract class, defined as follows. While not absolutely necessary, we'll be using inheritance to simplify the development of these types of applications:

```
private static abstract class Entity implements Runnable {

    public abstract void run();

}
```

2. Next, we will create two derived classes: `Player` and `Zombie`. These classes implement the `run` method and a `toString` method. The `run` method uses the `sleep` method to simulate the work performed. As expected, zombies are slower than humans:

```
private static class Player extends Entity {
    private final static AtomicInteger idSource =
        new AtomicInteger();
    private final int id = idSource.incrementAndGet();

    public void run() {
        System.out.println(toString() + " started");
        try {
            Thread.currentThread().sleep(
                    ThreadLocalRandom.current().nextInt(200,
                    600));
    }
    catch (InterruptedException ex) {
                ex.printStackTrace();
    }
            System.out.println(toString() + " stopped");
    }

        @Override
        public String toString() {
            return "Player #" + id;
    }
}

    private static class Zombie extends Entity {
        private final static AtomicInteger idSource = new
AtomicInteger();
```

```
                private final int id = idSource.incrementAndGet();

                public void run() {
                    System.out.println(toString() + " started");
                    try {
                        Thread.currentThread().sleep(
                                ThreadLocalRandom.current().nextInt(400,
                                800));
        }
        catch (InterruptedException ex) {
                        ex.printStackTrace();
        }
                    System.out.println(toString() + " stopped");
        }

                @Override
                public String toString() {
                    return "Zombie #" + id;
        }
        }
```

3. To make the example clearer, add the following `main` methoid to the `GamePhaserExample` class:

```
        public static void main(String[] args) {
            new GamePhaserExample().execute();
        }
```

4. Next, add the following `execute` method where we create a list of participants and then call the `gameEngine` method:

```
        private void execute() {
            List<Entity> entities = new ArrayList<>();
            entities = new ArrayList<>();
            entities.add(new Player());
            entities.add(new Zombie());
            entities.add(new Zombie());
            entities.add(new Zombie());
            gameEngine(entities);
        }
```

5. The `gameEngine` method follows. A `for each` loop creates a thread for each participant:

```
        private void gameEngine(List<Entity> entities) {
            final Phaser phaser = new Phaser(1);
            for (final Entity entity : entities) {
```

```
final String member = entity.toString();
System.out.println(member + " joined the game");
phaser.register();
new Thread() {
    @Override
    public void run() {
        System.out.println(member +
                " waiting for the remaining
                    participants");
        phaser.arriveAndAwaitAdvance();
          // wait for remaining entities
        System.out.println(member + " starting run");
        entity.run();
    }
}.start();
}

        phaser.arriveAndDeregister();
         //Deregister and continue
        System.out.println("Phaser continuing");
}
```

6. Execute the application. The output is non-deterministic, but should be similar to the following:

Player #1 joined the game

Zombie #1 joined the game

Zombie #2 joined the game

Player #1 waiting for the remaining participants

Zombie #1 waiting for the remaining participants

Zombie #3 joined the game

Phaser continuing

Zombie #3 waiting for the remaining participants

Zombie #2 waiting for the remaining participants

Zombie #1 starting run

Zombie #1 started

Zombie #3 starting run

Zombie #3 started

Zombie #2 starting run

Zombie #2 started

Player #1 starting run

Player #1 started

Player #1 stopped

Zombie #1 stopped

Zombie #3 stopped

Zombie #2 stopped

Notice that the `Phaser` object waits until all of the participants have joined the game.

How it works...

The `sleep` method was used to simulate the work involved by that entity. Notice the use of the `ThreadLocalRandom` class. Its `nextInt` method returned a random number between the values specified in its parameters. When using concurrent threads, this is the preferred way of generating random numbers as detailed in the *Supporting multiple threads using the ThreadLocalRandom class* recipe.

An instance of the `AtomicInteger` class was used to assign unique IDs to each object created. This is a safe way of generating numbers in threads. The `toString` method returns a simple string representation of the entity.

In the `execute` method, we created an `ArrayList` to hold the participants. Notice the use of the diamond operator in the creation of the `ArrayList`. This Java 7 language improvement is explained in the *Using the diamond operator for constructor type inference* recipe in *Chapter 1, Java Language Improvements*. One player and three zombies were added. The zombies always seem to outnumber the humans. The `gameEngine` method was then called.

A `Phaser` object was created with an argument of one and that represented the first participant. It is not an entity and simply served as a mechanism to help control the phaser.

In the for each loop, the number of parties in the phaser was incremented by one using the `register` method. A new thread was created using an anonymous inner class. In its `run` method, the entity was not started until all of the participants arrived. The `arriveAndAwaitAdvance` method resulted in the notification that a participant has arrived, and that the method should not return until all of the participants have arrived and the phase has finished.

At the start of each iteration of the `while` loop, the number of registered participants was one larger than the number of participants who have arrived. The `register` method incremented this internal count by one. The internal count was then two more than the number that had arrived. When the `arriveAndAwaitAdvance` method is executed, the number of participants who are waiting now will be one more than those who had registered.

After the loop terminated, there was still one more registered party than participants who had arrived. However, when the `arriveAndDeregister` method executed, the internal count of the number of participants who had arrived matched the number of participants, and the threads started. In addition, the number of registered parties was decreased by one. When all of the threads terminated, the application terminated.

There's more...

It is possible to register a group of parties using the `bulkRegister` method. This method takes a single integer argument specifying the number of parties to register.

Under some conditions, it may be desirable to force the termination of the phaser. The `forceTermination` method is used for this purpose.

During the execution of a phaser, there are several methods that will return information about the state of the phaser as detailed in the following table. If the phaser has terminated, then these methods will have no effect:

Method	Description
getRoot	Returns the root Phaser. Used with a tree of Phasers
getParent	Returns the parent of the Phaser
getPhase	Returns the current phase number
getArrivedParties	The number of parties that have arrived at this current phase
getRegisteredParties	The number of registered parties
getUnarrivedParties	The number of parties that have not yet arrived at this current phase

A tree of phasers can be constructed, where a phaser is created as a branch of the task. The `getRoot` method is useful in this situation. The phaser construct is discussed at `http://www.cs.rice.edu/~vs3/PDF/SPSS08-phasers.pdf`.

Using a phaser to repeat a series of tasks

We can also use the `Phaser` class to support a series of phases where tasks are executed, a possible intermediate action is performed, and then the series of tasks are repeated again.

To support this behavior, we will modify the `gameEngine` method. The modification will include:

- The addition of an `iterations` variable
- The overriding of the `Phaser` class' `onAdvance` method
- Using a `while` loop within each task's `run` method controlled by the `isTerminated` method

Add a variable called `iterations` and initialize it to 3. This is used to specify how many phases we will use. Also, override the `onAdvance` method shown as follows:

```
final int iterations = 3;

final Phaser phaser = new Phaser(1) {
        protected boolean onAdvance(int phase, int
registeredParties) {
                System.out.println("Phase number " + phase + "
completed\n")
                return phase >= iterations-1 || registeredParties ==
0;
        }
};
```

Each phase is uniquely numbered and starts at zero. A call to the `onAdvance` passes the current phase number and the current number of parties registered to the phaser. The default implementation of this method returns `true` when the number of registered parties becomes zero. This results in the phaser being terminated.

The implementation of this method resulted in the method returning `true` only if the phase number exceeded the `iterations` value, that is, minus 1, or there are no registered parties using the phaser.

Modify the `run` method as highlighted in the following code:

```
for (final Entity entity : entities) {
        final String member = entity.toString();
        System.out.println(member + " joined the game");
        phaser.register();
        new Thread() {

            @Override
            public void run() {
                do {
                    System.out.println(member + " starting run");
                    entity.run();
                    System.out.println(member +
                            " waiting for the remaining
participants during phase " +
                                phaser.getPhase());
                    phaser.arriveAndAwaitAdvance(); // wait for
remaining entities
}
while (!phaser.isTerminated());
}
}.start();
}
```

The entity is allowed to run first, and then it waits for the other participants to complete and arrive. As long as the phaser has not been terminated as determined by the `isTerminated` method, the next phase will be executed when everyone is ready.

The last step is to use the `arriveAndAwaitAdvance` method to advance the phaser to the next phase. Again, as long as the phaser has not terminated, the phaser will advance to the next phase when every participant has arrived. Use the following code sequence to accomplish this:

```
while (!phaser.isTerminated()) {
    phaser.arriveAndAwaitAdvance();
}

System.out.println("Phaser continuing");
```

Execute the program using only one player and one zombie. This will reduce the amount of output and should be similar to the following:

Player #1 joined the game

Zombie #1 joined the game

Player #1 starting run

Player #1 started

Zombie #1 starting run

Zombie #1 started

Player #1 stopped

Player #1 waiting for the remaining participants during phase 0

Zombie #1 stopped

Zombie #1 waiting for the remaining participants during phase 0

Phase number 0 completed

Player #1 starting run

Player #1 started

Zombie #1 starting run

Zombie #1 started

Player #1 stopped

Player #1 waiting for the remaining participants during phase 1

Zombie #1 stopped

Zombie #1 waiting for the remaining participants during phase 1

Phase number 1 completed

Zombie #1 starting run

Player #1 starting run

Zombie #1 started

Player #1 started

Player #1 stopped

Player #1 waiting for the remaining participants during phase 2

Zombie #1 stopped

Zombie #1 waiting for the remaining participants during phase 2

Phase number 2 completed

Phaser continuing

See also

See the *Using a random number generator isolated to the current thread* recipe for further information about generating random numbers for multiple threads.

Using the new ConcurrentLinkedDeque safely with multiple threads

The `java.util.concurrent.ConcurrentLinkedDeque` class, which is a member of the Java Collections Framework, offers the ability for multiple threads to safely access the same data collection concurrently. The class implements a double-ended queue, known as a **deque**, and allows for the insertion and removal of elements from both ends of the deque. It is also known as a head-tail linked list and, like other concurrent collections, does not allow the usage of null elements.

In this recipe we will demonstrate a basic implementation of the ConcurrentLinkedDeque class and illustrate the use of some of the most common methods.

Getting ready

To use a ConcurrentLinkedDeque in a producer/consumer framework:

1. Create an instance of a ConcurrentLinkedDeque.

2. Define the element to place into the deque.

3. Implement a producer thread to generate elements to be placed in the deque.

4. Implement a consumer thread to remove elements from the deque.

How to do it...

1. Create a new console application. Declare a private static instance of a ConcurrentLinkedDeque using a generic type of Item. The Item class is declared as an inner class. Include get methods and constructors, as shown in the following code, using two attributes, description and itemId:

   ```
   private static ConcurrentLinkedDeque<Item> deque = new
   ConcurrentLinkedDeque<>();

   static class Item {

       privateublic final String description;
       privateublic final int itemId;

       public Item() {
           "this(Default Item";, 0)
   }

       public Item(String description, int itemId) {
           this.description = description;
           this.itemId = itemId;
   }
   }
   ```

2. Then create a producer class to generate elements of the type Item. For this recipe's purposes, we are only going to generate seven items and then print out a statement to demonstrate that the item has been added to the deque. We use the ConcurrentLinkedDeque class' add method to add the elements. After each addition, the thread sleeps briefly:

   ```
   static class ItemProducer implements Runnable {
       @Override
       public void run() {
           String itemName = "";
   ```

```
                    int itemId = 0;
                    try {
                        for (int x = 1; x < 8; x++) {
                            itemName = "Item" + x;
                            itemId = x;
                            deque.add(new Item(itemName, itemId));
                            System.out.println("New Item Added:" +
itemName + " " + itemId);
                            Thread.currentThread().sleep(250);
                    }
                    }
                    catch (InterruptedException ex) {
                            ex.printStackTrace();
                    }
                    }
                    }
```

3. Next, create a consumer class. To ensure that the deque will have elements in it by the time the consumer thread tries to access it, we make the thread sleep for one second prior to retrieving elements. Then we use the `pollFirst` method to retrieve the first element in the deque. If the element is not null then we pass the element to a `generateOrder` method. In this method, we print out information about the item:

```
static class ItemConsumer implements Runnable {

        @Override
        public void run() {
            try {
                Thread.currentThread().sleep(1000);
        }
        catch (InterruptedException ex) {
                ex.printStackTrace();
        }

            Item item;
            while ((item = deque.pollFirst()) != null) {
        {
                    generateOrder(item);
        }
        }
        }


        private void generateOrder(Item item) {
            System.out.println("Part Order");
            System.out.println("Item description: " + item.
getDescriptiond());
            System.out.println("Item ID # " + item.getItemIdi());
```

```
              System.out.println();
              try {
                  Thread.currentThread().sleep(1000);
}
catch (InterruptedException ex) {
                  ex.printStackTrace();
}
}
}
```

4. Finally, in our `main` method, we start both threads:

```
      public static void main(String[] args) {
          new Thread(new ItemProducer());.start()
          new Thread(new ItemConsumer());.start()
}
```

5. When you execute the program, you should see output similar to the following:

New Item Added:Item1 1

New Item Added:Item2 2

New Item Added:Item3 3

New Item Added:Item4 4

Part Order

Item description: Item1

Item ID # 1

New Item Added:Item5 5

New Item Added:Item6 6

New Item Added:Item7 7

Part Order

Item description: Item2

Item ID # 2

Part Order

Item description: Item3

Item ID # 3

Part Order

Item description: Item4

Item ID # 4

Part Order

Item description: Item5

Item ID # 5

Part Order

Item description: Item6

Item ID # 6

Part Order

Item description: Item7

Item ID # 7

How it works...

When we started both threads, we gave the producer thread a head start to populate our deque with items. After a second, the consumer thread began retrieving elements. The use of the `ConcurrentLinkedDeque` class allowed both threads to safely access elements of the deque at the same time.

In our example, we made use of the methods `add` and `pollFirst` to add and remove elements of the deque. There are a number of methods available, many of which operate in essentially the same fashion. The *There's more...* section provides more detail about the various options for accessing the deque elements.

There's more...

We will cover several topics including:

- ▸ Problems with asynchronous concurrent threads
- ▸ Adding elements to the deque
- ▸ Retrieving elements from the deque
- ▸ Accessing a specific element of the deque

Problems with asynchronous concurrent threads

Due to the fact that multiple threads may be accessing the collection at any given moment, the `size` method is not always going to return an accurate result. This is also true when using the `iterator` or `descendingIterator` methods. Additionally, any bulk data operations, such as `addAll` or `removeAll`, are not always going to achieve the desired results. If one thread is accessing an item in the collection and another thread tries to pull all items, the bulk action is not guaranteed to function atomically.

There are two `toArray` methods available for retrieving all elements of the deque and storing them in an array. The first returns an array of objects representing all of the elements of the deque and can be cast to the appropriate data type. This is useful when the elements of the deque are of different data types. The following is an example of how to use the first form of the `toArray` method using our previous thread example:

```
Item[] items = (Item[]) deque.toArray();
```

The other `toArray` method requires an initialized array of a specific data type as an argument and returns an array of elements of that data type.

```
Item[] items = deque.toArray(new Item[0]);
```

Adding elements to the deque

The following table lists some of the methods available for adding elements to the deque. The methods that are grouped together in the following table perform essentially the same function. This variety of similar methods is the result of the `ConcurrentLinkedDeque` class implementing slightly different interfaces:

Method name	Adds an element to

`add(Element e)`
`offer(Element e)`
`offerLast(Element e)`
`addLast(Element e)`
	End of the deque

`addFirst(Element e)`
`offerFirst(Element e)`
`push(Element e)`
	Front of the deque

Retrieving elements from the deque

The following are some of the methods available for retrieving elements from the deque:

Method name	Error action	Function

`element()`
`getFirst()`
`getLast()`
	Throws exception if deque is empty	Retrieves but does not remove the first element of the deque

`peek()`
`peekFirst()`
`peekLast()`
	Returns null if deque is empty	

`pop()` `removeFirst()`	Throws exception if deque is empty	Retrieves and removes first element of deque
`poll()` `pollFirst()`	Returns null if deque is empty	
`removeLast()`	Throws exception if deque is empty	Retrieves and removes last element of deque
`pollLast()`	Returns null if deque is empty	

Accessing a specific element of the deque

The following are some of the methods available for accessing specific elements of a deque:

Method name	Function	Comments
`contains(Element e)`	Returns `true` if the deque contains at least one element that equals `Element e`	
`remove(Element e)` `removeFirstOccurrence(Element e)`	Removes the first occurrence of an element in the deque that equals `Element e`	If the element does not exist in the deque, the deque is unchanged. Throws exception if `e` is null
`removeLastOccurrence(Element e)`	Removes the last occurrence of an element in the deque that equals `Element e`	

Using the new LinkedTransferQueue class

The `java.util.concurrent.LinkedTransferQueue` class implements the `java.util.concurrent.TransferQueue` interface and is an unbounded queue that follows a **First In First Out** model for the queue elements. This class provides blocking methods and non-blocking methods for retrieving elements and is an appropriate choice for concurrent access by multiple threads. In this recipe we will create a simple implementation of a `LinkedTransferQueue` and explore some of the methods available in this class.

Getting ready

To use a `LinkedTransferQueue` in a producer/consumer framework:

1. Create an instance of a `LinkedTransferQueue`.
2. Define a type of element to place into the queue.
3. Implement a producer thread to generate elements to be placed in the queue.
4. Implement a consumer thread to remove elements from the queue.

How to do it...

1. Create a new console application. Declare a private static instance of a `LinkedTransferQueue` using a generic type of `Item`. Then create the inner class `Item` and include get methods and constructors, as shown in the following code, using two attributes, `description` and `itemId` as follows:

```
private static LinkedTransferQueue<Item>
        linkTransQ = new LinkedTransferQueue<>();

    static class Item {
  public final String description;
  public final int itemId;

  public Item() {
      this("Default Item", 0) ;
}

    public Item(String description, int itemId) {
        this.description = description;
        this.itemId = itemId;
}
}
}
```

2. Next, create a producer class to generate elements of the type `Item`. For this recipe's purposes, we are only going to generate seven items and then print out a statement to demonstrate that the item has been added to the queue. We will use the `LinkedTransferQueue` class' `offer` method to add the elements. After each addition, the thread sleeps briefly and we print out the name of the item added. We then use the `hasWaitingConsumer` method to determine if there are any consumer threads waiting for items to become available:

```
static class ItemProducer implements Runnable {
    @Override
    public void run() {
        try {
            for (int x = 1; x < 8; x++) {
                String itemName = "Item" + x;
                int itemId = x;
                linkTransQ.offer(new Item(itemName, itemId));
                System.out.println("New Item Added:" +
                    itemName + " " + itemId);
                Thread.currentThread().sleep(250);
                if (linkTransQ.hasWaitingConsumer()) {
                    System.out.println("Hurry up!");
    }
    }
    }
    catch (InterruptedException ex) {
                ex.printStackTrace();
    }
    }
    }
```

3. Next, create a consumer class. To demonstrate the function of the `hasWaitingConsumer` method, we make the thread sleep for one second prior to retrieving elements to ensure there is no waiting consumer at first. Then, within a `while` loop, we use the `take` method to remove the first item in the list. We chose the `take` method because it is a blocking method and will wait until the queue has an available element. Once the consumer thread is able to take an element, we pass the element to the `generateOrder` method, which prints out information about the item:

```
static class ItemConsumer implements Runnable {
    @Override
    public void run() {
        try {
            Thread.currentThread().sleep(1000);
    }
    catch (InterruptedException ex) {
                ex.printStackTrace();
```

```
        }
                    while (true) {
                        try {
                            generateOrder(linkTransQ.take());
        }
    catch (InterruptedException ex) {
                            ex.printStackTrace();
        }
        }
        }

            private void generateOrder(Item item) {
                System.out.println();
                System.out.println("Part Order");
                System.out.println("Item description: " +
                    item.description());
                System.out.println("Item ID # " + item.itemId());

        }
        }
```

4. Finally, in our `main` method, we start both threads:

```
        public static void main(String[] args) {
            new Thread(new ItemProducer()).start();
            new Thread(new ItemConsumer()).start();
        }
```

5. When you execute the program, you should see output similar to the following:

New Item Added:Item1 1

New Item Added:Item2 2

New Item Added:Item3 3

New Item Added:Item4 4

Part Order

Item description: Item1

Item ID # 1

Part Order

Item description: Item2

Item ID # 2

Part Order
Item description: Item3
Item ID # 3

Part Order
Item description: Item4
Item ID # 4

Hurry up!
New Item Added:Item5 5

Part Order
Item description: Item5
Item ID # 5

Hurry up!

Part Order
Item description: Item6
Item ID # 6

New Item Added:Item6 6
Hurry up!

Part Order
Item description: Item7
Item ID # 7

New Item Added:Item7 7
Hurry up!

How it works...

When we started both threads, we gave the producer thread a **head start** to populate our queue with items by sleeping for one second in the `ItemConsumer` class. Notice that the `hasWaitingConsumer` method returned `false` initially because the `take` method had not yet been executed by the consumer thread. After a second, the consumer thread began retrieving elements. With each retrieval, the `generateOrder` method printed out information about the element retrieved. After all elements in the queue were retrieved, notice a final *Hurry up!* statement, indicating there is still a consumer waiting. In this example, because the consumer is using a blocking method within a `while` loop, the thread will never terminate. In a real life situation, the thread should be terminated in a more graceful manner, such as sending a terminate message to the consumer thread.

In our example, we used the methods `offer` and `take` to add and remove elements of the queue. There are other methods available and these are discussed in the *There's more...* section.

There's more...

Here we will discuss the following:

- Problems with asynchronous concurrent threads
- Adding elements to the queue
- Retrieving elements from the deque

Problems with asynchronous concurrent threads

Due to the fact that multiple threads may be accessing the collection at any given moment, the `size` method is not always going to return an accurate result. Additionally, any bulk data operations, such as `addAll` or `removeAll`, are not always going to achieve the desired results. If one thread is accessing an item in the collection and another thread tries to pull all items, the bulk action is not guaranteed to function atomically.

Adding elements to the queue

The following are some of the methods available for adding elements to the queue:

Method name	Adds element to the	Comments
add(Element e)	End of the queue	Queue is unbounded, so the method will never return `false` or throw an exception
offer(Element e)		Queue is unbounded, so the method will never return `false`
put(Element e)		Queue is unbounded, so the method will never block

Method name	Adds element to the	Comments
offer(Element e, Long t, TimeUnit u)	End of the queue Wait for t time units of type u before giving up	Queue is unbounded, so the method will always return true

Retrieving elements from the deque

The following are some of the methods available for retrieving elements from the deque:

Method name	Function	Comments
peek()	Retrieves, but does not remove the first element of the queue	Returns null if the queue is empty
poll()	Removes the first element of the queue	Returns null if the queue is empty
poll(Long t, TimeUnit u)	Removes element from front of the queue, waiting time t (in units u) before giving up	Returns null if the time limit is up before an element is available
remove(Object e)	Removes element from the queue that equals Object e	Returns true if the element is found and removed
take()	Removes the first element of the queue	Throws an exception if interrupted while blocking
transfer(Element e)	Transfers an element to the consumer thread, waiting if necessary	Will insert an element at the end of the queue and wait for the consumer thread to retrieve it
tryTransfer(Element e)	Transfers an element immediately to the consumer	Returns false if the consumer is not available
tryTransfer(Element e, Time t, TimeUnit u)	Transfers an element to the consumer immediately, or within time specified by t (in units u)	Returns false if the consumer is not available when the time limit has elapsed

Supporting multiple threads using the ThreadLocalRandom class

The `java.util.concurrent` package has a new class, `ThreadLocalRandom`, which supports functionality similar to the `Random` class. However, the use of this new class, with multiple threads, will result in less contention and better performance as compared to their use with the `Random` class. When multiple threads need to use random numbers, the `ThreadLocalRandom` class should be used. The random number generator is local to the current thread. This recipe examines how to use this class.

Getting ready

The recommended way of using this class is to:

1. Use the static `current` method to return an instance of the `ThreadLocalRandom` class.
2. Use the methods of the class against this object.

How to do it...

1. Create a new console application. Add the following code to the `main` method:

```
System.out.println("Five random integers");
for(int i = 0; i<5; i++) {
    System.out.println(ThreadLocalRandom.current().
      nextInt());
}

System.out.println();
System.out.println("Random double number between 0.0 and
35.0");
System.out.println(ThreadLocalRandom.current().nextDouble(35.0));

System.out.println();
System.out.println("Five random Long numbers between
  1234567 and 7654321");
for(int i = 0; i<5; i++) {
    System.out.println(
            ThreadLocalRandom.current().nextLong(1234567L,
              7654321L));
}
```

2. Execute the program. Your output should appear similar to the following:

Five random integers

0

4232237

178803790

758674372

1565954732

Random double number between 0.0 and 35.0

3.196571144914888

Five random Long numbers between 1234567 and 7654321

7525440

2545475

1320305

1240628

1728476

How it works...

The `nextInt` method was executed five times with its return value being displayed. Notice that the method returns 0 initially. The `ThreadLocalRandom` class extends the `Random` class. However, the `setSeed` method is not supported. If you try to use it, it will throw an `UnsupportedOperationException`.

The `nextDouble` method was then executed. This version of the overloaded method returned a number between 0.0 and 35.0. The `nextLong` method was executed five times using two parameters, which specified its starting (inclusive) and ending (exclusive) range values.

There's more...

The methods of this class return uniformly distributed numbers. The following table summarizes its methods:

 When a range is specified, the start value is inclusive and the end value is exclusive.

Method	Parameters	Returns
current	None	The thread's current instance
next	Integer value representing the number of bits for the return value	An integer in the range specified by the number of bits
nextDouble	double	A double number between 0.0 and its argument
	double, double	A double number between its arguments
nextInt	int, int	An integer number between its arguments
nextLong	long	A long number between 0 and its argument
	long, long	A long number between its arguments
setSeed	long	Throws UnsupportedOperationException

See also

Examples of its use are found in the *Using the reusable synchronization barrier Phaser* recipe.

11
Odds and Ends

In this chapter, we will cover the following:

- ▶ Handling weeks in Java 7
- ▶ Using Currency in Java 7
- ▶ Using the NumericShaper.Range enumeration to support the display of digits
- ▶ JavaBean improvements in Java 7
- ▶ Handling locales and the Locale.Builder class in Java 7
- ▶ Handling null references
- ▶ Using the new BitSet methods in Java 7

Introduction

This chapter will address many new additions to Java 7 that do not fit into the previous chapters. Many of these enhancements have potentially widespread application, such as the `java.lang.Objects` class and `java.util.Locale` class improvements as discussed in the *Handling locales and the Locale.Builder class in Java 7* recipe. Others are more specialized, such as the improvements made to the `java.util.BitSet` class, which is covered in the *Using the new BitSet methods in Java 7* recipe.

There have been a number of improvements in the handling of weeks and currency. The calculation of the current week and the number of weeks per year is impacted by the locale. In addition, it is now possible to determine the currencies available on a platform. These issues are illustrated in the *Handling weeks in Java 7* and *Using Currency on Java 7* recipes.

A new enumeration has been added that eases the display of digits in different languages. The use of the `java.awt.font.NumericShaper` class for this endeavor is discussed in the *Using the NumericShaper.Range enumeration to support the display of digits* recipe. Improvements in the support of JavaBeans are discussed in the *JavaBean improvements in Java 7* recipe.

There are also a number of enhancements, which do not warrant separate recipes. The rest of this introduction is devoted to these topics.

Unicode 6.0

Unicode 6.0 is the newest revision of the Unicode standard. Java 7 supports this release with the addition of thousands of more characters and numerous new methods. In addition, regular expression pattern matching supports Unicode 6.0 using either **\u** or **\x** escape sequences.

Numerous new character blocks were added to the `Character.UnicodeBlock` class. The `Character.UnicodeScript` enumeration was added in Java 7 to represent the character scripts defined in the **Unicode Standard Annex #24: Script Names**.

 More information regarding Unicode Standard Annex #24: Script Names can be found at http://download.oracle.com/javase/7/docs/api/index.html.

Several methods have been added to the `Character` class in support of the Unicode operations. The following illustrates their use with the string 朝鲜圆, which is the display name for North Korean Won in Chinese based on the locale, and the simplified script as used in mainland China. Add the following code sequence to a new application:

```
int codePoint = Character.codePointAt("朝鲜圆", 0);
System.out.println("isBmpCodePoint: " + Character.
isBmpCodePoint(codePoint));
System.out.println("isSurrogate: " +
Character.isSurrogate('朝'));
System.out.println("highSurrogate: " + (int)Character.
highSurrogate(codePoint));
System.out.println("lowSurrogate: " + (int)Character.
lowSurrogate(codePoint));
System.out.println("isAlphabetic: " + Character.
isAlphabetic(codePoint));
System.out.println("isIdeographic: " + Character.
isIdeographic(codePoint));
System.out.println("getName: " + Character.
getName(codePoint));
```

When executed, your output should appear as follows:

isBmpCodePoint: true

isSurrogate: false

highSurrogate: 55257

lowSurrogate: 57117

isAlphabetic: true

isIdeographic: true

getName: CJK UNIFIED IDEOGRAPHS 671D

Since the character is not a Unicode surrogate code, the `highSurrogate` and `lowSurrogate` method results are not useful.

 More information regarding Unicode 6.0 can be found at `http://www.unicode.org/versions/Unicode6.0.0/`.

Primitive types and the compare method

Java 7 introduced new static methods for comparing primitive data types `Boolean`, `byte`, `long`, `short`, and `int`. Each wrapper class now has a `compare` method, which takes two instances of the data type as arguments and returns an integer representing the result of the comparison. For example, you would have previously needed to use the `compareTo` method to compare two Boolean variables, x and y as follows:

```
Boolean.valueOf(x).compareTo(Boolean.valueOf(y))
```

You can now use the `compare` method as follows:

```
Boolean.compare(x,y);
```

While this is new to Java for the Boolean data type, the `compare` method was previously available for `doubles` and `floats`. Additionally in 7, the `parse`, `valueof`, and `decode` methods, used for converting strings to numeric values, will accept a leading plus (+) sign with data types `Byte`, `Short`, `Integer`, `Long`, and `BigInteger`, in addition to `Float`, `Double`, and `BigDecimal`, which previously accepted the sign.

Global logger

The `java.util.logging.Logger` class has a new method, `getGlobal`, used for retrieving the global logger object named GLOBAL_LOGGER_NAME. The static field global of the `Logger` class is prone to deadlocks when the `Logger` class is used in conjunction with the `LogManager` class, as both classes will wait on each other to complete initialization. The `getGlobal` method is the preferred way to access the `global logger` object, in order to prevent such deadlock.

JavaDocs improvements

There have been significant improvements in JavaDocs as of Java 7. From a structural standpoint, the generation of the HTML pages is now accomplished by using the `HTMLTree` classes to create a document tree, which results in more accurate HTML generation and fewer invalid pages.

There have also been external changes to the JavaDocs, some of which were in order to comply with the new **Section 508** accessibility guidelines. These are developed to ensure screen readers, used for translating web-based text into audible output, are able to accurately translate an HTML page. Primarily, this has resulted in the addition of more captions and headings on the tables. JavaDocs now also use a CSS stylesheet to simplify changes to the appearance of the pages.

JVM performance enhancements

The performance of the Java HotSpotTM virtual machine has been improved. Most of these improvements are not under the control of the developer and are specialized in nature. The interested reader will find more details about these enhancements at `http://docs.oracle.com/javase/7/docs/technotes/guides/vm/performance-enhancements-7.html`.

Handling weeks in Java 7

Some applications are concerned with the number of weeks in a year and the current week of the year. It is common knowledge that there are 52 weeks in a year, but 52 weeks multiplied by 7 days per week equals 364 days per year, not the actual 365 days. A **week number** is used to refer to the week of the year. But how is that calculated? Java 7 has introduced several methods to support determining the week of the year. In this recipe we will examine these methods, and see how week-related values are calculated. The **ISO 8601** standard provides methods for representing dates and time. The `java.util.GregorianCalendar` class supports this standard, except as described in the following section.

Getting ready

To use these week-based methods we need to:

1. Create an instance of the `Calendar` class.
2. Use its methods as appropriate.

How to do it...

Some implementations of the abstract `java.util.Calendar` class do not support week calculations. To determine if the `Calendar` implementation supports week calculations, we need to execute the `isWeekDateSupported` method. It returns `true` if the support is provided. To return the number of weeks for the current calendar year, use the `getWeeksInWeekYear` method. To determine the week for the current date, use the `get` method with the `WEEK_OF_YEAR` as its argument.

1. Create a new console application. Add the following code to the `main` method:

```
Calendar calendar = Calendar.getInstance();

if(calendar.isWeekDateSupported()) {
        System.out.println("Number of weeks in this year: " +
calendar.getWeeksInWeekYear());
        System.out.println("Current week number: " + calendar.
get(Calendar.WEEK_OF_YEAR));
        }
```

2. Execute the application. Your output should appear as follows, but the values will be dependent upon the date the application was executed:

Number of weeks in this year: 53

Current week number: 48

How it works...

An instance of the `Calendar` class was created. This is normally an instance of the `GregorianCalendar` class. An `if` statement was controlled by the `isWeekDateSupported` method. It returned `true`, which resulted in the execution of the `getWeeksInWeekYear` and `get` methods. The `get` method was passed in the field `WEEK_OF_YEAR`, which returned the current week number.

There's more...

The date can be set using the `setWeekDate` method. This method has three arguments specifying the year, week, and day. It provides a convenient technique for setting the date based on weeks. The following illustrates this process by setting the year to 2012, the week to the 16th week of the year, and the day to the third day of the week:

```
calendar.setWeekDate(2012, 16, 3);
System.out.println(DateFormat.getDateTimeInstance(
    DateFormat.LONG, DateFormat.LONG).format(calendar.
getTime()));
```

When this code is executed, we get the following output:

April 17, 2012 12:00:08 PM CDT

The way that the first and last week of the year is calculated is locale-dependent. The `GregorianCalendar` class' `WEEK_OF_YEAR` field ranges from 1 to 53, where 53 represents a leap week. The first week of the year is:

- The earliest seven day period
- Starting on the first day of the week (`getFirstDayOfWeek`)
- That contains at least the minimal days in a week (`getMinimalDaysInFirstWeek`)

The `getFirstDayOfWeek` and `getMinimalDaysInFirstWeek` methods are locale-dependent. For example, the `getFirstDayOfWeek` method returns an integer representing the first day of the week for a locale. In the U.S., it is SUNDAY, but in France it is MONDAY.

The first and last week of a week year may have different calendar years. Consider the following code sequence. The calendar is set to the first day of the first week of 2022:

```
calendar.setWeekDate(2022, 1, 1);
System.out.println(DateFormat.getDateTimeInstance(
    DateFormat.LONG, DateFormat.LONG).format(calendar.
getTime()));
```

When executed, we get the following output:

December 26, 2021 12:15:39 PM CST

This shows that the week actually starts in the previous year.

In addition, the `TimeZone` and `SimpleTimeZone` classes have an `observesDaylightTime` method that returns `true` if the time zone observes daylight saving time. The following code sequence creates an instance of a `SimpleTimeZone` class and then determines if daylight saving time is supported. The time zone used is for **Central Standard Time (CST)**:

```
SimpleTimeZone simpleTimeZone = new SimpleTimeZone(
        -21600000,
            "CST",
            Calendar.MARCH, 1, -Calendar.SUNDAY,
            7200000,
            Calendar.NOVEMBER, -1, Calendar.SUNDAY,
            7200000,
            3600000);
System.out.println(simpleTimeZone.getDisplayName() + " - " +
        simpleTimeZone.observesDaylightTime());
```

When this sequence is executed, you should get the following output:

Central Standard Time – true

Using the Currency class in Java 7

The `java.util.Currency` class introduced four new methods for retrieving information about available currencies and their properties. This recipe illustrates the use of the following methods:

- `getAvailableCurrencies`: This method returns a set of currencies available
- `getNumericCode`: This method returns the ISO 4217 numeric code for the currency
- `getDisplayName`: This overloaded method returns a string representing the display name of the currency. One method is passed a `Locale` object. The string returned is specific for that locale.

Getting ready

The `getAvailableCurrencies` method is static, so it should be executed against the class name. The other methods execute against an instance of the `Currency` class.

How to do it...

1. Create a new console application. Add the following code to the `main` method:

```
Set<Currency> currencies =
    Currency.getAvailableCurrencies();
for (Currency currency : currencies) {
```

```
System.out.printf("%s - %s - %s\n",
    currency.getDisplayName(),
        currency.getDisplayName(Locale.GERMAN),
        currency.getNumericCode());
}
```

2. When the application is executed, you should get output similar to the following. However, the first part of each may differ depending on the current locale.

North Korean Won - Nordkoreanischer Won - 408

Euro - Euro - 978

Dutch Guilder - Holländischer Gulden - 528

Falkland Islands Pound - Falkland-Pfund - 238

Danish Krone - Dänische Krone - 208

Belize Dollar - Belize-Dollar – 84

How it works...

The code sequence begins with the generation of a `Set` of the `Currency` objects representing the current system's configuration. The overloaded `getDisplayName` methods were executed against each element of the set. The `Locale.GERMAN` argument was used to illustrate the use of this method. The last value displayed was the numeric code for the currency.

Using the NumericShaper.Range enumeration to support the display of digits

In this recipe we will demonstrate the use of `java.awt.font.NumericShaper.Range` enumeration to support the display of digits using the `java.awt.font.NumericShaper` class. Sometimes it is desirable to display numeric digits using a different language than is currently being used. For example, in an English language tutorial regarding the Mongolian language, we may want to explain the numeric system in English, but display numbers using the Mongolian digits. The `NumericShaper` class provides this support. The new `NumericShaper.Range` enumeration has simplified this support.

Getting ready

To display digits using the `NumericShaper.Range` enumeration:

1. Create a `HashMap` to hold display attribute information.

2. Create a `Font` object to define the font to use.

3. Specify the range of Unicode characters to display the text.

4. Create a `FontRenderContext` object to hold information about how to measure the text to be displayed.

5. Create an instance of `TextLayout` and use it in the `paintComponent` method to render the text.

How to do it...

We will illustrate the use of the `NumericShaper.Range` enumeration to display Mongolian digits. This is a simplified version of the example found at `http://download.oracle.com/javase/tutorial/i18n/text/shapedDigits.html`.

1. Create an application that extends the `JFrame` class, which is shown as follows. We will illustrate the use of the `NumericShaper` class in the `NumericShaperPanel` class:

```
public class NumericShaperExample extends JFrame {

    public NumericShaperExample() {
        Container container = this.getContentPane();
        container.add("Center", new NumericShaperPanel());

        this.setDefaultCloseOperation(JFrame.EXIT_ON_CLOSE);
        this.setTitle("NumericShaper Example");
        this.setSize(250, 120);

    }

    public static void main(String[] args) {
        new NumericShaperExample();.setVisible(true)
    }
}
```

2. Next, add the `NumericShaperPanel` class to the project as follows:

```
public class NumericShaperPanel extends JPanel {

    private TextLayout layout;

    public NumericShaperPanel() {
        String text = "0 1 2 3 4 5 6 7 8 9";
        HashMap map = new HashMap();
        Font font = new Font("Mongolian Baiti", Font.PLAIN, 32);
        map.put(TextAttribute.FONT, font);
        map.put(TextAttribute.NUMERIC_SHAPING,
```

```
                    NumericShaper.getShaper(NumericShaper.Range.
                        MONGOLIAN));
            FontRenderContext fontRenderContext =
                    new FontRenderContext(null, false, false);
            layout = new TextLayout(text, map, fontRenderContext);
    }

        public void paintComponent(Graphics g) {
            Graphics2D g2d = (Graphics2D) g;
            layout.draw(g2d, 10, 50);
    }
}
```

3. Execute the application. Your output should appear as follows:

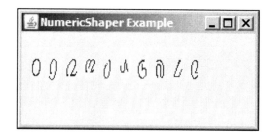

How it works...

In the `main` method, an instance of the `NumericShaperExample` class was created. Within its constructor, an instance of the `NumericShaperPanel` class was created and added to the center of the window. The title, default close operation, and size of the window were set. Next, the window was made visible.

In the constructor of the `NumericShaperPanel` class, a text string was created along with a `HashMap` to hold the essential features of the display. This map was used as an argument to the `TextLayout` constructor along with the string to be displayed and the map. The text was displayed in Mongolian using the Mongolian Baiti font and with the MONGOLIAN range. We used this font to demonstrate the new methods of the `NumericShaper` class.

The NumericShaper class has added new methods to make it easier to display numeric values in a different language. The getShaper method is overloaded with one version accepting a NumericShaper.Range enumeration value. The value specifies the language to use. The NumericShaper.Range enumeration has been added to represent a range of Unicode characters for digits in a given language.

In the paintComponent method, the Graphics2D object was used as an argument of the draw method to render the string to the window.

There's more...

The getContextualShaper method is used to control how digits are displayed when used with a different script. This means if Japanese script is used before digits, then Japanese digits are displayed. The method takes a set of NumericShaper.Range enumeration values.

The shape method also uses a range to specify the script to use for an array of char given a start and an end index in the array. The getRangeSet method returns a set of NumericShaper.Range used by the NumericShaper instance.

JavaBean enhancements in Java 7

JavaBean is a way of building reusable components for Java applications. They are Java classes that follow certain naming conventions. There have been several JavaBean enhancements added in Java 7. Here we will focus on the java.beans.Expression class, which is useful in executing methods. The execute method has been added to facilitate this capability.

Getting ready

To use the Expression class to execute a method:

1. Create an array of arguments for the method, if needed.
2. Create an instance of the Expression class specifying the object that the method is to be executed against, the method name, and any arguments needed.
3. Invoke the execute method against the expression.
4. Use the getValue method to obtain the results of the method execution, if necessary.

How to do it...

1. Create a new console application. Create two classes: `JavaBeanExample`, which contains the `main` method and a `Person` class. The `Person` class contains a single field for a name along with constructors, a getter method, and a setter method:

```
public class Person {
    private String name;

    public Person() {
        this("Jane", 23);
    }

    public Person(String name, int age) {
        this.name = name;
    }

    public String getName() {
        return name;
    }

    public void setName(String name) {
        this.name = name;
    }
}
```

2. In the `main` method of the `JavaBeanExample` class, we will create an instance of the `Person` class, and use the `Expression` class to execute its `getName` and `setName` methods:

```
public static void main(String[] args) throws Exception {
    Person person = new Person();
    String arguments[] = {"Peter"};
    Expression expression = new Expression(null, person,
        "setName", arguments);

    System.out.println("Name: " + person.getName());
    expression.execute();
    System.out.println("Name: " + person.getName());

    System.out.println();
    expression = new Expression(null, person,
        "getName", null);
    System.out.println("Name: " + person.getName());
    expression.execute();
    System.out.println("getValue: " +
        expression.getValue());
}
```

3. Execute the application. Its output should appear as follows:

Name: Jane

Name: Peter

Name: Peter

getValue: Peter

How it works...

The `Person` class used a single field, name. The `getName` and `setName` methods were used from the `main` method, where a `Person` instance was created. The `Expression` class' constructor has four arguments. The first argument was not used in this example, but can be used to define a return value for the method executed. The second argument was the object that the method would be executed against. The third argument is a string containing the name of the method, and the last argument was an array containing the parameters used by the method.

In the first sequence, the `setName` method was executed using an argument of `Peter`. The output of the application shows that the name was initially `Jane`, but was changed to `Peter` after the `execute` method was executed.

In the second sequence, the `getName` method was executed. The `getValue` method returns the results of the execution of the method. The output shows that the `getName` method returned `Peter`.

There's more...

There have been other enhancements to the classes of the `java.bean` package. For example, the `toString` method has been overridden in the `FeatureDescriptor` and `PropertyChangeEvent` classes to provide a more meaningful description.

The `Introspector` class provides a way of learning about the properties, methods, and events of a Java Bean without using the Reflection API, which can be tedious. The class has added a `getBeanInfo` method, which uses the `Inspector` class' control flags to affect the `BeanInfo` object returned.

The `Transient` annotation has been added to control what is included. A `true` value for the attribute means that the annotated feature should be ignored.

A new constructor has been added to the `XMLDecoder` class that accepts an `InputSource` object. Also, the `createHandler` method has been added, which returns a `DefaultHandler` object. This handler is used to parse XML archives created by the `XMLEncoder` class.

A new constructor has been added to the XMLEncoder class. This permits writing out JavaBeans to an OutputStream using a specific charset with a specific indention.

Handling locales and the Locale.Builder class in Java 7

The java.util.Locale.Builder class has been added to Java 7 and provides an easy way of creating a locale. The Locale.Category enumeration is also new and makes using different locales for display and formatting purposes easy. We will first look at the use of the Locale.Builder class and then examine other locale improvements and the use of the Locale.Category enumeration in the *There's more...* section.

Getting ready

To build and use a new Locale object:

1. Create an instance of the Builder class.

2. Use the relevant methods of the class to set up the attributes needed.

3. Use the Locale object as needed.

How to do it...

1. Create a new console application. In the main method, add the following code. We will create a new locale based on Eastern Armenian using Latin script as found in Italy. The locale is demonstrated by displaying the date for the third day of the 16th week in 2012 using the setWeekDate method. This method is discussed in more detail in the *Handling Weeks in Java 7* recipe:

```
Calendar calendar = Calendar.getInstance();
calendar.setWeekDate(2012, 16, 3);

Builder builder = new Builder();
builder.setLanguage("hy");
builder.setScript("Latn");
builder.setRegion("IT");
builder.setVariant("arevela");

Locale locale = builder.build();
Locale.setDefault(locale);

System.out.println(DateFormat.getDateTimeInstance(
        DateFormat.LONG,
            DateFormat.LONG).format(calendar.getTime()));
System.out.println("" + locale.getDisplayLanguage());
```

2. A second example builds a locale based on Chinese using the Simplified script, which is used in mainland China:

```
builder.setLanguage("zh");
builder.setScript("Hans");
builder.setRegion("CN");

locale = builder.build();
Locale.setDefault(locale);

System.out.println(DateFormat.getDateTimeInstance(
        DateFormat.LONG,
            DateFormat.LONG).format(calendar.getTime())));
System.out.println("" + locale.getDisplayLanguage());
```

3. When executed, the output should appear as follows:

April 17, 2012 7:25:42 PM CDT

Armenian

2012年4月17日 下午07时**25**分42秒

中文

How it works...

The `Builder` object was created. Using this object, we applied methods to set the language, script, and region for the locale. The `build` method was then executed and a `Locale` object was returned. We used this locale to display the date and the display language for the locale. This was performed twice. First, for the Armenian language, and then for Chinese.

There's more...

It is important to be able to label a piece of information to indicate the language being used. A tag is used for this purpose. A standard set of tags is defined by the **IETF BCP 47** standard. Java 7 conforms to this standard and has added several methods to handle tags.

The standard supports the concept of extensions to a tag. These extensions can be used to provide more information about the locale. There are two types:

▸ Unicode locale extension
▸ Private use extension

The Unicode locale extensions are defined by the **Unicode Common Locale Data Repository (CLDR)** (`http://cldr.unicode.org/`). These extensions are concerned with non-language information, such as currency and dates. The CLDR maintains a standard repository of locale information. Private use extensions are used to specify platform-specific information, such as that related to operating systems or programming languages.

 More information regarding the IETF BCP 47 standard can be found at `http://tools.ietf.org/rfc/bcp/bcp47.txt`.

An extension consists of a key/value pair. The key is a single character and the value follows the following format:

```
SUBTAG ('-' SUBTAG)*
```

A `SUBTAG` consists of a series of alphanumeric characters. For Unicode locale extensions, the value must be at least two characters, but not more than 8 characters in length. For private use extensions, 1 to 8 characters are permitted. All extension strings are case-insensitive.

The key for Unicode locale extension is **u**, and for private use extensions it is **x**. These extensions can be added to a locale to provide additional information, such as the calendar number types to use.

The keys that can be used are listed in the following table:

Key code	Description
ca	Calendar algorithm for determining dates
co	Collation type—the ordering used in a language
ka	Collation parameters—used to specify the ordering
cu	Currency type information
nu	Numbering system
va	Common variant type

Examples of key and types are found in the following table:

Key/Type	Meaning
nu-armnlow	Armenian lowercase numerals
ca-indian	Indian calendar

Several methods have been added to use these extensions. The getExtensionKeys method returns a set of Character objects of all keys used with the locale. Likewise, the getUnicodeLocaleAttributes and getUnicodeLocaleKeys methods return a set of strings listing the attributes and the Unicode keys available. The methods return an empty set if there are no extensions available. If the key is known, the getExtension method or getUnicodeLocaleType methods will return a string containing the value for that key.

For a given locale, the getScript, getDisplayScript, and toLanguageTag methods return the script, a displayable name for the script, and a well-formed **BCP 47** tag for the locale respectively. The getDisplayScript method will also return a displayable name for the script, given a locale as an argument.

The next section discusses the use of the setDefault method to control the display of information using two different locales at the same time.

Using the Locale.Category enumeration to display information using two different locales

The Locale.Category enumeration has been added to Java 7. It has two values, DISPLAY and FORMAT. This permits the default locale to be set for format type resources (dates, numbers, and currency) and for display resources (GUI aspects of an application). For example, part of an application may set the format to accommodate one locale, such as JAPANESE while displaying related information in another, such as GERMAN.

Consider the following example:

```
Locale locale = Locale.getDefault();
Calendar calendar = Calendar.getInstance();
calendar.setWeekDate(2012, 16, 3);

System.out.println(DateFormat.getDateTimeInstance(
    DateFormat.LONG,
        DateFormat.LONG).format(calendar.getTime()));
System.out.println(ocale.getDisplayLanguage());

Locale.setDefault(Locale.Category.FORMAT, Locale.JAPANESE);
Locale.setDefault(Locale.Category.DISPLAY, Locale.GERMAN);

System.out.println(DateFormat.getDateTimeInstance(
    DateFormat.LONG,
        DateFormat.LONG).format(calendar.getTime()));
System.out.println(locale.getDisplayLanguage());
```

When this code sequence is executed, you should get output similar to the following. The initial date and display language may differ depending on your default locale.

April 17, 2012 7:15:14 PM CDT

English

2012/04/17 19:15:14 CDT

English

The default locale was retrieved and the `setWeekDate` method was used to set a date. This method is discussed in more detail in the *Using Weeks in Java 7* recipe. Next, the date and the display language are printed. The display was repeated, except that the default locale is changed using the `setDefault` method. The display resources were changed to use `Locale.JAPANESE`, and the format type resources were changed to `Locale.GERMAN`. The output reflected this change.

Handling null references

A fairly common exception is the `java.lang.NullPointerException`. This occurs when an attempt is made to execute a method against a reference variable, which contains a value of null. In this recipe we will examine various techniques that are available to address this type of exception.

The `java.util.Objects` class has been introduced and provides a number of static methods that address situations where null values need to be handled. The use of this class simplifies the testing for null values.

The *There's more...* section examines the use of empty lists, which could be used instead of returning null. The `java.util.Collections` class has three methods that return empty lists.

Getting ready

To use the `Objects` class to override the `equals` and `hashCode` methods:

1. Override the methods in the target class.
2. Use the `Objects` class' `equals` method to avoid explicit code to check for null values in the `equals` method.
3. Use the `Objects` class' `hashCode` method to avoid the need for explicit code to check for null values in the `hashCode` method.

How to do it...

1. Create a new console application. We will create an `Item` class to demonstrate the use of the `Objects` class. In the `Item` class, we will override the `equals` and `hashCode` methods. These methods were generated by the NetBeans' insert code command. We use these methods, because they illustrate the `Objects` class' methods and are well structured. Start by creating the class as follows:

```java
public class Item {
    private String name;
    private int partNumber;

    public Item() {
        this("Widget", 0);
    }

    public Item(String name, int partNumber) {
        this.name = Objects.requireNonNull(name);
        this.partNumber = partNumber;
    }

    public String getName() {
        return name;
    }

    public void setName(String name) {
        this.name = Objects.requireNonNull(name);
    }

    public int getPartNumber() {
        return partNumber;
    }

    public void setPartNumber(int partNumber) {
        this.partNumber = partNumber;
    }
}
```

2. Next, override the `equals` and `hashCode` methods as follows. They provide code to check for null values:

```java
@Override
public boolean equals(Object obj){
    if (obj == null) {
        return false;
    }
}
```

```
        if (getClass() != obj.getClass()) {
            return false;
}

        final Item other = (Item) obj;
        if (!Objects.equals(this.name, other.name)) {
            return false;
}

        if (this.partNumber != other.partNumber) {
            return false;
}

        return true;
}

    @Override
    public int hashCode() {
        int hash = 7;
        hash = 47 * hash + Objects.hashCode(this.name);
        hash = 47 * hash + this.partNumber;
        return hash;
    }
}
```

3. Finish the class by adding a toString method:

```
    @Override
    public String toString() {
        return name + " - " + partNumber;
}
```

4. Next, add the following to the main method:

```
        Item item1 = new Item("Eraser", 2200);
        Item item2 = new Item("Eraser", 2200);
        Item item3 = new Item("Pencil", 1100);
        Item item4 = null;

        System.out.println("item1 equals item1: " +
          item1.equals(item1));
        System.out.println("item1 equals item2: " +
          item1.equals(item2));
        System.out.println("item1 equals item3: " +
          item1.equals(item3));
        System.out.println("item1 equals item4: " +
          item1.equals(item4));

        item2.setName(null);
        System.out.println("item1 equals item2: " +
          item1.equals(item2));
```

5. Execute the application. Your output should appear as follows:

item1 equals item1: true

item1 equals item2: true

item1 equals item3: false

item1 equals item4: false

Exception in thread "main" java.lang.NullPointerException

    at java.util.Objects.requireNonNull(Objects.java:201)

    at packt.Item.setName(Item.java:23)

    at packt.NullReferenceExamples.main(NullReferenceExamples.java:71)

As we will see shortly, the `NullPointerException` is the result of trying to assign a null value to an Item's name field.

How it works...

In the `equals` method, a test was first made to determine if the object passed was null. If it was, then `false` is returned. A test was made to ensure that the classes were of the same type. The `equals` method was then used to see if the two name fields were equal to each other.

The `Objects` class' `equals` method behaves as summarized in the following table. The meaning of equality is determined by the `equals` method of the first argument:

First argument	Second argument	Returns
Not null	Not null	`true` if they are the same object, otherwise `false`
Not null	null	`false`
null	Not null	`false`
null	null	`true`

The last test compared the two integer `partNumber` fields for equality.

In the `Item` class' `hashCode` method, the `Objects` class' `hashCode` method was applied to the name field. This method will return 0 if its argument is null otherwise it returns the hash code for the argument. The `partNumber` was then used to compute the final value for the hash code.

Notice the use of the `requireNonNull` method in the two argument constructors and the `setName` method. The method checks for a non-null argument. If the argument is null, it then throws a `NullPointerException`. This effectively catches a potential error earlier in the application.

The `requireNonNull` method is overloaded with a second version accepting a second string argument. This argument changes the message generated, when an exception occurs. Replace the body of the `setName` method with the following code:

```
        this.name = Objects.requireNonNull(name, "The name field
    requires a non-null value");
```

Re-execute the application. The exception message will now appear as follows:

Exception in thread "main" java.lang.NullPointerException: The name field requires a non-null value

There's more...

There are several other `Objects` class methods that may be of interest. In addition, the second section will examine the use of empty iterators to avoid null pointer exceptions.

Additional Objects class methods

The `Objects` class' `hashCode` method is overloaded. A second version takes a variable number of objects as arguments. The method will generate a hash code using this sequence of objects. For example, the `Item` class' `hashCode` method could have been written as:

```
    @Override
    public int hashCode() {
        return Objects.hash(name,partNumber);
    }
```

The `deepEquals` method compares two objects deeply. This means it compares more than just the reference values. Two null arguments are considered to be deeply equal. If both arguments are arrays, then the `Arrays.deepEqual` method is invoked. Equality of objects is determined by the `equals` method of the first argument.

The `compare` method is used to compare the first two arguments returning either a negative value, a zero, or a positive value depending on the relationship between the arguments. Typically, returning a 0 indicates that the arguments are the same. A negative value means that the first argument is less than the second argument. A positive value indicates that the first argument is greater than the second argument.

The method will return a zero if its arguments are identical, or if both arguments are null. Otherwise, the return value is determined using the `Comparator` interface's `compare` method.

The `Objects` class' `toString` method is used to guarantee that a string is returned even if the object is null. The following sequence illustrates the use of this overloaded method:

```
Item item4 = null;
System.out.println("toString: " + Objects.toString(item4));
System.out.println("toString: " + Objects.toString(item4,
    "Item is null"));
```

When executed, the first use of the method displays the word **null**. In the second version, the string argument is displayed as follows:

toString: null

toString: Item is null

Using empty iterators to avoid null pointer exceptions

One approach to avoid a `NullPointerException` is to return a non-null value, when the list could not be created. It could be beneficial to return an empty `Iterator` instead.

In Java 7, the `Collections` class has added three new methods that return an `Iterator`, a `ListIterator`, or an `Enumeration`, all of which are empty. By returning empty, they can be used without incurring a null pointer exception.

To demonstrate the use of an empty list iterator, create a new method that returns a generic `ListIterator<String>` as shown in the following code. An `if` statement is used to return either a `ListIterator` or an empty `ListIterator`:

```
public static ListIterator<String> returnEmptyListIterator() {
    boolean someConditionMet = false;
    if(someConditionMet) {
        ArrayList<String> list = new ArrayList<>();
        // Add elements
        ListIterator<String> listIterator = list.listIterator();
        return listIterator;
    }
else {

        return Collections.emptyListIterator();

    }
}
```

Use the following `main` method to test the behavior of the iterator:

```
public static void main(String[] args) {
    ListIterator<String> list = returnEmptyListIterator();
    while(()))String item: list {
        System.out.println(item);
    }
}
```

When it executes, there should be no output. This indicates that the iterator is empty. If we had returned null instead, we would have received a `NullPointerException`.

The `Collections` class' static `emptyListIterator` method returns a `ListIterator`, whose methods work as listed in the following table:

Method	Behavior
hasNext hasPrevious	Always returns `false`
next previous	Always throws `NoSuchElementException`
remove set	Always throws `IllegalStateException`
add	Always throws `UnsupportedOperationException`
nextIndex	Always returns 0
previousIndex	Always returns -1

The `emptyIterator` method will return an empty iterator with the following behavior:

Method	Behavior
hasNext	Always returns `false`
next	Always throws `NoSuchElementException`
remove	Always throws `IllegalStateException`

The `emptyEnumeration` method returns an empty enumeration. Its `hasMoreElements` will always return `false`, and its `nextElement` will always throw a `NoSuchElementException` exception.

Using the new BitSet methods in Java 7

The `java.util.BitSet` class gained several new methods with the latest release of Java. These are designed to simplify the manipulation of large sets of bits and provide easier access to information about bit location. Bit sets can be used for priority queues or compressed data structures. This recipe demonstrates some of the new methods.

Getting ready

To use the new `BitSet` methods:

1. Create an instance of a `BitSet`.
2. Execute methods against the `BitSet` object as needed.

How to do it...

1. Create a new console application. In the `main` method, create an instance of a `BitSet` object. Then declare an array of long numbers and use the static `valueOf` method to set our `BitSet` object to the value of this long array. Add a `println` statement, so we see the way our long numbers are represented in the `BitSet`:

   ```
   BitSet bitSet = new BitSet();
   long[] array = {1, 21, 3};
   bitSet = BitSet.valueOf(array);
   System.out.println(bitSet);
   ```

2. Next, use the `toLongArray` method to convert the `BitSet` back to an array of long numbers. Use a for loop to print out the values in the array:

   ```
   long[] tmp = bitSet.toLongArray();
   for (long number : tmp) {
       System.out.println(number);
   }
   ```

3. Execute the application. You should see the following output:

   {0, 64, 66, 68, 128, 129}

   1

   21

   3

How it works...

After creating our `BitSet` object, we created an array containing three `long` numbers, which serve as a representation of the sequence of bits that we wish to use in our `BitSet`. The `valueOf` method takes this representation and converts it to the sequence of bits.

When we printed out the `BitSet`, we saw the sequence {0, 64, 66, 68, 128, 129}. Each number in this `BitSet` represents the index of the bit that was set in our sequence of bits. For example, the 0 represents the `long` number 1 in our array, as the index of the bit used to represent the one was at position 0. Likewise, bits 64, 66, and 68 were set to represent our `long` number 21. The 128th and 129th bits in the sequence were set to represent our `long` number 3. We reversed the process in the next section, when we used the `toLongArray` method to return our `BitSet` to its original form.

In our example, we used an array of `long` numbers. Similar `valueOf` methods exist for `byte`, `LongBuffer`, and `ByteBuffer` arrays. When using a `LongBuffer` or `ByteBuffer` array, the buffers are not modified by the `valueOf` method, and the `BitSet` cannot be converted back to the buffer. Instead, the `BitSet` must be converted by using the `toLongArray` method, or the similar `toByteArray` method that converts a `BitSet` into an array of bytes.

There's more...

There are two new methods useful for locating a set or clearing bits in a `BitSet`. The method `previousSetBit` takes an integer representing a specific index as its argument and returns an integer representing the closest bit in the `BitSet` that is set. For example, add the following code sequence to our previous example (using `BitSet` represented by long numbers {1, 21, 3}):

```
System.out.println(bitSet.previousSetBit(1));
```

This would result in an output of integer 0. This is because we passed an argument of index 1 to the `previousSetBit` method and the closest previous bit set in our `BitSet` was at index 0.

The `previousClearBit` method operates in a similar fashion. If we were to execute the following code in our previous example:

```
System.out.println(bitSet.previousClearBit(66));
```

We would get output of integer 65. The bit sitting at index 65 is the closest clear bit to our argument 66. Both methods will return a -1 if no such bit exists in the `BitSet`.

Index

Symbols

? 169
[ ] 169
{} 169
* 169
** 169
\ 169
-D java command option 270
-D option 251
@SafeVarargs annotation 8, 36
  about 35, 36
  heap pollution, example 39, 40
  using, in Java core libraries 38
  working 37
@SuppressWarnings annotation 35

A

abort method 278
Abstract Window Toolkit. *See* **AWT**
accept method 283
Access Control List (ACL) 76
AclEntryPermission enumeration values
  APPEND_DATA 131
  DELETE 131
  DELETE_CHILD 131
  EXECUTE 131
  READ_ACL 131
  READ_ATTRIBUTES 131
  READ_DATA 131
  READ_NAMED_ATTRS 131
  SYNCHRONIZE 131
  WRITE_ACL 131
  WRITE_ATTRIBUTES 131
  WRITE_DATA 131
  WRITE_NAMED_ATTRS 131

  WRITE_OWNER 131
AclEntryType value
  ALARM 131
  ALLOW 131
  AUDIT 131
  DENY 131
AclFileAttributeView
  using, for file's ACL maintainance 101-103
  working 104, 105
ACL permissions, file
  setting 126-130
  working 130-132
actionPerformed method 237, 259, 260
addFirst() method 317
addLast() method 317
add() method 317
allocate method 107
AND operation 16
applet initialization status
  handling with event handlers 262-265
  loading status, using 262-264
ApplicationDriver class 214
ApplicationWindow class 238, 253, 255, 256
areExtraMouseButtonsEnabled method 248-251
ARM 17
Arrays.deepEqual method 350
arriveAndAwaitAdvance method 308, 311
arriveAndDeregister method 309
AssertionError class
  using, in Java 7 28, 29
AsynchronousChannelGroup class 182, 206
AsynchronousFileChannel class
  about 182
  file, reading from 206-208
  file, writing to 202-204
  working 204-210

L

lastAccessTime attribute 81
lastModifiedTime attribute
  arguments 81
launchWebStartApplication function 296
lightweight
  mixing, with heavyweight components 217-
    219
LinkedTransferQueue class
  asynchronous concurrent threads, issues
    323
  elements, adding to queue 323
  elements, retrieving from deque 324
  using 319-322
  working 323
listPermissions method 134
literals
  invalid underscore usages, examples 15
  underscores usage, mistakes 15
  underscores, using 13-15
  working 14, 15
Locale.Category enumeration
  using, for information display 345
LogManager class 332

M

main method 51, 274, 284
managed bean. *See* MBean
ManagementFactory class 283
ManagementFactory, Java 7
  methods 285
manipulateResource methods 23
MBean 283
method
  exists 86
  getTotalSpace 152
  getUnallocatedSpace 152
  getUsableSpace 152
  isDirectory 86
  isExecutable 86
  isReadable 86
  isReadOnly 152
  isRegularFile 86
  isWritable 87
  name 152
  notExists 86

type 152
MIME 79
mouse events
  handling 248-251
MouseListener 248
mousePressed event method 249
mousePressed method 251
move method
  uses 141
  using, with resolveSibling method 142
  working 140
MultipleExceptions class 25, 28
multiple exception types
  AssertionError class , using in Java 7 28
  caching 24, 25
  catch block, working 26
  common exception base class, using 27, 28
  ReflectiveOperationException, using 27
Multipurpose Internet Mail Extension. *See*
    MIME
MXBean
  accessing 283, 284
  working 284

N

name method 152
NetBeans 7.0.1 9
newBufferedWriter method 188
newBuilder method 130
newByteChannel method 191
newDirectoryStream method 171, 210
newFactory method 273
newFileSystem method 155, 178
new JLayer decorator
  component, decorating 241, 242
  using 240-244
  working 244
nextDouble method 327
nextIndex method 352
nextInt method 308, 326, 327
nextLong method 326, 327
next method 327, 352
Nimbus Look and Feel 217
NIO2 181
non-atomic method 87
non-reifiable data 37

using, for file event monitor 173-175
working 176, 177
weakly consistent 167
Web Start programs 265
week number 332
window
  color gradient, using 224-227
  displaying, focus controlling 252-255
  shape, managing 227
  transparency feature, using 224-227
window opacity
  about 222, 223
  working 223, 224
window types
  about 219
  example, Type.NORMAL 221
  example, Type.POPUP 220, 221
  example, Type.UTILITY 221, 222
  managing 219
  working 220

withCachedThreadPool 209
withFixedThreadPool 209
withThreadPool 209
WorkerThread class 258, 260
work-stealing 299
write method 107
write operations 202

X

X.509 certificate 269

Z

zip filesystem provider
  about 178
  working 179

Thank you for buying
Java 7 New Features Cookbook

About Packt Publishing

Packt, pronounced 'packed', published its first book "*Mastering phpMyAdmin for Effective MySQL Management*" in April 2004 and subsequently continued to specialize in publishing highly focused books on specific technologies and solutions.

Our books and publications share the experiences of your fellow IT professionals in adapting and customizing today's systems, applications, and frameworks. Our solution-based books give you the knowledge and power to customize the software and technologies you're using to get the job done. Packt books are more specific and less general than the IT books you have seen in the past. Our unique business model allows us to bring you more focused information, giving you more of what you need to know, and less of what you don't.

Packt is a modern, yet unique publishing company, which focuses on producing quality, cutting-edge books for communities of developers, administrators, and newbies alike. For more information, please visit our website: www.PacktPub.com.

About Packt Enterprise

In 2010, Packt launched two new brands, Packt Enterprise and Packt Open Source, in order to continue its focus on specialization. This book is part of the Packt Enterprise brand, home to books published on enterprise software – software created by major vendors, including (but not limited to) IBM, Microsoft and Oracle, often for use in other corporations. Its titles will offer information relevant to a range of users of this software, including administrators, developers, architects, and end users.

Writing for Packt

We welcome all inquiries from people who are interested in authoring. Book proposals should be sent to author@packtpub.com. If your book idea is still at an early stage and you would like to discuss it first before writing a formal book proposal, contact us; one of our commissioning editors will get in touch with you.

We're not just looking for published authors; if you have strong technical skills but no writing experience, our experienced editors can help you develop a writing career, or simply get some additional reward for your expertise.

Learning jQuery, Third Edition

ISBN: 978-1-84951-654-9   Paperback: 428 pages

Create better interaction, design, and web development
with simple JavaScript techniques

1. An introduction to jQuery that requires minimal
   programming experience

2. Detailed solutions to specific client-side problems

3. Revised and updated version of this popular
   jQuery book

Ext JS 4 First Look

ISBN: 978-1-84951-666-2   Paperback: 340 pages

A practical guide including examples of the new features
in Ext JS 4 and tips to migrate from Ext JS 3

1. Migrate your Ext JS 3 applications easily to Ext JS
   4 based on the examples presented in this guide

2. Full of diagrams, illustrations, and step-by-step
   instructions to develop real word applications

3. Driven by examples and explanations of how
   things work

Please check **www.PacktPub.com** for information on our titles

JBoss ESB Beginner's Guide

ISBN: 978-1-84951-658-7   Paperback: 320 pages

A comprehensive, practical guide to developing service-based applications using the Open Source JBoss Enterprise Service Bus

1. Develop your own service-based applications, from simple deployments through to complex legacy integrations

2. Learn how services can communicate with each other and the benefits to be gained from loose coupling

3. Contains clear, practical instructions for service development, highlighted through the use of numerous working examples

Liferay Portal Systems Development

ISBN: 978-1-84951-598-6   Paperback: 546 pages

Build dynamic, content-rich, and social systems on top of Liferay

1. Use Liferay tools (CMS, WCM, collaborative API and social API) to create your own Web sites and WAP sites with hands-on examples

2. Customize Liferay portal using JSR-286 portlets, hooks, themes, layout templates, webs plugins, and diverse portlet bridges

3. Build your own websites with kernel features such as indexing, workflow, staging, scheduling, messaging, polling, tracking, auditing, reporting and more

Please check **www.PacktPub.com** for information on our titles

CPSIA information can be obtained at www.ICGtesting.com
Printed in the USA
LVOW122035270212

270659LV00003B/25/P